GLOBAL FAITH BOOK SERIES

I0147242

STUDIES IN
BAHÁ'Í PHILOSOPHY

Selected Articles

STUDIES IN
BAHÁ'Í PHILOSOPHY

Selected Articles

Edited and with an Introduction
by Mikhail Sergeev

BOSTON • 2018

STUDIES IN BAHÁ'Í PHILOSOPHY
Selected Articles
(Global Faith Book Series. Vol. 1)

Editor: Mikhail Sergeev, *University of the Arts (Philadelphia)*

ISBN 978-1-940220901
Library of Congress Control Number 2018950130

Cover Image: Jules Heller (1919–2007), "Graceful Forms," c. 2005, unique ink-jet print. http://www.julesheller.net/

Published by M·GRAPHICS PUBLISHING
🖥 www.mgraphics-publishing.com
✉ info@mgraphics-publishing.com
   mgraphics.books@gmail.com

Printed in the U.S.A.

CONTENTS

The Sixth Wave: Bahá'í Scriptural Philosophy

MIKHAIL SERGEEV

University of the Arts

ABOUT THE BAHÁ'Í FAITH

The Bahá'í Faith is a modern religion, which was founded by Mírzá Ḥusayn-'Alí, a Persian prophet who is known under his religious name of Bahá'u'lláh (the "Glory of God" in Arabic).

Bahá'u'lláh was born in Iran in 1817. As a young man he joined a religious movement of Babism whose followers were expecting a new revelation that had to be delivered by the coming messenger of God. The group was initiated in Iran in 1844 and soon was suppressed by the government. Its leader, the Bab (whose religious name means the "Gate" in Arabic) was executed in 1850. After Bab's martyrdom, Bahá'u'lláh came to the forefront of the movement and in 1863 proclaimed himself to be the promised messenger.

The founder of the new religion that came to be known as the Bahá'í Faith preached for the next twenty-nine years of his life that he spent in exile. After Bahá'u'lláh's death, his eldest son, 'Abdu'l-Bahá (the "Servant of Glory"), became the head of the Bahá'í community. Later the leadership was passed on to 'Abdu'l-Bahá's grandson Shoghi Effendi and in 1963 — to the Universal House of Justice, whose first members were elected by the Bahá'í representatives.

1

The principles of the Bahá'í religion reflect its main purpose, namely, the global unity of humankind. According to Bahá'u'lláh, such a unity cannot be secured without a spiritual revival and human unification under the guidance of one faith. This is a necessary but not sufficient condition for the success of globalization, however. In the sphere of politics, as Bahá'u'lláh argues, it is imperative to create a world federation and an international tribunal that would represent the interests of all nations and maintain universal peace. In the social domain there is a need for balanced economic development of different countries, protection of human rights regardless of religion, race, ethnicity, social status or gender. In the sphere of culture, one needs obligatory universal education, acceptance of a common script as well as harmonious development of science and religion. Finally, on the existential level, every individual must independently strive for truth and overcome prejudices, especially those that lead to conflict or any form of intolerance and fanaticism.

The administrative structure of the Bahá'í Faith is built on the democratic foundations. Members of the local community, 21 years and older, once a year elect a Local Spiritual Assembly that consists of nine members and governs the affairs of its locality. Delegates from Local Spiritual Assemblies every year elect nine members of the National Spiritual Assembly. Every five years the members of National Spiritual Assemblies of all countries elect the Universal House of Justice. The Universal House of Justice is located in Haifa, Israel, and is the supreme governing body of the faith. Its decisions, which have been invested with infallibility by Bahá'u'lláh, are made on the basis of consensus or, if such a consensus cannot be reached, by the simple majority vote.

According to statistical data, "[t]here are more than 5 million Bahá'ís in the world. The Bahá'í Faith is established in virtually every country and in many dependent territories and overseas epartments of countries. Bahá'ís reside in well over 100,000 localities. About 2,100 indigenous tribes, races, and ethnic groups are represented in the Bahá'í community." ("Statistics," Bahá'í World

News Service. Media Information, http://news.bahai.org/media-infor-
mation/statistics.)

BAHÁ'Í PHILOSOPHY

Depending upon their epistemological foundations philosophical systems can be divided into five types: empiricist (Locke),
rationalist (Descartes), intuitivist (Bergson), traditionalist (Confucius), and scriptural (Aquinas). Hindu thinkers should be credited with the invention of scriptural philosophy.

The beginning of Hindu religious philosophy could be traced
back to the seventh century before Christ — to Kapila (c. 700), a
legendary founder of Samkhya school of Hindu thought. Sāmkhya
was one of the six traditional schools of Hindu religious philosophy. Tradition considers Kapila to be the originator of the school
and attributes to him the authorship of The Sāmkhya-pravacana
Sūtra. The essence of the Sāmkhya system consisted in reducing
the variety of objects in the universe to two basic elements —
spirit and matter — different combinations of which produce the
world's colorful multiplicity.

The purpose of Hindu philosophy was to defend the validity and truth of Hindu scriptural texts by means of rational arguments. That was, for example, the task of Jaimini
(c. 400 B.C.) — the author of Mīmānsā Sutra, which belonged to
Pūrvā-Mīmānsā school of Hinduism. One of the six traditional
schools of Hindu philosophy, Pūrvā-Mīmānsā was preoccupied
with religious obligations, as they have been outlined in the
Vedas and other scriptural texts. Philosophical arguments of the
mīmānsikas reflected their pragmatic concerns and focused on
the proofs of the validity of scriptures.

In Western philosophical tradition Philo (Judaeus) of
Alexandria (B.C. 20) is considered the first scriptural philosopher. An Orthodox Jewish thinker, Philo was strongly influenced
by the ancient Greek intellectual tradition. These dual loyalties
determined the peculiar character of Philo's thought that can be
described as "scriptural philosophy." Philo interpreted Hebrew

Scriptures allegorically in his effort to synthesize Jewish wisdom and Hellenistic thought. More specifically, he tried to support the revelation of Moses by the philosophical arguments of Plato and the Stoics. Philo taught, for instance, that God first created man in His own mind (Logos) and only then as a person possessing body and soul. The highest human aspiration, according to Philo, consists in overcoming physical limitations and returning to divine origins by means of intellectual contemplation.

In the history of philosophy there were five major waves of scriptural reasoning — Hindu, Buddhist, Jewish, Christian, and Muslim. In this context Bahá'í philosophy represents the sixth wave, and it finds itself in a fruitful dialogue not only with the traditional forms of religious philosophy but also with modern Western thought which is based solely on reason and empirical observation.

In this collection the reader will find articles on various aspects of Bahá'í philosophy — philosophical anthropology, philosophy of science, philosophy of culture, epistemology, ethics, philosophy of religion, comparative and political philosophy, and, finally, history of philosophy. The authors of those articles — Bahá'í and non-Bahá'í scholars — reflect global aspirations of this religion by representing diverse countries of the world — USA, Canada, France, Italy, and Sweden. This collection of articles also introduces a Global Faith Book Series which publishes works on various aspects of the Bahá'í Faith and globalization.

Human Nature And World Religion: Toward A Bahá'í-Inspired Philosophical Anthropology

HAROLD ROSEN

University of British Columbia (Canada)

INTRODUCTION: INSPIRING VOICES ECHOING ACROSS THE AGES

How do the major religions depict human nature? A coherent and composite picture of our human station emerges from a sympathetic study of four representative scriptural traditions — the Buddhist faith, the Christian faith, the Islamic faith and the Bahá'í faith. In these religious worldviews, human beings are situated dramatically between the natural and spiritual realms — higher than earth, but lower than heaven. We are given a privileged place with unique capacities and a range of choices. In this essay, four levels of reality are briefly described — the natural, the human, the spiritual and the divine — using key quotes from four sets of scriptures. A consistent religious metaphysic is presented using these sources.

Some insights from the Western intellectual tradition — including classical Greek thought and Renaissance humanism, philosophical anthropology and virtue theory — complement and enrich this composite view of human nature. Key points from Plato, Aristotle, Marsilio Ficino, Giovanni Pico della Mirandola, Max Scheler, and H. B. Danesh are especially relevant to the present study. Themes of creative freedom, civilization-building and self-transcendence emerge from a study of these fields and figures, offering positive alternatives to the prevailing secular and materialistic concepts of human nature. In this Bahá'í-inspired perspective, the primary human capacities of loving, knowing and willing are accented; and Bahá'í teachings are shown to integrate and enhance a wide range of scriptural and philosophical sources, with powerful implications for change in many fields of study and action.

Several lofty views of human nature have resounded through the centuries and millennia, inspiring confidence in those who contemplate their beautiful and oracular imagery. About 3000 years ago, David's Psalm 8 depicted human beings with a profoundly dignified role in the cosmos:

> "When I look at Thy heavens, the work of Thy fingers, the moon and the stars which Thou has established; what is man that Thou art mindful of him, and the son of man that Thou dost care for him? Yet Thou hast made him little less than God, and dost crown him with glory and honor. Thou hast given him dominion over the works of Thy hands; Thou hast put all things under his feet..."[1]

This expresses deep wonder at our human station in the creation as a whole, marveling at our lofty responsibilities and our extensive powers.

In 1486, Pico della Mirandola's "The Dignity of Man" offered a powerful portrayal of human capacity and privilege, establishing a theme for the European Renaissance. God is presented as saying to humanity:

> "O Adam... you may have and possess... whatever place, whatever form, and whatever functions you shall de-

---

[1] Psalm 8, *The New Oxford Annotated Bible* (Revised Standard Version), editors H. G. May and B. M. Metzger (New York: Oxford University Press, 1973).

sire... You who are confined by no limits, shall determine for yourself your own nature, in accordance with your own free will... I have set you at the center of the world, so that from there, you may more easily survey whatever is in the world. We have made you... the moulder and maker of yourself."[2]

Again, human freedom, capacity and responsibility are intensely evoked in this famous passage.

In about the year 1600, Shakespeare described human beings as the 'paragon of animals'. The term 'paragon' was drawn from Italian and Greek roots, meaning 'whetstone for sharpening', a model or pattern of excellence, the perfection of its kind, peerless example, or touchstone of comparison. Shakespeare summarized the God-given capacities of human beings in a seemingly oracular utterance. "What a piece of work is man! how noble in reason! how infinite in faculties! in form and moving, how express and admirable! in action, how like an angel! in apprehension, how like a god! the beauty of the world! the paragon of animals!" (Hamlet, Act 2, Scene 2)[3] Yet again, the creative endowment of humanity is placed before us in exalted and memorable language.

The Bahá'í Faith claims a revelation that serves as an 'eye to past ages', enabling humanity to integrate many religious and philosophical views, as well as to discern their common Source. "As the human race in all its diversity is a single species, so the intervention by which God cultivates the qualities of mind and heart latent in that species is a single process."[4] This statement points to the underlying oneness of the various conceptions of God, humanity and religion. This essay attempts to identify some of these conceptions of unity, which are specifically focused on

---

[2] *The Portable Renaissance Reader*, editors J.B Ross and M. M. McLaughlin (New York: The Viking Press, 1967), 478.

[3] *The Works of William Shakespeare (Complete)*, William Shakespeare (Roslyn, NY: Black's Readers Service, 1972), 1141.

[4] *One Common Faith, The Universal House of Justice.* (Thornhill, Ontario: Bahá'í Canada Publications, 2005), 23.

human nature, and to integrate them with related theoretical fields and disciplines, hopefully serving as a contribution to a Bahá'í-inspired philosophical anthropology.

PHILOSOPHICAL ANTHROPOLOGY AND ITS RELIGIOUS THEMES

Though human nature had been an important theme for classical Greek and foundational Christian thinkers and had received attention by such modern thinkers as Kant and Hegel, it became an independent discipline in Western philosophy in the 1920s. Max Scheler and Helmut Plessner are considered the founders of modern philosophical anthropology. Its primary focus has been with these questions: What is human nature? What are the most essential qualities of human beings? What are our most characteristic capacities and limitations? What are the primary self-images of humanity? What is our place in the nature of things? And it is with this latter question, along with its religious aspects, that this essay is most concerned.

This field has generally depicted man as capable of surpassing natural limits, but also as self-defeating and mysterious. We are seen as a choosing creature, both within and above nature, both individual and social, and both creative and destructive. Since we are able to forge our destiny to a degree, we are not fully amenable to scientific investigation. The primary 'works' of man — including consciousness, language, religion, art, science, technology, commerce and governance — are interpreted as arising from our nature. Five general concepts of human nature have been identified but interpreted as inconsistent, calling for intellectual reconciliation in a higher synthesis or a breakthrough to a new and more adequate conception: 1) the Judeo-Christian view that we are sinful and graced beings; 2) the Greek and Enlightenment view that we are rational beings; 3) the modern scientific view that we are highly developed animals; 4) the pessimistic view that we are at an evolutionary dead-end, having wasted our potential and become dissolute; and 5) the optimistic view that we are self-transcending beings with great potential in the areas of power, creativity and love.

Modern Western religious thinkers such as Kierkegaard, Buber and Brunner have accented the theological and faith-related dimensions of the human condition. Created in the image of God, we are viewed as spiritual beings longing to serve and become closer to God. We can be loving and just on one hand, with divine guidance and inspiration; but we can also misuse our freedom and sink into sin and destruction. From the religious perspective, human nature is best understood from the inside, and is illumined with revelation — which is best understood with the 'logic of the heart' transcending that of the mind. The maturing of humanity is understood as growing toward God through humble acceptance of our creatureliness, combined with strengthening of conscience as well as decisive and loving action. In the religious view, love is usually understood as a value hierarchy, progressing from physical to social to divine. Faith is the condition of the whole person rooted in God. Human life is essentially a creative struggle in the context of body and soul, freedom and necessity, temporality and eternity. To this theological portrayal of human nature, the Bahá'í faith adds the affirmation that ultimate fulfillment is offered to humanity by all the Divine Revealers.

FOUR LEVELS OF REALITY: A COMMON METAPHYSIC FOR LOCATING OUR PLACE IN THE GRAND SCHEME

An exciting and hopeful discovery can be made through a sympathetic study of world religions. It appears that all major scriptural traditions offer a similar map of ultimate reality. In very comparable ways they proclaim the same basic metaphysical 'big picture' with four distinguishable levels. We will attempt to illustrate this metaphysical commonality with a brief look at the way Buddhist, Christian, Islamic and Bahá'í scriptures depict four levels of reality. Because sincere multi-scriptural study is rare, and because the key terms for each faith tradition arise from different cultural and historical settings, this deeply significant truth about humanity's common philosophical ground is not often glimpsed. Among the benefits of a study like this is the invitation to see and appreciate the unified reality to which most of the scriptural symbols and parables point.

According to the world's scriptures collectively, our human condition is described as being both in and above the material world. Below us and around us is the realm of nature and matter, in which we can discover three major sub-levels: elements, plants and animals. We have reasoning, discerning souls capable of directing themselves in both material and spiritual directions. We have a privileged and dignified place in the grand scheme of things. Above us in a higher realm is the revelatory world of the Spirit or Word, made accessible to us by the foundational Revealers, Messengers and Enlightened Ones. And above these revered figures is a realm that even they cannot penetrate — God or the Infinite Divine Realm. This coherent metaphysic provides the context for elaborate teachings on the proper development of the human soul.

Some of the key terms for the Divine or Ultimate Reality in the collective body of world scriptures include: God, the Creator, the Unborn Transcendent Power, the Absolute and Un-manifest, and the Eternal Mystery. Some of the key terms for the spiritual or revelatory realm include: The Holy Spirit, the Creative Word, the Dharma or Truth, and the Revealers or Founders. This realm is generally believed to be "inhabited" by variously conceived celestial beings, angels and archangels. Some of the key terms for the human realm include: the soul, the mind, the heart, the spirit, as well as the domain of choice, self-observation, virtues and aspirations on one hand, and vices and temptations on the other. And some of the key terms for natural reality include: the physical creation, the material world, containing elemental bodies (with their powers of attraction and integration), plants (with their powers of adaptation and growth), and animals (with their powers of sensation and mobility). In sum, four interacting but distinguishable levels of reality are presented in the world religions, with human beings placed dramatically between the natural and spiritual realms.

DIVINE OR ULTIMATE REALITY: BEYOND ALL REACH AND COMPREHENSION, SOURCE OF ALL POWER AND GOODNESS

How do our four representative faiths view God or the Highest Realm? The terms used seem to refer to the same One Source of all power and goodness, beyond direct access and comprehension, and so these terms may be regarded as functionally equivalent. It is true that in the Eastern religions, the preferred terms for Divine Reality are more impersonal and the images are more abstract than those preferred in the Western Religions. But if God is beyond our comprehension, this difference between impersonal and personal terms is not substantive, but rather a matter of cultural preference and psychological temperament.

In Buddhist scriptures the Ultimate or Transcendent Realm is referred to as the Unborn and the Unconditioned, the Formless Realm, and the Dharmakaya or Eternal Truth. "Because there is an Unborn, a not-become, a not-made, a not-compounded Reality, therefore there is an escape from the born, the become, the made, the compounded."[5] And:

> What is meant by the Eternally-Abiding Reality? The ancient road of Reality... has been here all the time, like gold or silver preserved in the mine. The Dharmadatu (Absolute Truth) abides forever... (like the) Reason of all things. Reality forever abides, Reality keeps its order, like the roads in an ancient city." (Lankavatara Sutra 61)[6]

Or: "The Absolute is unlimited and unceasing."[7] This Absolute and Eternally-Abiding Reality is clearly an impersonal concept of God.

In Christian scriptures the Highest Realm is called God the Father, the Creator, He Who is and was and is to be, the Alpha and Omega or the Beginning and End. "There is... one God and

---

[5] Udana 80, quoted in *World Scripture: A Comparative Anthology of Sacred Texts*, edited by Andrew Wilson, et al, (New York: Paragon House), 48.
[6] Lankavatara Sutra 61, quoted in *World Scripture*, 102.
[7] Lion's Roar of Queen Srimala 5, quoted in *World Scripture*, 466.

Father of all, who is above all and through all and in all."[8] "There is one God, the Father, from whom are all things and from whom we exist."[9] "I am the Alpha and the Omega, says the Lord God, who is and who was and who is to come, the Almighty."[10] For Christians, God is referred to in these passages in terms that are both personal and impersonal.

In Islamic scriptures the Highest Power is referred to as Allah, the one and only God, the Creator of the heavens and the earth, the Eternal and Absolute, the Incomprehensible and Unseen Reality. "No vision can grasp Him, but His grasp is over all vision: He is above all comprehension, yet is acquainted with all things."[11] "He is the First and the Last, the Evident and the Immanent: and He has full knowledge of all things."[12] "God is He, than Whom there is no other god — the Sovereign, the Holy One, the Source of Peace... Whatever is in the heavens and on earth doth declare His praises and Gory."[13] Muslims — like Jews, Christians and Bahá'ís — refer to God in both personal and impersonal terms.

In Bahá'í scriptures God is termed the Creator of all worlds and realms of being, the Unknowable Essence, the Central Orb of the Universe, the Ancient Being and the Fathomless Mystery. "Know thou that every created thing is a sign of the revelation of God."[14] As exalted as the Manifestations of God are deemed to be, there are aspects of Divine Reality that are unknown and inaccessible even to them. "The way is barred and to seek it is impiety."[15] And:

---

[8] Ephesians 4.6, *Oxford Annotated Bible*, op cit.

[9] 1st Corinthians 8.6, ibid.

[10] Revelation 1.8, ibid.

[11] Qur'an 6.103, translated by Abdullah Yusuf Ali, (Elmhurst, NY: Tahrike Tarsile Qur'an, Inc, 2001).

[12] Qur'an 57.3, ibid.

[13] Qur'an 59.23–24, ibid.

[14] Baha'u'llah. *Gleanings from the Writings of Baha'u'llah*, (Wilmette, IL: Bahá'í Publishing, 2005), section 93.1.

[15] Baha'u'llah. *The Seven Valleys and the Four Valleys*, (Wilmette, IL: Bahá'í Publishing, 1991), 37.

Far be it from His glory that human tongue should adequately recount His praise, or that human heart comprehends His fathomless mystery. He is, and hath ever been, veiled in the ancient eternity of His Essence, and will remain in His Reality everlastingly hidden from the sight of men." (Gleanings 19.1)[16]

These passages depict God as to some degree discernible in every part of creation, but most essentially above and beyond all things visible and invisible.

SPIRITUAL OR REVELATORY REALITY: INTERMEDIARY BETWEEN CREATOR AND CREATED, REVELATORY GUIDANCE AND ETERNAL LIFE

How do our four representative faiths view the spiritual or revelatory level of reality? Again, it is apparent that the major world religions offer comparable teachings about the level of reality below God and above humanity. The Revealers, Prophets and Founders are believed to have originated in an eternal realm. Though the Spiritual and Revelatory level contains sub-levels and beings that are differently named in the various scriptural traditions, the sublime realities to which these terms point appear to be the same. Together these realities traverse much of the distance between the ultimately unknowable Creator and the created order. They serve an intermediary function between God and human beings, and they are the direct source of the revelatory guidance and written scriptures that have been delivered to humanity periodically.

Buddhist scriptures speak of the Realm of Form, the Dharma or Spiritual Path, as well as past, present and future Buddhas assisted by a variety of celestial beings who have attained the desire-less and un-describable realm of Nirvana. The Realm of Form (Rupadhatu) is described as heavens occupied by celestial beings,

---

[16] Gleanings 19.1, op cit.

higher states of awareness and exalted meditative states.[17] The Buddha represents the Wisdom and Compassion of this realm. "He who sees the Dharma sees me; and he who sees me sees the Dharma."[18] "The Tathagata (Path-Maker or Way-Shower) is the victor unvanquished, the absolute seer, the perfectly self-controlled one."[19] "The Buddha will not die; the Buddha will continue to live in the holy body of the law."[20] The 'holy body of the law' and the Word of God appear to be identical.

Christian scriptures refer to the Word of God, the Logos, Holy Spirit, Christ the Son of God, and the kingdom of heaven not of this world. The people who seek to grow closer to God should heed "every word that proceeds from the mouth of God."[21] Christ explained that his words did not come from him alone, but God. "What I say, therefore, I say as the Father has bidden me."[22] He also declared, "My kingship is not of this world."[23] The author of Hebrews wrote that through the Son, God "created the world. He reflects the glory of God and bears the very stamp of his nature, upholding the universe by his word of power."[24] The terms Spirit, Word and Wisdom in the Jewish and Christian scriptures refer to the power and guidance of the heavenly kingdom, and they appear to be equivalent to the Eastern term Dharma.

Islamic scriptures are revered as the Source of Bounty and Grace, the Mother of the Book, the Word of God, and the realm from which the Divine Messengers are sent to humanity. Those who are obedient to the *Qur'an* are believed to be following "a Revelation from the Lord of the worlds."[25] Such Holy Books are

---

[17] *Encyclopedia of Religion.* 1st ed., Mircea Eliade, editor (New York: Macmillan, 1987).

[18] Samyutta Nikaya 3.120, quoted in *World Scripture*, 465.

[19] Digha Nikaya 3.135, quoted in *The God of Buddha*, J. M. Fozdar (New York: Asia Publishing House, 1973), 26.

[20] Digha Nikaya 1.46, quoted in *The God of Buddha*, 23.

[21] Matthew 4.4, *Oxford Annotated Bible*, op cit.

[22] John 12.50, ibid.

[23] John 18.36, ibid.

[24] Hebrews 1.3, ibid.

[25] Qur'an 56.80, op cit.

said to come to humanity at intervals: "for each period is a Book (revealed)."[26] Acceptance of the Messenger is understood as following the will of God. "He who obeys the Messenger, obeys God."[27] God sends Prophets and Messengers because human beings easily forget and regress to superstition. "It is He that hath sent His Messenger with Guidance and the Religion of Truth, to proclaim it over all religion."[28] For Muslims the spiritual or revelatory Realm is the Source of the Book, and appears to be equivalent to the Word, the Law and the Truth (or Dharma) as understood by Hindus and Buddhists.

Bahá'í scriptures affirm that divine attributes are perfectly reflected by the Manifestations of God — including Moses, Zoroaster, Krishna, Buddha, Christ, Muhammad and Baha'u'llah — in ways that human beings cannot fully grasp. The spiritual realm is the Source of the Word of God, as well as the heavenly realms, some of which can be attained by the human soul in its never-ending spiritual progress. In Bahá'í Writings the revelatory realm is described as having three sub-levels: 1) *Malakut* — the order of souls completely free and detached from bodily existence, the companions of the light who dwell in the Concourse on High; at this level the Manifestations of God are said to be 'distinct'; 2) *Jabarut* — the higher order of Exalted Beings or Eternal Spiritual Guides in which the revealed God acts and makes commands; at this level the Manifestations are said to be 'united or one'; and 3) *Lahut* — the names and attributes of Divine Consciousness, the Tongue of Grandeur, also called the Word, the Logos, the Holy Spirit or the Primal Will.[29] The Manifestations traverse the levels of the spiritual realm, but also exemplify the human realm during their historic missions on earth. They have a 'dual-station' and can be described as both human and beyond-human, both in the world and above the world, both historically distinct and

---

[26] Qur'an 13.38, op cit.
[27] Qur'an 4.80, op cit.
[28] Qur'an 9.33, op cit.
[29] AdibTaherzadeh. *The Revelation of Baha'u'llah: Baghdad 1853–63*, Vol. 1 (Oxford: George Ronald, 1980), 55–60.

united in divine purpose. These teachings add significant details to the previous revelations, and they cast light on the pattern of progressive revelation in the world's religious history.

NATURAL REALITY: THE WORLD OF TIME/SPACE, FORM/ENERGY, CHANGE/STRUGGLE, LIFE/DEATH

How do our four representative faiths view the natural order? The major scriptural traditions claim that humanity is called to a position above nature, but we can slip backward into its lower domain, depending on the moral and spiritual quality of our choices. Nature itself is a world of time and space, bodily form and physical energy, struggle and development, causal determination, life and death. Traces of the Creator can be found in the created realm, and we are to discern these evidences and make good use of them.

Buddhist scriptures refer to the transient Realm of Desire, 'myriads of things', 'causal actions', as well as the realm of 'impermanent' processes'. The Realm of Desire consists of elements, plants, animals and unenlightened human beings. All physical realities are impermanent and transitory processes but ordered by causal relations. "The world exists because of causal actions; all things are produced by causal actions and all beings are governed and bound by causal actions. They are fixed like the rolling wheel of a cart, fixed by the pin of its axle."[30] Impermanent and transitory are all phenomenal realities.[31] "As the bee takes the essence of a flower and flies away without destroying its beauty and perfume, so let the sage wander in this life."[32] Wisdom requires respectful use of nature.

Christian scriptures speak of the 'world of flesh' as full of material temptations, but nature is also viewed as Providence, the

---

[30] Sutta Nipata 654, quoted in *World Scripture*, op cit, 102.

[31] John Powers. *A Concise Encyclopedia of Buddhism* (Oxford: Oneworld Books, 2000), article on Anitya, 21.

[32] Dhammapada 49, translated by Juan Mascaro (London: Penguin Books, 1973).

'handiwork' and the 'footstool' of God. Divine power is evident in things made visible. "Ever since the creation of the world (God's) invisible nature, namely, his eternal power and deity, have been clearly perceived in the things that have been made."[33] "Be fruitful and multiply, and fill the earth and subdue it... have dominion over... every living thing that moves upon the earth."[34] Dominion is the moral quality of good stewardship, rather than the license to dominate arbitrarily as sometimes interpreted. Each creature is ultimately dependent on God for its life and growth.

Islamic scriptures mention frequently the created and providential order, and 'signs for those who discern'. The natural world is described as designed in detail by God, with limitations assigned to each creature. "In the creation of the heavens and the earth... in the beasts of all kinds... are Signs for a people that are wise."[35] "It is God Who causeth the seed-grain and the date-stone to split and sprout."[36] "And among His Signs is this, that heaven and earth stand by His Command; then when He calls you, by a single call, ye (straightway) come forth."[37] For the early Muslims who pondered their scriptures, there was considerable encouragement for the development of the sciences.

Bahá'í scriptures describe the physical creation in some detail as interdependent and evolutionary, as well as subject to frailty and limitation. The material world can be a temptation to unproductive attachment, but it is also the means of all progress. Nature is a system of interconnections among the mineral, plant, animal and human kingdoms. "All beings, whether large or small, were created perfect and complete from the first, but their perfections appear in them by degrees. The organization of God is one; the evolution of existence is one, the divine system is one."[38] "Every

---

[33] Romans 1.20, *Oxford Annotated Bible*, op cit.
[34] Genesis 1.38, ibid.
[35] Qur'an 2.164, op cit.
[36] Qur'an 6.95, ibid.
[37] Qur'an 30.25, ibid.
[38] Abdul-Baha. *Some Answered Questions*, compiled and translated by Laura Clifford Barney, (Wilmette, IL: Bahá'í Publishing, 2004), 198.

part of the universe is connected with every other part by ties that are very powerful and admit of no imbalance, nor any slackening whatever."[39] "Arts, crafts and sciences uplift the world of being, and are conducive to its exaltation."[40]

HUMAN REALITY: BETWEEN HEAVEN AND EARTH, SPIRIT AND NATURE; BOTH IN AND ABOVE, CREATIVE AND DESTRUCTIVE

Now we come to the central theme of this essay: how our four representative faiths have depicted human nature? According to the collective body of world scriptures, "the human being is a microcosm of the universe, having the essences of all things in him- or herself. As the microcosm, human beings have the foundation to know, use and enjoy all things. Of all creatures, humans have the widest scope of thought and action, encompassing all things, knowing and appreciating all things, guiding and prospering all things, and transcending all things."[41] We occupy a privileged place between heaven and earth, poised for moral and spiritual progress. But we have the choice to embellish and grow beyond the world of nature, and to join the Creator in the building of a better world, or, on the other hand, to regress to an animal-like condition, to be obstructive to the processes of advancement, and destructive of the divine bounty offered to us.

Specifically, as regards human relations with the natural world: "The religions give a two-fold teaching, for the human being is both a part of nature, and yet qualitatively distinct as the highest and central entity in nature... The scriptures teach, in various ways, that the human being is the crown of creation." Our dominion over nature "means to contribute to and enhance the

---

[39] Abdul-Baha. *Selections from the Writings of Abdul-Baha*, Universal House of Justice and Marzieh Gail (Wilmette, IL: Bahá'í Publishing, 2010), section 137.2.

[40] Baha'u'llah. *Epistle to the Son of the Wolf*, (Wilmette, IL: Bahá'í Publishing, 1988), 26.

[41] *World Scripture*, op cit, 212.

harmony and beauty of the natural world. When human beings are at one with Absolute Reality, they emit a luster and a spiritual fragrance that perfects their environment."[42]

Prophecies of humanity's moral and spiritual maturation abound in the world's scriptures, and they paint an inspiring picture of harmony between the natural, human and spiritual realms. The Buddhist image of the Pure Land is described as a coming era that will be prosperous, delightful, filled with many beautiful gardens and spiritually advanced souls. Humanity will be unified in thought and aspiration, raising their hearts to their Lord with resolve and serene faith.[43] In the Christian prophecy of the 'new heaven and new earth', the sea will disappear as nations befriend one another and all travel becomes free of fear. 'All things will be made new' as all learning is shared and all obstacles to advancement are removed. The glory of God will be the light by which the nations walk.[44] Islamic prophecies envision a 'second creation' and a Day of Renewal, when the world will be filled with justice, the roads will be completely safe, and the earth will show forth its bounties in splendor.[45] Bahá'í scriptures declare that the Cycle of Fulfillment has begun. "This is the Day in which God's most excellent favors have been poured out upon men, the Day in which His most mighty grace hath been infused into all created things."[46]

On our central theme of human nature itself, Buddhist scriptures refer to an inner agent of awareness and effort, to the limitless depths of our human endowment, and to the seat of mindfulness by which moral and spiritual progress can be made. "We say that the Essence of Mind is great because it embraces all things,

[42] Ibid, 203.
[43] Sukhavativyuha, summarized from *Buddhist Scriptures*, edited by Edward Conze (New York: Penguin Putnam, 1959), 232–36.
[44] Revelation 21, *Oxford Annotated Bible*, op cit.
[45] Qur'an 21.104, op cit and *Kitab al-Irshad*, quoted in Moojan Momen, *The Phenomenon of Religion: A Thematic Approach* (Oxford: Oneworld Publishing, 1999), 253.
[46] Gleanings 4.1, op cit.

since all things are within our nature."[47] We are also described as prone to selfishness and attachment, which is the most basic cause of our suffering. But the Third Noble Truth declares that suffering can be overcome through intentional practices. "Guard well your mind. Uplift yourself from your lower self, even as an elephant draws himself out of a muddy swamp."[48] "Even as rain breaks not through a well-thatched house, passions break not through a well-guarded mind."[49] "Let no man endanger his duty (to the Path of Truth), the good of his soul, for the good of another (choice), however great. When he has seen the good of his soul, let him follow it with earnestness."[50]

Christian scriptures refer to the human spirit as 'made in the image of God' and capable of reflecting the heavenly virtues. "The fruit of the Spirit is love, joy, peace, patience, kindness, goodness, faithfulness, gentleness, self-control."[51] But we are also creatures of choice and bodily limitation, capable of sin. "I see in my (bodily) members another law at war with the law of my mind and making me captive to the law of sin which dwells in my members."[52] The choice between higher aspiration and lower temptation is always ours. "For those who live according to the flesh set their minds on the things of the flesh, but those who live according to the Spirit set their minds on the things of the Spirit."[53] We are called to contribute to the creation, using our unique gifts fruitfully. "Having gifts that differ according the grace given to us, let us use them."[54]

Islamic scriptures also accent the privileged condition of the human soul or heart, gifted with special divine favor, but also having a tendency to forget our obligations to God, making our-

---

[47] Sutra of Hui Neng 2, quoted in *World Scripture*, op cit, 212.
[48] Dhammapada 327, op cit.
[49] Dhammapada 14, ibid.
[50] Dhammapada 166, ibid.
[51] Galatians 5.23, *Oxford Annotated Bible*, op cit.
[52] Romans 7.23, ibid.
[53] Romans 8.5, ibid.
[54] Romans 12.6, op cit.

selves the center all things. "Do ye not see that God has... made His bounties flow to you in exceeding measure, (both) seen and unseen?"[55] "It is He Who hath made thee (His) agents, inheritors of the earth: He hath raised you in ranks, some above the others: that He may try you in the gifts He hath given you."[56] Though we are all children of God, we have been created diverse in languages, colors, tribes and nations, as a challenge to our growth and development. Often, we squander this endowment and fail these tests. "The (human) soul is certainly prone to evil, unless my Lord do bestow His Mercy."[57] "We test you by evil and by good, by way of trial."[58]

Bahá'í scriptures develop an elaborate set of teachings on the human spirit as a 'luminous reality' selected "out of all created things for this supernal grace..." and able "to encompass all things, to understand their inmost essence, and to disclose their mysteries." We are able to "hear the hidden truths that are written and embedded into the heart of all that is."[59] "Man — the true man — is soul, not body."[60] "Upon the reality of man... (God) hath focused the radiance of all of His names and attributes and made it a mirror of His own Self. Alone of all created things, man hath been singled out for so great a favor, so great a bounty."[61] The main purpose of individual human existence is to know and love God, and to develop our divinely-given virtues. Our collective purpose is to co-fashion an ever-advancing civilization, implementing the guidance of the most recent Manifestation, Baha'u'llah.

The terms 'soul', 'human reality', 'human spirit', 'rational faculty', 'mind' and 'heart' are used somewhat interchangeably in Bahá'í scriptures. What endowments, capacities and responsi-

---

[55] Qur'an 31.20, op cit.
[56] Qur'an 6.165, op cit.
[57] Qur'an 12.53, op cit.
[58] Qur'an 21.35, op cit.
[59] Abdul-Baha in *Bahá'í Prayers* (Wilmette, IL: Bahá'í Publishing, IL, 1991), 103.
[60] Abdul-Baha *in Paris Talks* (Wilmette, IL: Bahá'í Publishing, 2006), section 28.6.
[61] Gleanings 27.2, op cit.

bilities are pointed to with these key terms? God is said to have created each soul with its own individuality, having the divine image engraved upon it. It is the first of all created things to declare the glory of its Creator — to recognize His glory, to cleave to His truth, and to bow down in adoration. It is a mystery that no mind can fully fathom. The soul lifts us above the rest of nature; it is a 'heavenly gem' and a harbinger proclaiming the reality of all the worlds of God. "Consider carefully... these concepts, this knowledge, these technical procedures and philosophical systems, these sciences, arts, industries and inventions — all are emanations of the human mind."[62] The soul is our human essence, and God elevates it to ever-higher stations after casting off its earthly frame.

How is the relationship between the soul and the body explained in Bahá'í teaching? The body, including the brain, is viewed as a magnificent tool of the soul. The body is a set of highly evolved instruments to implement the volitional choices and purposes of the soul. "The lamp needs the light, but the light does not need the lamp. The spirit does not need a body, but the body needs spirit or it cannot live. The soul can live without the body, but the body without a soul dies."[63] As a rational faculty, the soul initiates the motion or stillness of the body — including such functions as seeing, hearing and speaking — for better and for worse. The soul both receives messages from and directs the brain; and so the brain functions as a site of interaction between the soul/mind and the body. But the soul is also able to reflect the higher Spiritual or Revelatory realm. Therefore, the soul is intermediary between the body and the Spirit, just as the tree is intermediary between the seed and the fruit. In other words, Bahá'í teachings confirm the other major scriptures in viewing the soul as intermediary between 'heaven and earth', and between 'Spirit and nature'. This description of the soul helps explain the human condition as both 'in' and 'above' the world.

---

[62] Abdul-Baha in *The Secret of Divine Civilization* (Wilmette, IL: Bahá'í Publishing, 1990), 2.

[63] *Paris Talks* 28.15–16, op cit.

> There are in the world of humanity three degrees; those
> of the body, the soul and spirit... When man allows the
> spirit, through his soul, to enlighten his understanding,
> then does he contain all creation; because man, being
> the culmination of all that went before... contains all
> the lower world within himself. Illumined by the spir-
> it through the instrumentality of the soul, man's radi-
> ant intelligence makes him the crowing-point of cre-
> ation. ...If... the spiritual nature of the soul has been
> so strengthened that it holds the material side in sub-
> jection, then does the man approach the Divine; his
> humanity becomes so glorified that the virtues of the
> Celestial Assembly are manifested in him... he stimu-
> lates the spiritual progress of mankind.[64]

The observation that human beings can waste their God-given potential and opportunity is characterized in a unique way in Bahá'í scriptures. It is as if very loving parents had provided their children with "a library of wonderful books", but the children continually amuse themselves with "pebbles and playthings." The parents long for their children's "eternal glory," but the children are content with "blindness and deprivation."[65] Though we are born holy and pure, it is possible for human beings through their own negligence and poor choices to become increasingly defiled. Our moral-spiritual capacities and creative potential can only be manifested through volition. Instead of rising to higher levels of awareness and service, we can allow lower, degraded activities to monopolize our attention. But our life in this world is, in part, a preparation for the spiritual life after the death of our bodies, for "indispensable forces of divine existence must be potentially attained in this world."[66]

---

[64] *Paris Talks* 31.1–6, ibid.

[65] Abdul-Baha in *The Promulgation of Universal Peace*, compiled by Howard McNutt, (Wilmette, IL: Bahá'í Publishing, 2007), 222.

[66] Ibid, 226.

If we ask why it is necessary for the soul, which had its origin in God, to make an often-painful journey back to God, the Bahá'í scriptures answer that we are in need of divine education as we pass from degree to degree in our progressive spiritual unfolding.

> Man must walk in many paths and be subjected to various processes in his evolution upward... He would not know the difference between young and old without experiencing the old... If there were no wrong, how would you recognize the right? If it were not for sin, how would you appreciate virtue? If sickness did not exist, how would you understand health?.. Briefly, the journey of the soul is necessary. The pathway of life is the road, which leads to divine knowledge and attainment. Without training and guidance, the soul could never progress beyond the conditions of its lower nature, which is ignorant and defective.[67]

Contrasting conditions of what we ordinarily consider 'desirable' and 'undesirable' are crucial aspects of our moral and spiritual progress in this life.

INSIGHTS FROM CLASSICAL GREEK AND RENAISSANCE THOUGHT

Having surveyed the place of human nature in the scriptures of representative world religions and seeing how they offer a four-level metaphysic in which human beings occupy a privileged and responsible place, we now turn to complementary views in some of the greatest minds of Classical Greece and Renaissance Europe. Plato and Aristotle offer insights on the tripartite nature of the soul, while Marsilio Ficino and Pico della Mirandola offer universal and synthetic perspectives on the soul in the context of spiritual progress in the cosmic hierarchy. These views all seem to

---

[67] Ibid, 295–96.

complement, integrate and develop the foundational teachings of revelatory systems.

Might we consider Plato (427–347 BCE) and Aristotle (384–322 BCE) the recipients of materials and teachings from a 'primal revelation' passed on to them through ancient Egyptian, Hermetic, Zoroastrian, Hebrew, Pythagorean and Orphic sources — as believed by Ficino and Pico? This hypothesis seems consistent with Islamic and Bahá'í teachings about the one God Who manifested the transformative Word or Spirit, which in turn produced a diverse but unified creation, and revealed divine guidance to humanity at intervals from the very beginnings of our earthly history. It is also consistent with the methods of Plato and Aristotle in gathering knowledge and opinions from very wide-ranging sources. If these two seminal figures absorbed spiritual ideas and monotheistic wisdom from lands such as Egypt, Israel and Persia, this would help explain their high-minded critique of Greek polytheism and their utility for subsequent Jewish, Christian, Islamic and Bahá'í thinkers. The hypothesis of a 'primal revelation' is another way of saying that divine revelation has been progressive and offered to humanity in varying times and places, going back into the very distant and largely untraceable past.

Plato's views on the soul probably had roots in previous traditions and revelations, combined with fresh philosophical insight and imaginative metaphors. In "The Phaedrus" he offered his famous concept of the soul as like the activities and relations among a charioteer, a white horse and a black horse. The white horse represents the positive, spiritual aspiration of the soul, and is called a 'lover of honor', a 'follower of glory' that is 'heaven-bound', manifesting the qualities of obedience to the charioteer, guided by his word and a 'maker of sacred pledges'. On the other hand, the black horse is pleasure-seeking and physically desirous, very disobedient to the charioteer, the 'mate of insolence and pride', while also opposing the white horse. The charioteer himself has the challenge of training the white horse and reining in the black horse simultaneously — determining the overall direction, waiting appropriately, reasoning, controlling the horses according to immediate conditions, and ultimately wishing to 'live in the light' like the white horse.[68] The soul, then, for Plato, has structural agencies along with dynamic processes consisting of spirit, desire and reason. More than two millennia later, Freud interpreted these human functions as the superego, the id and the ego respectively.

Aristotle is often interpreted as inconsistent with Plato on almost every topic, but from the perspective of this essay, their differences have been exaggerated and their commonality is deep and readily apparent. Though Aristotle's terminology is more scientifically and empirically oriented, and his temperament is less mystical and religious, his conclusions about the structure and processes of the soul are quite compatible. Aristotle, too, offers a tripartite description of the soul, in which Plato's white horse is cast as the 'theoretical intellect' contemplating the Highest Good; the black horse is cast as the natural functions of 'sensation and nutrition' attending to bodily needs and preferences; and the charioteer is cast as the 'practical intellect' making experience-based decisions that are compatible with knowledge and reason. For Plato and Aristotle, our primary human capacities manifest as three interacting functions of the soul: 1) spiritual aspiration, seeking reunion with the divine beloved, and contemplating the Highest Source of goodness and power; 2) bodily needs and material attachments, seeking physical satisfaction; and 3) practical learning and volitional control, seeking appropriate balance. A Bahá'í perspective on these three parts of the soul might emphasize their similarity to the primary capacities of spiritual 'loving' aimed at unity; social and intellectual 'learning' aimed at truth; and materially effective 'willing' aimed at service to the world of humanity.

---

[68] From Plato's "The Phaedrus," quoted and summarized in *Real Philosophy: An Anthology of the Universal Search for Meaning*, edited by J. Needleman and J. Appelbaum (London: Arkana Penguin, London, 1990), 24–28.

Marsilio Ficino (1433–1499) was, with Pico, among the most influential Renaissance thinkers. As an Italian translator and commenter on the complete works of Plato and Plotinus, he established a well-developed platonic theology of love and immortality, and integrated Plato with Christian thought more thoroughly than had Augustine (354–430). Ficino might be viewed as a pre-Reformation reformer who tried to offer a more spiritual, contemplative and deeply grounded faith than the hyper-rational and secular tendencies he saw developing in his day. He saw a divinely guided continuity from the distant ancients such as the 'Thrice-Great Hermes' (who was called Enoch in Jewish tradition, Thoth in Egyptian tradition, Houshang in Persian tradition, and Idris in Islamic tradition) to the culminating faith in Christ as the exemplar of divine love in action.

Ficino proposed a metaphysical hierarchy of which dramatized the central and unifying role of the human soul in creation. God is viewed as the highest level, below which is the angelic order, followed by the souls of humanity, who are above the qualitative level and the material order, which serves as the lowest level of the cosmic hierarchy. Above the soul are eternal, intelligible realms; below it are temporal and sensible realms. The soul, then, is drawn in two directions in its unifying activity — upward to the source of its being, downward to care for lower things. Yet all true experiences of love, no matter what the objects of this love may be, awaken us to the natural desire of the soul for union with God. All experiences of beauty and goodness are reflections, however faint or bright, of divine beauty and goodness. On this point, Bahá'ís believe that Baha'u'llah spoke for God and revealed a related truth: "I created thee... engraved on thee Mine image and revealed to thee My beauty."[69]

Pico (1463–1494) was another Italian philosopher, theologian and mystic who not only attempted an integration of Plato and Aristotle, but an integration of Greek classicism and mythology

---

[69] Baha'u'llah. *The Hidden Words*. Arabic section, Number 3 (Wilmette, IL: Bahá'í Publishing, 2002), 7.

with the 'primal revelation' — as conveyed and developed in the traditions of Hermeticism, Zoroastrianism, Pythagoreanism, Orphism and Kabbalism — combined with Christian scholasticism and humanism, as well as Islamic philosophy, theology and mysticism. He quoted the author of the Hermetic literature as teaching: "A great miracle is man."[70] This declaration was part of the 'man as microcosm' philosophy that helped pave the way toward the Scientific Revolution of the sixteenth century. A parallel teaching of Baha'u'llah was: "Man is the supreme Talisman... Regard man as a mine rich in gems of inestimable value. Education can, alone, cause it to reveal its treasures, and enable mankind to benefit therefrom."[71] Pico's vision was an interdisciplinary and universal-minded synthesis of the major philosophical and religious sources known in his day. He used allegorical interpretation to reconcile diverse texts and belief systems and viewed philosophy as preparatory to the higher fulfillment of religion.

In Pico's metaphysical system, he considered 'unity' to be a higher station than 'participatory being' — suggesting that all existing things grow toward an ultimate dynamic oneness. However, his most influential and enduring teaching concerned the freedom and powers of the human station. We are created by God as appreciators of the magnitude and splendor of creation, and as the 'moulder and maker' of ourselves, placed at the 'center of creation' so that we may survey, have and become whatever we choose. This view calls attention to the depth of our moral responsibility, because "to whom much is given, of him will much be required."[72] Pico envisioned a regenerative peace that would reconcile all philosophies and religions of the world and may have anticipated a revelation such as the Bahá'í faith, which began in 1844 in Persia with the central theme of world unity.

---

[70] Pico della Mirandola, quoted in *The Portable Renaissance Reader*, op cit, 476.
[71] Gleanings 122.1, op cit.
[72] Luke 12.48, *Oxford Annotated Bible*, op cit.

INSIGHTS FROM MAX SCHELER'S
PHILOSOPHICAL ANTHROPOLOGY[73]

Another figure offering very useful insights on human nature is Max Scheler (1874–1928), a German philosopher who is usually considered the founder of modern philosophical anthropology. Spiritual and religious themes played central roles in his system of thought. He viewed humans as valuing, loving, communal and aspiring beings, who in their essential nature are 'beside', 'outside' or 'beyond' the physical world. Scheler saw 'values' as objective and essentially good qualities that can be directly perceived and conceived. Value development, however, was viewed as relative to individual and social experience. We feel our way toward more positive and higher values.

He identified five sets of value-ranks that were placed in a hierarchy; 1) the lowest order of values are sensual, ranging from pain to pleasure; 2) then come utilitarian or pragmatic values, ranging from useless to useful; 3) vital values, ranging from the common or base to the noble or lofty; 4) intellectual and spiritual values, seeking ever-higher forms of truth, beauty and justice; and 5) eternal or religious values, seeking ever-more exalted encounters of holiness. God was conceived as a Being of ultimate goodness and power, meant to fill our 'mind-sphere' with faith; but an individual's mind-sphere may become filled with idols, pseudo-religions or nothingness. Mind was seen as a 'tether' between human existence and the Absolute, and in some respects, we are co-creators with God.

Scheler considered the feeling and aspiring 'heart' to be more essential to our human nature than our reasoning and willing functions. He called this view the 'emotional a priori': all values are feel-able phenomena that can be increasingly understood and appreciated as 'good'. The goodness of an object is measured by

---

[73] This section is drawn from Max Scheler: *A Concise Introduction to the World of a Great Thinker* (Pittsburgh, PA: Duquesne University Press, 1965).

how positive it is directly perceived to be, and how high it is on the value-hierarchy. An ethical choice is movement from less to more positive value, or from lower to higher value. True love is said to open our eyes to ever-higher values in the beloved. The act of love is a creative movement of the heart, bringing about and fostering ever-higher values in the beloved. Following Augustine, Scheler saw our key choices as ranging between forms of guided and misguided love. All of the positive values that he labeled 'vital', 'intellectual', 'spiritual' and 'religious' might be considered 'virtues' in the traditional sense.

The social application of this perspective led Scheler to describe the dangers and evils of Nazism, Capitalism and Communism. He advocated a 'United State of Europe' and was a strong advocate of international universities and continuing studies programs available to all persons everywhere. The highest form of knowledge was said to be 'knowledge for salvation' or moral-spiritual knowing in an ever widening 'community of love'. Human beings are the reconcilers of the material and spiritual realms, and love of the Eternal Being is the highest form of love. These basic affirmations in Scheler's philosophy seem generally consistent with how the scriptures of major religions depict human nature.

INSIGHTS FROM VIRTUE THEORY: PRAISEWORTHY QUALITIES AND CULTIVATING BEAUTIFUL CHARACTER

Further insights about human nature can be gleaned from a brief review of modern ethical theory. Three major ethical systems vie with one another in the Western world — the ethics of Duty or right principle, the ethics of Utility or good result, and the ethics of Virtue or beautiful character. From the late eighteenth century to the middle of the twentieth century, the Duty ethics of Immanuel Kant (1724–1804) and the Utility ethics of John Stuart Mill (1806–73) dominated most serious ethical discourse; but now a third approach has been recognized.

About five decades ago, the Virtue ethics of Aristotle was rediscovered, providing a needed alternative or supplement to the ethics of Duty and Utility. However, it becomes clear to any fair investigator of the major world religions that the moral standards found there can be properly understood as Virtue ethics. Therefore, the ancient and traditional guidance humanity has received over the ages emphasizes such ideals and virtues as: loving-kindness, devotion, gratitude, steadfastness, justice, mercy, humility, wisdom, honesty, respect, service, peace and unity. Such virtues are understood to be praiseworthy human qualities and God-given capacities of the human soul. They mirror spiritual powers of a higher world, requiring in this world ongoing nurture and education over the lifespan of the individual, as well as revelatory renewal over the millennia for societies and their leading institutions. "It is religion... which produces all human virtues, and it is these virtues which are the bright candles of civilization."[74]

Kantian ethics places the emphasis on duty, rational obligation and observing right principle. Its slogan might be formulated as 'trust the mind', as it entails making a rational analysis of the principles and rules relevant to the case at hand. The central principle of Duty ethics is: 'Act only on maxims that can be universalized for all persons in similar circumstances'. We are enjoined to consider rational duty above personal and interpersonal consequences; and we are to ask: 'What if everyone in similar circumstances were to do what I am about to do now?' This perspective has been associated with conservative temperaments and policies.

Utilitarian ethics places the emphasis on the interpersonal results of our actions and their social consequences. Its slogan might be 'trust the senses', as it entails an empirical investigation into the concrete benefits and injuries that are at stake. The central principle of Utility ethics is: 'Act so as to bring about the greatest good for the greatest number of persons involved.' We are to consider ultimate consequences more than formal obligations; and we are to ask: 'How much positive effect and how much harm would result from the action I am currently plan-

---

[74] *The Secret of Divine Civilization*, 98, op cit.

ning?' This perspective has been associated with liberal temperaments and policies.

Plato and Aristotle spoke of four 'cardinal virtues': wisdom, courage, temperance and justice. Augustine and Aquinas added and elaborated upon the three 'theological virtues': love, faith and hope. But as stated above, Virtue ethics is the ancient and traditional form of moral guidance, placing emphasis on cultivating beautiful character in oneself and others. Its most well-known and foundational sources have been the Manifestations of God — Moses, Zoroaster, Krishna, Buddha, Christ, Muhammad and Baha'u'llah. Its slogan might be 'trust the soul', as it entails attuning to and respectfully observing the virtuous guidelines that have facilitated humanity's character development down through the ages. The central principle of Virtue ethics is: 'Act in ways that cultivate virtues in ourselves and others.' We are to consider the higher longings and aspirations of humanity as having much higher authority than rationally conceived duties and empirically derived benefits; and we are to ask: 'What virtues call and command me, and what guidance is offered by traditional wisdom?' Though this perspective has been associated with both conservative and liberal temperaments and policies, it is more deeply grounded and universally applicable than the merely human attempts to justify our behavior morally.

PRIMARY HUMAN CAPACITIES: LOVING, KNOWING AND WILLING

We now move toward the conclusion of our survey, using H. B. Danesh's contemporary Bahá'í-inspired account of human nature.[75] He identifies our three primary human capacities as: loving, knowing, and willing. These capacities sound intrinsically positive and valuable, but their quality depends upon the quality of their objects, and each of them can be mis-used. For

---

[75] H. B. Danesh. *The Psychology of Spirituality: From Divided Self to Integrated Self* (Hong Kong: Juxta Publishing Ltd, 1997).

example, our loving capacity can be directed to the glorification of war; our knowing capacity can be directed to the efficiency of crime; and our willing capacity can be directed to discrimination against a certain ethno-cultural group or religious community. The soul is like a mirror and can be faced toward both creative and destructive purposes.

Our 'loving' capacity is variously termed emotion, feeling, affection, relating, caring, appreciating, aspiring and revering. As a God-given capacity it is meant to function as an active force of attention to beauty, growth and unity; and it can be the cause of closeness, intimacy and nurturance. Its main action is creating — bringing people, ideas and things together. Love affirms one's self-worth and forms friendships, creates families and rears children, feeds the hungry and shelters the homeless, removes strangeness and prejudice, fashions works of art and literature, and nurtures our own and others' spiritual growth. The ultimate purpose of our loving capacity is Unity-seeking.

Our 'knowing' capacity is variously termed cognition, learning, wondering, thinking, reasoning, investigating and discerning. As a God-given capacity it is meant to function as consciousness and self-awareness, thinking and problem solving, symbol using and language, intuiting and imagining, as well as higher insight and inspiration. Its various means include experience and reflection, logic and other forms of reasoning, creative work and discovery, study and intellectual pursuit, research and scientific investigation, as well as meditation and prayerful problem solving. The ultimate purpose of our knowing capacity is Truth-seeking.

Our 'willing' capacity is variously termed volition, choosing, deciding, committing, contributing, making and creating. As a God-given capacity it is meant to function as an agent of conscious choice and responsibility for our own and others' well-being. It sets our directions or keeps us passive in the face of options. If a boat is likened to the body, then the captain may be likened to the soul in its willing capacity, and the wind and water represent the conditions in the world. Our willing capacity provides motivation, the courage to act and the wherewithal to be creative. This capacity accounts more for the diversity of worldviews than does our knowing capacity. The ultimate purpose of our willing capacity is Service-seeking.

From Danesh's perspective, what is called the 'self' is the essence of one's being and an integration body, mind and soul. The self is our awareness that we exist now, have existed in the past, and will exist in the future. This experience is usually continuous and whole, for it includes feelings that link the body and the mind, as well as conscious and unconscious content. The self is the unique result of soul-body interface and interaction. But as social beings, the self must also be understood as our own being as perceived by others. The self, then, is a unifying concept.

> [The human reality] is the same reality which is given different names, according to the different conditions wherein it becomes manifest. Because of its attachment to matter and the phenomenal world, when it governs the physical functions of the body, it is called the soul. When it manifests itself as the thinker, the comprehender, it is called the mind. And when it soars into the atmosphere of God, and it travels in the spiritual world, it becomes designated the spirit.[76]

The self and soul then are unified, though their functions may be distinguished.

A significant observation regarding our three primary capacities is that a universal code of ethics seems to be derivable from the ideals toward which they strive: unity, truth and service. All religions and cultures might eventually agree that these aims could be used to co-fashion a coherent ethical basis for a global legal system. 'Unity' is here understood not to mean 'sameness' or 'domination' by any single group or perspective, but rather, integrative oneness among diverse views, dynamic balance and

---

[76] Abdul-Baha quoted in H. B. Danesh's *The Psychology of Spirituality*, 39, op cit, citing "The Star in the West" 7.19 (March 1917), 190.

interdependence among diverse groups, world-consciousness and compassion, mutual empowerment of all individuals, and universal justice and peace. Unity means that previous tendencies to uphold national sovereignties are gradually transcended. 'Truth', in terms of its role in everyday life, means openness to investigation, consultative problem-solving, replacing ignorance with education and knowledge, rooting out the sources of all prejudices, as well as equal receptivity to scientific research and revelatory guidance. 'Service' is here understood as the highest expression of will and suggests contributing to the well-being of others in ever wider circles. Service implies that self-centeredness has yielded to care for humanity, domination has yielded to more egalitarian participation, and competition has yielded to cooperation toward an ever-advancing global civilization.

In Bahá'í teachings, 'spiritual growth' is a term more associated with individuals, whereas 'spiritual evolution' has a collective connotation, referring more to humanity as whole. Our personal spiritual growth is a process of reflecting divine virtues ever more perfectly and allowing spiritual radiance to illumine the soul ever more completely. Humanity's spiritual evolution comes in response the series of Revealers or Manifestations of God and will gradually lead to achieving on earth an ever more heavenly civilization.

CREATIVE FREEDOM, CIVILIZATION-BUILDING, AND SELF-TRANSCENDENCE: POSITIVE ALTERNATIVES TO SECULAR MATERIALISM

In this essay we have tried to discern and distill general truths about human nature from a survey of representative world religions as well as some influential thinkers in Western philosophy. We have sought useful insights from a fairly broad range of spiritual and intellectual views, attempting to see clearly the 'forests' of wisdom about the soul, and not get lost in the 'trees' of historical and theoretical details. From this perspective, three features of human nature stand out from the myriad of qualities described here and elsewhere in the related literature. Human beings, unlike other observable creatures, can be seen to exercise creative freedom, build complex social institutions, and undergo transformation toward higher levels of being. In other words, we have a pronounced degree of choice, we fashion lofty civilizations, and we consciously evolve in a moral and spiritual sense. Our fulfillment as human beings requires these activities. Yet these undeniably human capacities are ignored or curtailed by the prevailing worldview of secular materialism, which presupposes that we are primarily comfort-seeking, technologically adept animals, mechanically adapting to changing environments.

Most of the world's operative economic, political and educational systems — as they have developed from the sixteenth century onwards — presuppose that we are predominantly material and non-spiritual beings competing for limited resources. Though an analysis and critique of the secular and material worldview is beyond our present scope, we offer a few comments that emerge from within this survey. Among the powers of revelation and religion are the generating of new and higher civilizations. When religious systems are in decline, when spiritual aspiration has become weak, when virtues diminish so that vices become prominent, and when institutional leadership becomes corrupt — then civilization as a whole declines as materialistic ideologies fill the spiritual void, and humanity drifts and sinks and desperately awaits a new revelation. The darkest periods of the twentieth century — two world wars, financial and environmental crises, humanitarian atrocities — show the results of filling the moral-spiritual void with arrogant and materialistic ideologies. Such is the general condition of humanity today — adrift in the absence of a consciously embraced and divinely guided global civilization — though we can identify universal sources of inspiration and wisdom because new light has come into our world.

As we have tried to show, foundational religious and philosophical sources teach that we can choose to develop our higher nature, which makes us creative contributors to the institutions of a growing or reformed civilization. We can devise social systems that empower us individually and collectively. We can seek ever-higher dimensions of the spiritual and revelatory realm. We are fashioned for self-transcendence and for making the earth ever more heavenly. We have arrived at the point where our evolution can become intentional — whether approached biologically, psychosocially or spiritually. We live in a developmental, evolutionary and progressive universe, as shown both by the sequential scriptures of major religions and the discoveries of modern science. This seems to be the summary testimony of the world religions, the wisest philosophical observers of our human condition, and the methods and contents of the sciences. This view provides hopeful alternatives to the prevailing but fated perspective of secular materialism.

INTERPRETIVE SUMMARY: BAHÁ'Í TEACHINGS INTEGRATE MANY TRADITIONS ON HUMAN NATURE

To conclude, we attempt to state explicitly the most important questions addressed in, and arising from, this essay — providing very brief and clear responses that seem consistent with a sympathetic study of world religions and Western thought, especially as guided and interpreted by Bahá'í teachings. By this means, the most significant and suggestive principles of this study might be lifted up for consideration. Responses to key questions are written in italics.

Can we discern a common metaphysic in the scriptures of major religions? *Yes: authoritative Buddhist, Christian, Islamic and Bahá'í sources together paint a 'big picture' of a four-leveled interactive and developmental universe — the Divine or Ultimate realm, the Spiritual or Revelatory realm, the human realm, and the natural realm.* What place is assigned to human beings in the traditional religious worldview? *We are both in and above nature, poised for never-ending spiritual progress toward God.*

Are Greek Classical philosophy and Renaissance thought compatible with the way world religions depict human nature? *Yes: the greatest minds of ancient Greece and Renaissance Europe also depict the soul as occupying a privileged place in the cosmic hierarchy, linking the material and spiritual realms.* Are there any versions of modern philosophical anthropology, which complement both the religious worldview and traditional Western philosophy? *Yes: this is illustrated by Max Scheler's view that values have an objective pole, can be rank ordered, and that love and co-creativity are key descriptors of the human condition.* Is virtue ethics compatible with the traditional religious worldview, with Western classical thought, and with Scheler's philosophical anthropology? *Yes: virtue ethics have been taught by the major religious systems, and elaborated upon by Plato, Aristotle, Augustine, Aquinas, Ficino, Pico and Scheler.*

Do we have an essential human nature, and if so, what is it? *Yes: we are spiritually developing beings.* Do we have the limitations of animal nature? *Yes, but we are endowed with higher capacities.* Is there an immortal or eternal dimension to our nature? *Yes: we begin in the physical world and grow beyond it.* Can we become one with and identical to God? *No, but we can make indefinite progress in likeness to God.* What is the purpose of human life as individuals? *To love and know God, and to develop our virtues.* Are there key virtues in the Bahá'í Revelation? *Unity, peace, justice, love, wisdom, truthfulness, service, and covenantal obedience.*

Can we be fulfilled by material means alone? *No, but material means are essential for all progress.* Which are the primary human capacities? *The loving heart, the learning mind, and the noble will.* What is the Bahá'í understanding of the loving heart? *We are to love all God's children as He loves us.* What is the Bahá'í understanding of the learning mind? *We are to discover higher truth and make continual progress.* What is the Bahá'í understanding of the noble will? *We are to align our will with God's will, and to serve humanity.* What is the Bahá'í concept of the self? *Integration of body, mind and soul, both conscious and unconscious.* Is the self tripartite in some respects, but ultimately one? *Yes: this is another instance of unity-in-diversity.* Must we grow and develop in order to fulfill our human nature? *Yes, as is the case with all parts of creation.* What is humanity's collective purpose? *To fashion together an ev-*

er-advancing global civilization. Is a universal code of ethics possible and desirable? *Yes: it will aim toward unity, truth and service.*

Are Bahá'í teachings on the soul compatible with all the previously mentioned perspectives and fields? *It certainly appears so, for their overall theme is dynamic unity of all faith traditions, peoples and reputable fields of study and action.* What are the core themes of these fields and the Bahá'í faith as regards human nature? *Creative freedom, civilization-building and self-transcendence have been central themes and affirmations of world religions and philosophies of human nature.*

Do these themes provide a viable alternative to the prevailing worldview of secular materialism? *Yes, for they call us to re-fashion education, governance and commerce so as to foster the development of our higher moral-spiritual capacities.* Is there hope for humanity's future, and can we make of earth a heaven? *Yes: with our collective human effort and with God's guidance and grace.*

We close with guidance from Baha'u'llah, touching on several themes we have addressed and clothing them in language both poetic and injunctive.

Be an ornament to the countenance of truth,
> a crown to the brow of fidelity,
> a pillar of the temple of righteousness,
> a breath of life to the body of mankind,
> an ensign of the hosts of justice,
> a luminary above the horizon of virtue,
> a dew upon the soil of the human heart,
> an ark upon the ocean of knowledge,
> a sun in the heaven of bounty,
> a gem on the diadem of wisdom,
> a shining light in the firmament of thy generation,
> a fruit upon the tree of humility.[77]

---

[77] Gleanings 130.1, op cit.

Macrocriticism: A Comparison of Nicolai Berdyaev and Shoghi Effendi

ZAID LUNDBERG

Lund University, Lund (Sweden)

INTRODUCTORY OBSERVATIONS

Some perceptive authors[1] have recognized points of similarities between the writings of Nicolai Berdyaev[2] (1874–1948) and the corpus of the Bahá'í Faith but, as this paper will show, more work needs to be done in this field.

While Colin Chant states that Berdyaev is "the most widely read of the Russian religious philosophers,"[3] Oliver Fielding Clarke writes that Berdyaev "is *par excellence* the Christian philosopher."[4] Boris Jakim even refers to Berdyaev as "one of the greatest religious thinkers of the 20th century."[5] Yet, his biogra-

---

[1] Sergeev, Mikhail 1996. The Sophiology of Nicholas Berdyaev and the Bahá'í Teachings, presentation at the annual conference of the American Academy of Religion, New Orleans, November 1996. Kluge, Ian 2002. The Call into Being: Introduction to Bahá'í Existentialism. http://irfancolloquia.org/44/kluge_being, retrieved on July 4, 2018.

[2] Also spelled Nicolas or Nikolay, and Berdyayev or Berdiaev.

[3] S. Brown, D. Collinson, and R. Wilkinson eds. *Biographical Dictionary of Twentieth-Century Philosophers* (London: Routledge, 1996), 62.

[4] Oliver Fielding Clarke. *Introduction to Berdyaev* (London: Geoffrey Bles, 1950), 6, italics original.

[5] Boris Jakim. *A Brief Overview of Nikolai Berdyaev's Life and Works*, in N. Berdyaev The Meaning of History (CA: Semantron Press, 2009), 225. S. Brown, D. Collinson, and R. Wilkinson eds. *Biographical Dictionary of Twentieth- Century Philosophers* (London: Routledge, 1996) has an entry on Berdyaev.

phers have not noticed the recognition of Berdyaev as a major macrocritic of the 20th century.

Although *Encyclopedia Britannica* has an entry on Shoghi Rabbaní Effendi[6] (1897–1957) his "religious thinking" has not been acknowledged *outside* of the Bahá'í community. Even *within* the Bahá'í Community, Shoghi Effendi is mainly known as a religious *leader* ("Guardian of the Cause of God")[7] and his role as *a major macrocritic* of the 20th century has not been fully recognized.[8]

Before we delve into the field of macrocriticism a few words should be said about the similarities and differences of the lives of Berdyaev and Shoghi Effendi.

On a geopolitical and historical level Berdyaev and Shoghi Effendi both lived through crumbling and chaotic empires. Berdyaev was born during the 19th century Russian and Tsarist Empire and lived through its end during WWI and the Bolshevik Revolutions of 1917. Berdyaev further witnessed the establishment of the Soviet Union in 1922 and the reign of Stalinism until his death in Paris in 1948. Shoghi Effendi was born in 'Akka, Palestine, and witnessed not only the rule of the British Mandate in Palestine (1920) but also the end of the Ottoman Empire in 1922. Shoghi Effendi also experienced the dismantling of the British Mandate in 1948 and the creation of the State of Israel in 1948 until his sudden death in London in 1957.

Another similarity is that Berdyaev and Shoghi Effendi were both exiles. Berdyaev was imprisoned in 1898 for his participating in an anti-governmental student demonstration and in 1901–1902 he was exiled to Vologda. His final expulsion, however, was in 1922 when Lenin finally put him — together with 160 other

---

[6] Shoghi Effendi was born Shoghi Rabbaní. Effendi is a title of respect which means "Sir."

[7] Encyclopedia Britannica online, https://www.britannica.com/biography/Shoghi-Effendi-Rabbani, retrieved on July 4, 2018.

[8] For an in-depth discussion on this theme see my PhD dissertation — Zaid Lundberg. *Ominous Signs of End Times: Shoghi Effendi's Apocalyptic Jeremiad, Macro-critique, and Rhetorical Vision as Theodicy in the Age of Catastrophe* (Lund: Lund University Press, forthcoming).

intellectuals — on the "philosopher's ship." After that he lived two years in Berlin (where he established a Religio-Philosophic Academy) but eventually settled down in Paris in 1924 and where he lived during the rest of his life. Besides working for the YMCA and working as an editor for a journal in Paris, it is important to notice is that all his major works were written in exile. Shoghi Effendi, on the other hand, was never imprisoned, but he was a descendant of Iranian exiles (the Báb, Bahá'u'lláh and 'Abdu'l-Bahá) where the former had been imprisoned and executed and the latter had both been imprisoned and banished several times during their lives.[9] Although Shoghi Effendi had studied in Lebanon/Syria, and the UK, he traveled several times to Europe (mainly Switzerland and France) and traveled twice through the continent of Africa, but he never visited Iran.

Other similarities are that both Berdyaev and Shoghi Effendi were deeply religious and prolific writers. Linguistically too, Berdyaev spoke Russian, German and French and Shoghi Effendi was fluent in Persian, Arabic, English and French. Even though Berdyaev was a Marxist for a brief period he has was a critical Russian orthodox and refers to himself a "Christian socialist."[10] In his youth Shoghi Effendi was studying in different Christian schools[11] but he was literally raised in the Bahá'í Faith and, from 1922 until his death in 1957, he was its appointed leader. Although Berdyaev and Shoghi Effendi entered matrimony both their marriages remained childless.

In comparing Berdyaev and Shoghi Effendi it is also important to note some differences. Berdyaev was an intellectual academic,[12] a philosopher and a theologian. Shoghi Effendi, although

---

[9] E.g., W. S. Hatcher, & J. D. Martin. *The Bahá'í Faith: The Emerging Global Religion* (SF: Harper & Row, 1989), 28–56.

[10] Nicolai Berdyaev *The End of Our Time* (1924) (CA: Semantron Press, 2009), 204.

[11] In Haifa he attended Collège des Frères (a French Jesuit school) and in Beirut he studied at the Syrian Protestant College (later known as the American University of Beirut).

[12] Chair of Philosophy at the University of Moscow although he never earned an official degree.

educated at Oxford,[13] was primarily a full-time religious leader. Whereas Berdyaev wrote about 50 books and numerous articles, Shoghi Effendi only published two books.[14] Yet, it should be mentioned that Shoghi Effendi translated some of the major works by Bahá'u'lláh and the Báb[15] and, most importantly in the context of this paper, is that he wrote about 16000–26000 letters to Bahá'ís around the globe.[16] Some of these letters have subsequently been compiled and published as books.[17]

Yet, as this paper will show, Berdyaev and Shoghi Effendi were also major macro-critics of the 20th century and the main purpose of this paper is to show that their macro critique is not only comparable but also, in many respects, similar.

MACROCRITICISM

Macrocriticism is a neologism and an umbrella term for the following theoretical[18] areas of criticism: *Cultural* criticism, including concepts like "counter-culture"[19] and "cultural pessimism;"[20]

---

[13] Riaz Khadem Shoghi Effendi in Oxford (Oxford: George Ronald, 1999).

[14] *God Passes By* (1944) (Wilmette, IL: Bahá'í Publishing Trust, 1979) is the only book that Shoghi Effendi wrote in English. He also composed a shorter version of it in Persian, known as *Lawh-i-Qawm*.

[15] Morten Bergsmo (ed) *Studying the Writings of Shoghi Effendi* (Oxford: George Ronald, 1991), 29–30.

[16] Ibid, 25. These letters were privately addressed to individuals or collectively addressed to local, national ssemblies and Bahá'í communities.

[17] E.g., The Promised Day is Come (1941) (Wilmette, IL: Bahá'í Publishing Trust, 1980), which is about 100 pages in length, and The World Order of Baháá'u'lláh — Selected Letters (1929–36) (Wilmette, IL: Bahá'í Publishing Trust, 1991), which is a collection of major letters sent to North America.

[18] I state that these areas are "theoretical" since in practice, i.e., in the actual texts, these areas are intermingled.

[19] Theodor Roszak. *The Making of a Counter Culture: Reflections on the Technocratic Society and Its Youthful Opposition* (LA: University of California Press, 1968).

[20] Oliver Bennett. *Cultural Pessimism: Narratives of Decline in the Postmodern World* (Edinburgh: Edinburgh Press, 2001).

Social criticism;[21] and *Civilizational* criticism.[22] It also includes related areas such as *Anti-modernism;*[23] *Orientalism/Occidentalism;*[24]
Postcolonial criticism;[25] *Dystopianism;*[26] *Counter-Enlightenment;*[27]
Eco criticism[28] and *Gender* criticism.[29]In other words, macrocriticism is a field which looks at critique directed not only at *one*
aspect or dimension of a social entity (technology, politics, economics, ecology etc) but it includes *several* dimensions or critique
directed towards "society-at-large" or "the-world-at-large."

In my readings of both Berdyaev and Shoghi Effendi, and inspired by Kenneth Burke's concept of the "Pentad,"[30] I have divided the field of macrocriticism into five dimensions or clusters:

---

[21] Michael Walzer. *Interpretation and Social Criticism* (Cambridge, MA:
Harvard University Press, 1987), and *The Company of Critics: Social
Criticism and Political Commitment in the Twentieth Century* (NY: Basic
Books, 1988).

[22] John Zerzan. *Against Civilization: Readings and Reflections* (LA: Feral
House, 2005).

[23] T. J. Jackson. *Lears No Place of Grace: Antimodernism and the Transformation of American Culture*, 1880–1920 (Chicago: The University of
Chicago Press, 1983).

[24] E. W. Said. *Orientalism* (NY: Pantheon Books, 1978). I. Buruma, &
A. Margalit. *Occidentalism: A Short History of Anti-Westernism* (London:
Atlantic Books, 2004).

[25] B. J. Moore-Gilbert, G. Stanton, & W. Maley (eds). *Postcolonial Criticism*
(Harlow Essex: Longman, 1997).

[26] M. K. Booker. *The Dystopian Impulse in Modern Literature: Fiction as
Social Criticis*m (London: Greenwood Press, 1994).

[27] Isaiah Berlin. *Against the Current: Essays in the History of Ideas* (London:
Pimlico, 1979).

[28] C. Glotfelty & H. Fromm (eds). *The Ecocriticism Reader: Landmarks in
Literary Ecolog*y (London: The University of Georgia Press, 1996).

[29] Judith Spector (ed) Gender Studies: New Directions in Feminist Criticism
(OH: Bowling Green State University Popular Press, 1986). In this paper
I will focus only on Cultural, Social, and Civilizational criticism.

[30] Kenneth Burke. *A Grammar of Motives* (Berkeley: University of
California Press, 1945). Burke's "Pentad" is inspired from Dramatism and
includes the following five areas and questions: 1) scene (Where is the
act happening?), 2) act (What happened?), 3) agent (Who is involved in
the action?), 4) agency (How do the agents act?), and 5) purpose (Why
do the agents act?).

1) The World/Society/Civilization;[31]
2) History/The Age/Times;
3) Mankind/Humanity;
4) Progress/Science/Technology;
5) Ethics/Religion/Secularization.

This paper is delimited to dimensions 1, 2 and 5.[32]

THE WORLD/SOCIETY/CIVILIZATION

Although it should be clear that all dimensions or clusters of macrocriticism are intimately intertwined in the actual texts, the identification of five clusters is used here as a theoretical and heuristic device. For example, Berdyaev's expression "this doomed world of modern times"[33] and Shoghi Effendi's concept of a "New World Order" have both a temporal and spatial dimension. Yet, it is possible to locate passages in the writings of both Berdyaev and Shoghi Effendi where they directly criticize *the state* of the *world,* or *society*-at-large, or *civilization.* Sometimes they are more specific in their criticism, which they direct towards e.g., the West/East, certain continents, empires and countries. Berdyaev writes, for example, in 1923 of "the calamities which not only *Russia* but the whole of *Europe* and of *the whole world* have undergone."[34] In lengthier passage from the same year Berdyaev describes "The old worn-out world to which we can never go back" as a world of rationalist prophets, of individualism and Humanism, Liberalism and democratic theories, of imposing national monarchies and imperialist politics, of a monstrous economic system compounded of Industrialism and Capitalism, of vast technical apparatus, of exterior conquests and practical

---

[31] This dimension also includes such areas as continents and countries.
[32] For a more detailed description of these dimensions/clusters see my PhD dissertation.
[33] Nicolai Berdyaev. *The End of Our Time*, 78–79.
[34] Ibid, 75–76, italics added.

achievements; a world of unbridled and endless covetousness in its public life, of atheism and supreme disdain for the soul, and, at last, of Socialism, the end and crown of all contemporary history. We gladly echo the words of the revolutionary song, "Down with the old world!" — but we understand by that term this doomed world of modern times.[35]

In another passage Berdyaev writes that the "world is in confusion" and that it tends towards the construction of a spiritual order analogous to that of the Middle Ages. Decay precedes a middle age, and it is needful to mark the course of those elements that are dying and those that are coming to birth... Individualism, the "atomization" of society, the inordinate acquisitiveness of the world, indefinite over-population and the endlessness of people's needs, the lack of faith, the weakening of spiritual life, these and other are the causes which have contributed to build up that industrial capitalist system which has change the face of human life and broken its rhythm with nature. The power of the machine and the chronic "speeding-up" that it involves have created myths and phantoms and directed man's life towards these figments which, nevertheless, give an impression of being more real than realities... monstrous manufactories of useless things or of weapons for the destruction of life, in the ostentation of their luxury... The whole economic system of Capitalism is an offshoot of a devouring and overwhelming lust... It is the result of a secularization of economic life, and by it the hierarchical subordination of the material to the spiritual is inverted. The autonomy of economics has ended in their dominating the whole life of human societies: the worship of Mammon has become the determining force of the age.[36]

Berdyaev's critique of the world in these two passages are good examples of macrocritique since he enumerates not only *one* area of society but a very wide range of critique: individualism and humanism, liberalism, industrialism and capitalism, atheism,

---

[35] Ibid, 78–79.
[36] Ibid, 91–92.

secularization and the lack of faith, socialism, over-population, weapons of destruction, luxury etc. Although Berdyaev singles out a few political-economic systems above, he writes elsewhere *"All systems* of ideas and political and social forms throughout the world are going through a period of crisis. They are all in practice worn out and there is no longer anything that rouses the enthusiasm of civilized peoples."[37]

As early as 1923 Shoghi Effendi elaborates on the "Condition of the World" where he describes the world as being in a state of cataclysm. In another letter from the same year he writes of "world's evil plight" and "the ever-increasing confusion of the world, threatened as never before with disruptive forces, fierce rivalries, fresh commotions and grave disorder."[38] In the same compilation of letters Shoghi Effendi writes of "these days of world-encircling gloom, when the dark forces of nature, of hate, rebellion, anarchy and reaction are threatening the very stability of human society, when the most precious fruits of civilization are undergoing severe and unparalleled tests."[39]

In a letter of 1934 Shoghi Effendi writes, "The world is drawing nearer and nearer to a universal catastrophe which will mark the end of a bankrupt and of a fundamentally defective civilization."[40] In another passage from 1936 Shoghi Effendi writes:

> As we view the world around us, we are compelled to observe the manifold evidences of that universal fermentation which, in every continent of the globe and in every department of human life, be it religious, social, economic or political, is purging and reshaping humanity in anticipation of the Day when the wholeness of the human race will have been recognized and its unity

[37] Ibid, 200, italics added.
[38] Shoghi Effendi (1922–32) *Bahá'í Administration* (Wilmette, IL: Bahá'í Publishing Trust, 1974), 50.
[39] Ibid, 51.
[40] Shoghi Effendi. *The Light of Divine Guidance*, Vol. 1. (1922–39) (Hofheim-Langenhain: Bahá'í-Verlag, 1982), 53.

established. A twofold process, however, can be distinguished, each tending, in its own way and with an accelerated momentum, to bring to a climax the forces that are transforming the face of our planet.[41]

Like Berdyaev, Shoghi Effendi also states that the crisis of the world is not limited to a specific compartment, but it is truly macroscopic (global) and pervasive. Hence, he writes that it is in "every continent of the globe and in every department of human life" and that it also includes the "religious, social, economic or political."

Other passages in the writings of both Berdyaev and Shoghi Effendi testify to a critique towards specific continents, empires and countries. For example, Berdyaev states that "Europe is spending her strength extravagantly, she is exhausted"[42] and that "We are now taking part in the beginnings of the barbarization of Europe."[43] Similarly, Shoghi Effendi is highly critical towards especially the Qájar Dynasty in Iran and its "Unbridled Barbarism"[44] and the Ottoman Empire (which he calls "The Ottoman Ramshackle").[45] Shoghi Effendi,[46] and especially Berdyaev, also directs relentless critique towards Russia and the Soviet Union.[47]

Although Shoghi Effendi is generally praising especially N. America, he also highly critical towards its "excessive and enervating materialism" which is "now prevailing in their country"[48] and the "racial prejudice, the corrosion of which, for well-nigh a century, has bitten into the fiber, and attacked the whole social

---

[41] Shoghi Effendi. *The World Order of Baháá'u'lláh*, 169.
[42] Nicolai Berdyaev. *The End of Our Time*, 27.
[43] Ibid, 57–58.
[44] Shoghi Effendi. *Bahá'í Administration*, 133–134.
[45] Shoghi Effendi. *The Promised Day is Come*, 62.
[46] Shoghi Efendi. *Bahá'í Administration*, 160.
[47] Nicolai Berdyaev. *The End of Our Time*, 209–258.
[48] Shoghi Effendi (1939) *The Advent of Divine Justice* (Wilmette, IL: Bahá'í Publishing Trust, 1990), 16–17.

structure of American society."[49] He further criticizes N. America for its "corrupt and pleasure-seeking generation," "the deceitfulness and corruption that characterize the political life of the nation and of the parties and factions that compose it," and "the moral laxity and licentiousness which defile the character of a not inconsiderable proportion of its citizens."[50]

ETHICS/RELIGION/SECULARIZATION

This dimension of cluster of macrocriticism looks at the critique directed towards ethics/morality as well as critique directed towards religious *and* secular ideologies and institutions (or the process of secularization). Above it was stated that Berdyaev and Shoghi Effendi were deeply religious authors, yet it will be seen that they also direct sharp critique towards religious institutions. We will start by looking at Berdyaev's and Shoghi Effendi's critique towards ethics/morality, and then continue with their critique towards religion, secularization and secular ideologies.

In the spirit of macrocritique Berdyaev writes that "The decline and crisis of humanism are likewise manifest in the sphere of *moral life*" and that "There can be no shadow of doubt that we are living in an epoch marked by *the bankruptcy of that humanist morality* which had been the guiding light of modern history." But Berdyaev goes on to write "the close of the nineteenth and the beginning of the twentieth centuries [have] demonstrated its final collapse. The Great War in particular, and its lasting consequences, dealt a death-blow to its illusions."[51] Writing about the dehumanization and "the mechanization of human life, turning man into a machine" Berdyaev also writes, "This proves that the

---

[49] Ibid, 19.
[50] Ibid, 23.
[51] Nicolai Berdyaev (1923). *The Meaning of History* (CA: Semantron Press, 2009), 166, italics and clarification added.

whole of our social organism is afflicted with a terrible spiritual and *moral disease,* a truly bestial attitude of man to man."[52]

Similarly, Shoghi Effendi distinguishes between "The signs of moral downfall, as distinct from the evidences of decay in religious institutions." In this passage, entitled "Signs of Moral Downfall," Shoghi Effendi elaborates on "The perversion of human nature, the degradation of human conduct," and he goes on to write that when "the light of religion is quenched in men's hearts" then

> human character is debased, confidence is shaken, the nerves of discipline are relaxed, the voice of human conscience is stilled, the sense of decency and shame is obscured, conceptions of duty, of solidarity, of reciprocity and loyalty are distorted, and the very feeling of peacefulness, of joy and of hope is gradually extinguished.[53]

Shoghi Effendi continues in this passage to enumerate several areas of macro-criticism, which are all pertinent to the ethical dimension (or the effects of irreligious life):

> The recrudescence of religious intolerance, of racial animosity, and of patriotic arrogance; the increasing evidences of selfishness, of suspicion, of fear and of fraud; the spread of terrorism, of lawlessness, of drunkenness and of crime; the unquenchable thirst for, and the feverish pursuit after, earthly vanities, riches and pleasures; the weakening of family solidarity; the laxity in parental control; the lapse into luxurious indulgence; the irresponsible attitude towards marriage and the consequent rising tide of divorce; the degeneracy of art and music, the infection of literature, and the corruption of the press; the extension of the influence and activities of those "prophets of decadence" who advocate

---

[52] Nicolai Berdyaev (1934). *The Fate of Man in the Modern World* (CA: Semantron Press, 2009), 81, italics added.
[53] Shoghi Effendi. *The World Order of Bahá'u'lláh,* 187.

companionate marriage, who preach the philosophy of
nudism, who call modesty an intellectual fiction, who
refuse to regard the procreation of children as the sacred and primary purpose of marriage, who denounce
religion as an opiate of the people, who would, if given
free rein, lead back the human race to barbarism, chaos,
and ultimate extinction.[54]

When it comes to a critique of religion Berdyaev writes,
"Our time is a time of spiritual decadence, not of ascent"[55] and
that modern man "has lost his eternal spiritual bearings and so
there he is today — a prey to the devastating forces of our time."[56]
Berdyaev even states, "Man without God is no longer man."[57]

In several places in his writings Berdyaev refers to the "decay-
ing West" as "a soulless and atheistic civilization,"[58] that "Modern
capitalist civilization is essentially atheistic and hostile to the idea
of God" and that "The crime of killing God must be laid at its
[modern capitalist civilization] door rather than at that of revolutionary socialism."[59]

In a lengthier passage Berdyaev clarifies the difference between the atheism of socialism and capitalism:

The popularity of pragmatism in America, the classical
land of civilization, need cause no surprise. Socialism,
on the other hand, repudiated pragmatical religion; but
it pragmatically defends atheism as being more useful
for the development of life forces and worldly satisfaction of the larger masses of mankind. But the pragmatical and utilitarian approach of Capitalism had been the
real source of atheism and spiritual bankruptcy.[60]

---

[54] Ibid, 187–188.
[55] Nicolai Berdyaev. *The End of Our Time*, 15.
[56] Ibid, 45.
[57] Ibid, 55.
[58] Nicolai Berdyaev. *The Meaning of History*, 207, 208, 218.
[59] Ibid, 218, clarification added.
[60] Ibid, 219.

In a later work Berdyaev writes about the "wolf-like life of capitalist society" and "the false civilization of capitalism."[61] Besides criticizing socialism and capitalism Berdyaev is critical towards "all Communists, all Fascists, all National-Socials and all others possessed by the demon of the will to power" since "In the dictatorial states, fascist or communist, there is a development of thirst for power and violence, a desire for bloodshed and cruelty."[62] Yet, it is important to notice that Berdyaev states that

> From the Christian point of view, Hitlerism [Nazism] is more dangerous than Communism, since the latter struggles openly and directly against Christianity as against all religion, while Hitlerism demands a violent deformation of Christianity from within, altering the Christian faith itself in favour of the racialist theory and the dictatorship of the Third Reich.[63]

In addition to writing about socialism, capitalism, fascism and Nazism, Berdyaev also writes about "The pagan tendencies of our times."[64]

On the one hand Berdyaev writes that "Christianity is the greatest of religions"[65] and that "Christianity has gone on living in man in a secularized form" and "it is she [Christianity] who has kept him from disintegrating completely."[66] On the other hand Berdyaev also writes about "the failure of Christianity" which is not "the failure of God, as the adversaries of Christianity maintain, but of man."[67] Thus, he writes, "Europe has not made its Christianity real, but has distorted and betrayed it."[68] In a later work Berdyaev writes, "now Christianity, in its old age, is old

---

[61] Nicolai Berdyaev. *The Fate of Man in the Modern World*, 15–16, 18.

[62] Ibid, 45, 47. See also pp. 60–64.

[63] Ibid, 102, clarification added.

[64] Nicolai Berdyaev. *The End of Our Time*, 36.

[65] Nicolai Berdyaev. *The Meaning of History*, 72.

[66] Nicolai Berdyaev. *The End of Our Time*, 27, clarification added.

[67] Nicolai Berdyaev. *The Meaning of History*, 200–201.

[68] Nicolai Berdyaev. *The End of Our Time*, 61.

and burdened, with a long history in which Christians have often sinned and betrayed their ideal."[69] He continues to write that "All too often Christianity has been anti-human" and that "The religion of love and mercy has been transformed into a proclamation of cruel and relentless attitudes toward men."[70]

Whereas Berdyaev writes of spirituality/religion in general and of Christianity in particular, Shoghi Effendi writes of religion in general, and he specifically writes about the decline of Christianity *and* Islam. As an example of the first case Shoghi Effendi writes of "an unbelieving world"[71] and of "the decline of religion as a social force, of which the deterioration of religious institutions is but an external phenomenon, is chiefly responsible for so grave, so conspicuous an evil."[72]

In that same work Shoghi Effendi writes that "the forces of irreligion, of a purely materialistic philosophy, of unconcealed paganism have been unloosed, are now spreading, and, by consolidating themselves, are beginning to invade some of the most powerful Christian institutions of the western world, no unbiased observer can fail to admit."[73]

Shoghi Effendi thus seems to be in agreement with Berdyaev of the resurging paganism. Shoghi Effendi continues to write, "the chill of irreligion creeps relentlessly over the soul of mankind"[74] and that the "forces of irreligion are weakening the moral fiber and undermining the foundations of individual morality."[75] Hence Shoghi Effendi sees an intimate relation between ethics/morality and religion. In another work and in a lengthy passage, Shoghi Effendi writes of the results of "A world, dimmed by the steadily dying-out light of religion" as

---

[69] Nicolai Berdyaev. *The Fate of Man in the Modern World*, 23.
[70] Ibid, 122.
[71] Shoghi Effendi. *Bahá'í Administration*, 34.
[72] Shoghi Effendi. *The World Order of Baháá'u'lláh*, 186.
[73] Ibid, 180.
[74] Shoghi Effendi. The Advent of Divine Justice, 25.
[75] Ibid, 29.

heaving with the explosive forces of a blind and trium-
phant nationalism; scorched with the fires of pitiless
persecution, whether racial or religious; deluded by the
false theories and doctrines that threaten to supplant
the worship of God and the sanctification of His laws;
enervated by a rampant and brutal materialism; disintegrating through the corrosive influence of moral and
spiritual decadence; and enmeshed in the coils of economic anarchy and strife — such is the spectacle presented to men's eyes, as a result of the sweeping changes which this revolutionizing Force, as yet in the initial
stage of its operation, is now producing in the life of the
entire planet.[76]

More specifically, Shoghi Effendi writes of Islam and
Christianity. For example he writes of "The Decline of Islam"[77]
and the "Collapse of Islam"[78] as well as the "Deterioration of
Christian Institutions."[79] In Islam this process includes both
"The collapse of the power of the Shi'ih hierarchy"[80] as well as
"The overthrow of the Sultanate and the Caliphate, the twin
pillars of Sunni Islam."[81] With regard to Christianity Shoghi
Effendi writes of the "de-Christianization of the masses," "a
notable decline in the authority, the prestige and power of the
Church"[82] and that the "Christian Religion... has now fallen into
such a state of impotence."[83] Continuing to write about "the rapid dechristianization of the masses in many Christian countries"
Shoghi Effendi surveys "the fortunes of Christian ecclesiastical
orders" as follows:

---

[76] Ibid, 47.
[77] Shoghi Effendi. *Bahá'í Administration*, 169.
[78] Shoghi Effendi. *The World Order of Baháá'u'lláh*, 97.
[79] Ibid, 102.
[80] Ibid, 172.
[81] Ibid, 173.
[82] Ibid, 182.
[83] Ibid, 185.

to appreciate the steady deterioration of their influence, the decline of their power, the damage to their prestige, the flouting of their authority, the dwindling of their congregations, the relaxation of their discipline, the restriction of their press, the timidity of their leaders, the confusion in their ranks, the progressive confiscation of their properties, the surrender of some of their most powerful strongholds, and the extinction of other ancient and cherished institutions.[84]

Shoghi Effendi is especially critical towards Christianity during WWII:

What a sorry spectacle of impotence and disruption does this fratricidal war, which Christian nations are waging against Christian nations — Anglicans pitted against Lutherans, Catholics against Greek Orthodox, Catholics against Catholics, and Protestants against Protestants — in support of a so-called Christian civilization, offer to the eyes of those who are already perceiving the bankruptcy of the institutions that claim to speak in the name, and to be the custodians, of the Faith of Jesus Christ![85]

Writing on the phenomenon of secularization Berdyaev writes of "the secularization of society at large."[86] More elaborately he states "Science, art, political and economic life, society and culture now become autonomous" and that this "processes of differentiation is synonymous with the secularization of human culture. Even religion is secularized. Art and science, the state and society, enter the modern world along a secular path." Continuing on this theme Birdie writes:

The bonds holding together the various spheres of social and cultural life now become relaxed, and these spheres

[84] Shoghi Effendi. *The Promised Day is Come*, 103–104.
[85] Ibid, 105.
[86] Nicolai Berdyaev. *The End of Our Time*, 84.

become independent. That is the essential character of modern history. The transition from mediaeval to modern history is synonymous with one from the divine to the human aspects of the world, from the divine depths, interior concentration and the inner core, to an exterior cultural manifestation. This divorce from the spiritual depths, in which man's forces had been stored and to which they had been inwardly bound, is accompanied not only by their liberation, but by their passage from the depths to the periphery and the surface of human life, from the mediaeval religious to secular culture; and it implies the transference of the centre of gravity from the divine depths to purely human creation. The spiritual bond with the centre of life grows gradually weaker. Modern history therefore conducts European man along a path, which removes him ever further from the spiritual centre. It is the path of man's free experience and the trial of his creative forces.[87]

In a later work Berdyaev writes that "Apostasy from the Christian faith, abandonment of spiritual principles and disregard of the spiritual ends of life, must necessarily lead first to the stage called Capitalism and then to the stage called Socialism."[88]

Although it was seen above that Berdyaev is more positive towards socialism than capitalism he also writes that "The worship of Mammon instead of God is a characteristic of Socialism as well as of Capitalism"[89] and that "The socialist state... is a government by Satan."[90] To further clarify Berdyaev's view on communism he describes it as "anti-individualist, anti-liberal, anti-democratic, anti-humanist," that it is "hierarchical in its way; it denies modern formal liberties and equalities and builds up its

---

[87] Nicolai Berdyaev. *The Meaning of History*, pp. 130–131. See also Berdyaev's *The Fate of Man in the Modern World,* 70.

[88] Nicolai Berdyaev. *The End of Our Time*, 192.

[89] Ibid, 192.

[90] Ibid, 191.

satanist order of subordination," and that it is "a false church, a communion of lies."[91]

Shoghi Effendi similarly, writes of "the slow and hidden process of secularisation" that is "invading many a government department under the courageous guidance of the Governors of outlying provinces" and he continues to state that "in all of these a discerning eye can easily discover the symptoms that augur well for a future that is sure to witness the formal and complete separation of Church and State."[92] In a later work Shoghi Effendi writes of "the wave of secularisation,"[93] "the rising tide of secularism"[94] and the "menace of secularism"

> that has attacked Islam and is undermining its remaining institutions, that has invaded Persia, has penetrated into India, and raised its triumphant head in Turkey, has already manifested itself in both Europe and America, and is, in varying degrees, and under various forms and designations, challenging the basis of every established religion, and in particular the institutions and communities identified with the Faith of Jesus Christ. It would be no exaggeration to say that we are moving into a period, which the future historian will regard as one of the most critical in the history of Christianity.[95]

Thus, it is important to notice that although both Berdyaev and Shoghi Effendi are writing of the social pervasiveness and its global spread of secularisation, Shoghi Effendi states that it is challenging not only Christianity and Islam but "the basis of *every* established religion" and he also writes of "a world... whose religious systems have become anemic and lost their virtue."[96] It is because these processes that Shoghi Effendi also writes

---

[91] Ibid, 110.
[92] Shoghi Effendi. *Bahá'í Administration*, 148.
[93] Shoghi Effendi. *God Passes By*, 229–230.
[94] Shoghi Effendi. *The World Order of Baháá'u'lláh*, 186.
[95] Ibid, 181.
[96] Ibid, 195.

that "the lights of religion are fading out,"[97] and that "the bright flame of religion is fast dying out."[98] More specifically, Shoghi Effendi sees a relationship between secularism and irreligion in that "flagrant secularism" is "the direct offspring of irreligion."[99] In the same work Shoghi Effendi continues to write of "irreligion and its monstrous offspring" as a "triple curse that oppresses the soul of mankind in this day... responsible for the ills which are so tragically besetting it. . ."[100] Shoghi Effendi identifies this triple curse as "The chief idols in the desecrated temple of mankind" which are

> none other than the triple gods of Nationalism, Racialism and Communism, at whose altars governments and peoples, whether democratic or totalitarian, at peace or at war, of the East or of the West, Christian or Islamic, are, in various forms and in different degrees, now worshiping. Their high priests are the politicians and the worldly-wise, the so-called sages of the age; their sacrifice, the flesh and blood of the slaughtered multitudes; their incantations outworn shibboleths and insidious and irreverent formulas; their incense, the smoke of anguish that ascends from the lacerated hearts of the bereaved, the maimed, and the homeless.[101]

In the same work Shoghi Effendi enumerates another set of forces as "the forces of nationalism, paganism, secularism and racialism."[102] Berdyaev also writes that "Racialism is worse than communism since its ideology includes eternal hatred; communism, on the other hand, decrees hatred as a way. . ."[103] and he further writes, "Racialism is a ruder form of material-

---

[97] Shoghi Effendi, *The Advent of Divine Justice*, 29.
[98] Shoghi Effendi. *The Promised Day is Come*, 16.
[99] Ibid, 16.
[100] Ibid, 114.
[101] Ibid, 114.
[102] Ibid, 106.
[103] Nicolai Berdyaev. *The Fate of Man in the Modern World*, 29.

ism."[104] Berdyaev also writes that "Modern nationalism bears marks of bestial inhumanity," that "nationalism and racialism are worse than communism" and that "modern Nationalism means the dehumanisation and bestialization of human societies."[105]

Thus, whereas Berdyaev identifies communism and capitalism as responsible for the rise of materialism and atheism (and other social ills) he clearly sees capitalism, Nazism, nationalism and racialism as greater evils. Yet, Berdyaev ultimately admits that "The roots of all this must be sought in the plane of the spiritual, in the crisis of Christianity and of religious consciousness in general, in the decline of spirituality."[106] Thus, according to Berdyaev "Dechristianization led to dehumanization."[107]

Although Shoghi Effendi writes of "unbridled capitalism"[108] he also states, "There is nothing in the teachings against some kind of capitalism."[109] Another difference is that whereas Berdyaev is highly critical towards both fascism and Nazism, Shoghi Effendi just mentions them in passing.[110]

Their macrocritical emphasis is thus somewhat different but both Berdyaev and Shoghi Effendi identify the following modern phenomena as conjointly evil and responsible for, or as manifestations of, social ills or crises: nationalism, racism, paganism, secularism/atheism and communism (capitalism).

Despite all the critique towards religion and, particularly Christianity, Berdyaev also writes that "There is no possibility of a perfect society and a perfect culture without... real spiritual life,

---

[104] Ibid, 98.
[105] Ibid, 21, 83. See also p. 107.
[106] Ibid, 109.
[107] Ibid, 126.
[108] Shoghi Effendi (1947–57). *Citadel of Faith* (Wilmette, IL: Bahá'í Publishing Trust, 1980), 154.
[109] Shoghi Effendi qtd in Helen Hornby (ed) *Lights of Guidance: A Bahá'í Reference File* (New Delhi: Bahá'í Publishing Trust, 1994), 550.
[110] Shoghi Effendi. *Citadel of Faith*, 36–37.

that is, without a religious rebirth."[111] Thus, Berdyaev believes that "Christianity is coming back to its pre-Constantinian situation... that is the position in which the Russian Orthodox Church is already" while admitting that "It may well be that Christians are being called to go further back yet, to the catacombs, and from there to conquer the world anew."[112] Berdyaev consequently writes that "modern history" on the one hand "draws to an end," while "giving place to a new era" which he refers to as "a new Christian renaissance."[113] Thus, Berdyaev writes that "Only Christianity holds the resolution to the problem of the relationship of man and God, only in Christ is the image of man preserved, only within the Christian spirit are there created both society and culture, non-destructive to man."[114] In a later work Berdyaev states that "Only in the second coming of Christ, in the form of Christ, the coming One, will the perfection of man appear in its fullness."[115] In this context of Christian renaissance it is significant that Berdyaev also schematically portrays "four periods or states in man's historical destiny" as "barbarism, culture, civilization and religious transfiguration."[116]

Rather than looking *back* to a pristine state of Christianity, or looking *forward* to the Second Coming of Christ, Shoghi Effendi views the Bahá'í Faith "in the course of its sure yet toilsome march towards the salvation of the world"[117] and he endorses Bahá'u'lláh 's (the prophet-founder of the Bahá'í Faith) claim as *the fulfillment* of the Second Coming of Christ,

> the Judge, the Lawgiver and Redeemer of all mankind, as the Organizer of the entire planet, as the Unifier of the

---

[111] Nicolai Berdyaev. *The End of Our Time*, 199.

[112] Ibid, 201.

[113] Nicolai Berdyaev. *The Meaning of History*, 181.

[114] Nicolai Berdyaev (1932). The Spiritual Condition of the Contemporary World, Journal Put', Sept. No. 35: 68.

[115] Nicolai Berdyaev (1941). *The Beginning and the End* (NY: Harper Torchbook, 1957), 250.

[116] Ibid, 222.

[117] Shoghi Effendi. *Bahá'í Administration*, 60.

children of men, as the Inaugurator of the long-awaited millennium, as the Originator of a new "Universal Cycle," as the Establisher of the Most Great Peace, as the Fountain of the Most Great Justice, as the Proclaimer of the coming of age of the entire human race, as the Creator of a new World Order, and as the Inspirer and Founder of a world civilization.[118]

HISTORY/THE AGE/TIMES

This final dimension or cluster of macrocriticism is critique directed towards the *Zeitgeist* or the Spirit of the Age. It is significant that both Berdyaev and Shoghi Effendi refer to the epochal changes by using *volcanic* metaphors. For example, in 1923 — four years after WWI and six years after the Russian revolutions — Berdyaev writes that:

> There can be little doubt, I think, that not only Russia but Europe and the world as a whole are now entering upon *a catastrophic period* of their development. We are living at a *time of immense crisis,* on *the threshold* of *a new era.* The very structure or historical development has suffered a profound change. It is now essentially different from what it was prior to the World War and the Russia and the European revolutions. This change can only be regarded as catastrophic. *Volcanic sources* have opened in the historical substrata. Everything is tottering, and we have the impression of a particularly intense and acute movement of historical forces.[119]

In 1924 Berdyaev writes in a similar vein that "It would indeed seem that *the old, secular foundations of the West are trembling,* things apparently stabilized by use and wont are shifting.

---

[118] Shoghi Effendi. *God Passes By*, 93–94.
[119] Nicolai Berdyaev. *The Meaning of History*, 1–3, italics added. See also p. 168 and Nicolai Berdyaev. *The End of Our Time*, 12.

Nowhere and in no single matter is solid earth felt underfoot: *we are on volcanic ground* and any eruption is possible, material or spiritual."[120]

A year before (1923) Shoghi Effendi writes that:

> Four years of unprecedented warfare and *world cata-clysms* followed by another four years of bitter disap-pointment and suffering, have stirred deeply the con-science of mankind, and opened the eyes of an unbeliev-ing world to the Power of the Spirit that alone can cure its sicknesses, heal its wounds.[121]

Berdyaev continues to write in 1924, "the world is undergo-ing *a gigantic revolution;* not the communist revolution which, at bottom is everything that is most reactionary, a mess of all *the rotten elements of the old world,* but a true spiritual revolution. To call to a new middle age is a call to this spiritual revolution, to a complete renewal of consciousness."[122] In 1931 Shoghi Effendi writes of *"that transformation of unparalleled majesty and scope* which humanity is in this age bound to undergo. That the forces of *a world catastrophe* can alone precipitate such *a new phase* of human thought is, alas, becoming increasingly apparent."[123] After WWII, in 1947, Shoghi Effendi writes of "The *steadily deepening crisis* which mankind is traversing, on the morrow of the severest ordeal it has yet suffered, and the attendant tribulations and com-motions which *a travailing age* must necessarily experience, as a prelude to the birth of the *new World Order,* destined to rise upon the ruins of *a tottering civilization...*"[124]

Note that although Berdyaev and Shoghi Effendi write that "everything is tottering" or that civilization is defective, bank-rupt, and tottering, that it is "a time of immense crisis" or "a "steadily deepening crisis," a "gigantic revolution," and a "univer-

---

[120] Nicolai Berdyaev. *The End of Our Time,* 12, italics added.
[121] Shoghi Effendi. *Bahá'í Administration,* 34–35, italics added.
[122] Nicolai Berdyaev. *The End of Our Time,* 80, italics added.
[123] Shoghi Effendi. *The World Order of Baháá'u'lláh,* 45, italics added.
[124] Shoghi Effendi. *Citadel of Faith,* 29, italics added.

sal catastrophe," they are also in agreement that humanity, and the whole world, is entering a "threshold of a new era" or a "new World Order." These two processes, one destructive (the old, death) and one creative (the new, birth) are seen not as excluding or contradictory but as parallel and simultaneous phenomena.

Both Berdyaev and Shoghi Effendi argue that the current modern phase of history is *transitional.* Berdyaev describes it above that "We are living at a time of immense crisis, on the threshold of a new era" and Shoghi Effendi writes that "this Age of Transition" and its tribulations "are the precursors of that Era of blissful felicity."[125] Similarly, both Berdyaev and Shoghi Effendi utilize the metaphor of darkness/light in connection with the ages. Berdyaev writes for example that "we have passed from an era of light to an era of darkness"[126] and "Now night is on us. We are going into a period of senility and decay."[127] Similarly, Shoghi Effendi writes of "that turbulent Age, into the outer fringes of whose darkest phase we are now beginning to enter."[128]

It is important to notice that Both Berdyaev and Shoghi Effendi synoptically view the current phase of history as analogous to that of the fall of the Roman Empire and the beginning of the Middle Ages. For example, Berdyaev writes that "Our age resembles that of the fall of the Roman Empire, the failure and drying-up of Greco-Roman culture. . ."[129] and that "our epoch is the end of modern times and the beginning of a new middle age."[130] Berdyaev does not see this as a "renaissance but the dark beginnings of a middle age, and that we have got to pass through a new civilized barbarism."[131]

Berdyaev continues to write in 1924 "The beginning of *this new era* was marked by a general barbarization" and that:

---

[125] Shoghi Effendi. *The World Order of Baháʼuʼlláh*, 171.

[126] Nicolai Berdyaev. *The End of Our Time*, 70.

[127] Ibid, 57–58.

[128] Shoghi Effendi. *The World Order of Baháʼuʼlláh*, 171.

[129] Nicolai Berdyaev. *The End of Our Time*, 57–58.

[130] Ibid, 69.

[131] Ibid, 33.

the whole historical order that had built up the past was overrun by a torrent of disordered forces. And here we may well remind ourselves that the most terrible wars and revolutions, *wrecking of civilizations, fall of empires*, are not due solely to man's will but are also in a measure the work of divine providence. *Our age is like that, which saw the passing of the ancient world.* [132]

Ten years later (1934) Shoghi Effendi writes in a similar vein and asks the following:

Might we not look upon the momentous happenings which, in the course of the past twenty years, have so deeply agitated every continent of the earth, as ominous signs simultaneously proclaiming *the agonies of a disintegrating civilization*... the signs of an impending catastrophe, *strangely reminiscent of the Fall of the Roman Empire in the West,* which threatens to engulf the whole structure of present-day civilization... a tumult which will grow in scope and in intensity as the implications of this constantly evolving Scheme are more fully understood and its ramifications more widely extended over the surface of the globe. [133]

Notice that both Berdyaev and Shoghi Effendi write of "a torrent of disordered forces" or "signs of an impending catastrophe," and the wrecking of civilizations" and "the agonies of a disintegrating civilization." External barbaric tribes do not — like the Roman Empire — bring about the wrecking and disintegration of modern civilization but it is *civilization itself*, which is barbaric. Thus, both authors view not only the age but also the current civilization as highly dysfunctional, obsolete and ultimately dying.

---

[132] Nicolai Berdyaev. *The End of Our Time*, 74, italics added. See also pp. 144, 155.

[133] Shoghi Effendi. *The World Order of Baháá'u'lláh*, 155, italics added.

Consequently, both Berdyaev and Shoghi Effendi see "this constantly evolving Scheme" as part of a greater historical cycle. Berdyaev, for example, writes of "the destinies of peoples, societies, cultures," and that "they all pass through the clear-cut stages of *birth, infancy, adolescence, maturity, efflorescence, old age, decay* and *death.*"[134] Berdyaev hence consider peoples and societies as "living organisms" that exist "within the framework of history," that they "are doomed to whither, decay and dies as soon as their efflorescence is past," that "No great culture has been immune from decadence" and that "Every great national society and culture has been subject to this process of decay and death."[135]

Similarly, Shoghi Effendi writes of

The long ages of *infancy* and *childhood*, through which the human race had to pass, have receded into the background. Humanity is now experiencing the commotions invariably associated with the most turbulent stage of its evolution, the stage of *adolescence*, when the impetuosity of *youth* and its vehemence reach their climax, and must gradually be superseded by the calmness, the wisdom, and the *maturity* that characterize the stage of *manhood*. Then will the human race reach that stature of ripeness, which will enable it to acquire all the powers and capacities upon which its ultimate development must depend.[136]

Although both authors include the stages of infancy, adolescence, and maturity, only Berdyaev includes in this scheme birth, efflorescence, old age, decay and death.

What is then, the goal of the next stage or age? Here again, both Berdyaev and Shoghi Effendi seem to be in agreement. Berdyaev writes that "We are entering an epoch which at many points makes one think of the age of Hellenic universalism," and

---

[134] Nicolai Berdyaev. *The Meaning of History*, 194, italics added.

[135] Ibid, 194.

[136] Shoghi Effendi. *The World Order of Baháʼuʼlláh*, 117, italics added.

65

although there been previous "attempts at world-unification," he continues to write that

> Today the organization of each people affects the state of the whole world; what happens in Russia has repercussions in every country and upon every race. There has never before been such a close contact between the Eastern and Western worlds, which have lived so markedly separate. Civilization is ceasing to be European and becoming "of the world": Europe will have to renounce her pretension to a monopoly of culture.[137]

Berdyaev continues in the same work to write of "The modern world, rent by the violent quarrels of countries, classes, and individuals, prone to suspicion and hate," and yet that it "is drawn from every side towards a universal unification, to a conquest over that national exclusivism which has been responsible for the fall of nations." Thus, he continues to write of "if we examine deeply enough there certainly can be discerned a stirring towards a world-wide unification more vast than a unified Europe."[138]

Similar ideas of "globalization" can be found in later writings were Berdyaev writes, "Only progress in the direction of lessening sovereignty of national states and toward a world-federation of peoples will save us. . ." and "Along the bursting forth of militant Nationalism we see the universalization of mankind."[139]

Similar pioneering ideas of "globalization" can also been seen in the early writings of Shoghi Effendi.[140] In a chapter entitled "The Goal of the New World Order" Shoghi Effendi refers to "political and economic unification of the world" as "a principle that

---

[137] Nicolai Berdyaev. *The End of Our Time*, 98.

[138] Ibid, 99–100.

[139] Nicolai Berdyaev. *The Fate of Man in the Modern World*, 107, 108.

[140] For a more detailed discussion on Shoghi Effendi and Globalization see Zaid Lundberg 'Global Claims, Global Aims: An Analysis of Shoghi Effendi's *The World Order of Bahá'u'lláh*,' in M. Warburg (ed) *Bahá'í and Globalisation* (Aarhus: Aarhus Press, 2005).

has been increasingly advocated in recent times" but he continues to write that "the unification of mankind in this age" is part of "God's divinely appointed scheme." Shoghi Effendi continues to write that "It is towards this goal — the goal of a new World Order, Divine in origin, all-embracing in scope, equitable in principle, challenging in its features — that a harassed humanity must strive."[141] In a later letter Shoghi Effendi writes of "the political unification of the Eastern and Western Hemispheres," but he views this process as a prelude to "the emergence of a world government, and the establishment of the Lesser Peace."[142]

In a more elaborate way Shoghi Effendi describes the goal of the Bahá'í Faith "is none other but the achievement of this organic and spiritual unity of the whole body of nations" which is "signalizing... the coming of age of the entire human race." Shoghi Effendi continues to state that the unification of mankind is "marking the last and highest stage in the stupendous evolution of man's collective life on this planet" and that

> The emergence of a world community, the consciousness of world citizenship, the founding of a world civilization and culture — all of which must synchronize with the initial stages in the unfoldment of the Golden Age of the Bahá'í Era — should, by their very nature, be regarded, as far as this planetary life is concerned, as the furthermost limits in the organization of human society.[143]

Although Shoghi Effendi is writing in 1941 that the present state of the world and "indeed even its immediate future, is dark, distressingly dark," he continues to write, "Its distant future, however, is radiant, gloriously radiant — so radiant that no eye can visualize it."[144] Thus, it should be clear that despite their se-

---

[141] Shoghi Effendi. *The World Order of Baháá'u'lláh*, 33.
[142] Shoghi Effendi. *Citadel of Faith*, 25.
[143] Shoghi Effendi. *The World Order of Baháá'u'lláh*, 163.
[144] Shoghi Effendi. *The Promised Day is Come*, 116.

vere macrocritique, Berdyaev and Shoghi Effendi are both ultimately optimistic about the future collective life of humanity on
this planet.

CONCLUSIONS

The main purpose of this paper was to portray and compare
Berdyaev and Shoghi Effendi as major macrocritics of the 20th
century. I have thus introduced the novel concept of macrocriticism and used three dimensions of their macrocritique: 1) The
World/Society/Civilization; 2) Ethics/Religion/Secularisation;
and 3) History/The Age/Times. From the passages quoted and
examined it is clear that not only do Berdyaev and Shoghi Effendi
direct severe critique within all three dimensions, but also their
criticisms are also very similar.

In addition, both authors also portray a revival of religion/
spirituality beyond the current secular, chaotic and critical phase
of history. Berdyaev puts his hopes on a Christian renaissance
or the Second Coming of Christ. Shoghi Effendi believes in the
Messianic claims of Bahá'u'lláh and the present and future re-
demptive role of the Bahá'í Faith.

Finally, even though both authors reveal a highly critical picture of an obsolete and dying civilization or era, they simultaneously depict the birth of an emerging *global* civilization or era
beyond the cataclysmic crises of dysfunctional nationalist states.

The Concept of Nature in Bahá'í Philosophy[1]

JEAN-MARC LEPAIN

Independent scholar

Bahá'í philosophy, also named Divine Philosophy by 'Abdu'l-Bahá, is called to fulfil an essential role in the intellectual development of the Bahá'í Faith similar to theology in Christianity and Islamic philosophy in Islam. Within Bahá'í philosophy, philosophy of nature occupies a prominent place, as it combines metaphysics with philosophy of science and provides the foundations on which all other branches of Bahá'í philosophy will develop. After defining what philosophy of nature is in relation to philosophy of science and metaphysics, we will show that definitions and functions of nature that can be identified in the Bahá'í writings cannot be understood without reference to what we call the metaphysical framework of Bahá'í philosophy and its accompanying implicit ontology.

PHILOSOPHY OF NATURE WITHIN THE FRAMEWORK OF BAHÁ'Í PHILOSOPHY

We have suggested in some other works that Bahá'í philosophy can be divided into three main branches: (a) the philosophy of

---

[1] This paper is made of some extracts of a much longer paper entitled "Bahá'í philosophy of nature and its metaphysical framework."

the human person (covering topics such as anthropology, psychology, sociology, political science, etc. as well as the principles of our spiritual development); (b) the philosophy of nature (describing both the way in which the cosmos works and its finality and meaning); and (c) the philosophy of divine revelation (expressing how God communicates with humankind and how to interpret the Holy Writings).[2] As a consequence, philosophy of nature should be seen as a fundamental constituent of Bahá'í philosophy.

PHILOSOPHY OF NATURE AND PHILOSOPHY OF SCIENCE

Philosophy of nature plays the same role in Bahá'í philosophy as philosophy of science in the contemporary western philosophic tradition. It is therefore important to understand the differences between the two approaches. Most philosophers of science view their principal activity as the analysis of the method of enquiry used in the various sciences. They assume that science exists as a unified human activity based on a common purpose and an objective method with the aim of providing a comprehensive description of nature. However, they consider the question of why nature operates the way it does as totally irrelevant and unscientific and as having no meaningful answer. This refusal to consider the why-question is what leads to what we call ontological confusion. The why-question can only be answered if we know 'how' things exist. This is what defined modern ontology when applied to philosophy of science or nature. While classical ontology was primarily concerned with the identification of primitive entities in the universe (entities whose existence cannot be explained by other entities), modern ontology considers that all natural objects have ontological dimensions because they have a mode of existence that can be distinct from other objects, as we see in quantum mechanics. This is the reason for which we believe that each field of science must have a distinct ontology, even if these different ontologies ought to be reconciled in

---

[2] Lepain. *Tractatus: A Logical Introduction to Bahá'í Philosophy*, 2011, 6.

a broader metaphysical theory. However, many scientists think that science should only be concerned with a precise description of natural objects and of their properties and eschew the how and why questions. For them, science advances our understanding of nature by formulating theories based on observation and tested through experiment. As a consequence, defining scientific methodology is of paramount importance to philosophers of science as it provides the criteria for distinguishing science from non-science and good science from bad science. Philosophy of science rests on the assumption that science can be unified under one single methodology and that objective criteria capable of defining that methodology exist. The metaphysical assumption that underpins that view is that nature is continuous and homogeneous and that objects that are investigated by the different fields of science are relatively similar. Additionally, most philosophers of science operate within a larger philosophical framework, namely the naturalist framework. Naturalism says that nothing exists outside of nature, with the consequence that all explanations of nature must be sought within nature itself and its various physical constituents. They consequently see no role for metaphysics in scientific investigation.

By contrast, Bahá'í philosophy of nature, while recognizing philosophy of science as a legitimate and imminently useful activity, considers the fact that science alone cannot tell us everything about reality in general and nature in particular. It makes a sharp distinction between '*reality*' and '*nature*', seeing the latter only as an aspect of the former. Logical positivism's objective of banning metaphysics from philosophy of science is seen as illusory. During the past two decades, there has been a growing consensus that metaphysical issues could not be ignored. John Dupré writes: "*It is now widely understood that science itself cannot progress without powerful assumptions about the world it is trying to investigate that is to say a prior metaphysics.*"[3] Ian Thompson simi-

---

[3] Duprès, John. *The Disorder of Things; Metaphysical Foundation of the Disunity of Science.* Cambridge, MA: Harvard University Press, 1993, p. 1.

larly advocates a return to philosophy of nature and ontology. He writes: "*The problem, in modern times, is precisely that our maps are fragmented, confused and often appear in contradiction to each other*",[4] while Anjan Chakravartty claims that metaphysics should be regarded as "*a precursor to its epistemology*".[5] Miguel Espinoza considers physics and metaphysics to be part of the same process of understanding nature and that there cannot be any strict separation between the two.[6]

Metaphysical confusion leads to epistemological confusion. Understanding the reasons for this confusion might help us understand the role that a Bahá'í philosophy of nature could play. Many examples can be found in physics, biology and other sciences. Ian Thompson, for example, identifies six interpretations of quantum mechanics based on different ontologies. First, comes the so-called textbook interpretation based on **wave-particle complementarity ontology** of Niels Bohr and Werner Heisenberg, also called the Copenhagen interpretation. **Particle ontology** believes that quantum objects are corpuscles but with counterintuitive behaviors that must be accepted as facts of nature. The **wave ontology** of Schrödinger reverses the previous interpretation and considers that quantum objects are instead waves, with behaviours that make them appear like particles under certain circumstances. The **process ontology** of Whitehead and Russell declares that there is no constituting substance in nature and that what appear to us as waves or particles are in reality processes. The **ontology of propensity** builds potentialities and/or dispositions into the very nature of substance itself to explain quantum physics paradoxes. Finally, Born's **statistical interpretation** eliminates all ontology of particulars and says that quantum theory only describes general phenomena and cannot apply

---

4   Thompson, Ian J. *Philosophy of Nature and Quantum Reality*. Pleasanton, CA: Eagle Pearl Press, 2010, p. 3.
5   Chakravarty, Anjan. *Metaphysics for Scientific Realism: Knowing the Unobservable*. Cambridge: Cambridge University Press, 2007, p. 26.
6   Espinoza, Miguel. *Philosophie de la nature*, Paris: Ellipses, 2000, p. 7.

to individual systems.[7] With new theories such as the different forms of quantum gravity there are accordingly more than six different ontologies in fundamental physics. It looks like any new theory requires a new ontology.

It is not only quantum mechanics that is affected by ontological confusion. The mathematical formalism of physics manipulates abstract entities whose existence and nature remain highly speculative. Physicists consider that as long as these abstract entities are quantified, there is no problem. However, physics is unable to tell what energy, forces, fields, and the like really are.

Other examples of metaphysical confusion can be found in biology, with for example difficulty of defining the concepts of life, gene and genome, among others. Ten years after the completion of the Human Genome Project, it appears that a wrong ontology of genetics, more based on naturalist ideology than scientific observation, has been responsible for the project's inability to deliver promised curative therapies. This is because a wrong ontology of genes led to wrong assumptions regarding the relationship between genes and disease. Since then, it has become increasingly difficult to think of a gene as a function unit. We see diverging interpretations between the structural and functional understanding of the gene because structural understanding does not depend so much on molecular structure of the gene but rather, on the type of relationship that a particular gene establishes with other genes or with introns (non-coding segments of DNA) and how the gene expresses itself within a certain environment. In turn, this crisis of genetics ontology threatens the neo-Darwinian synthesis that for decades had offered an apparently stable model for understanding evolution. It has, however, become difficult to believe in a direct causal relation between molecular variations in a specific sequence of DNA and a phenotype trait. Putting in doubt this causal relation has devastating consequences for theories like evolutionary psychology that considers human nature and behavior to be the product of evolution and of our genet-

---

[7] Thompson, pp. 39–44.

ic make-up.[8] Morange believes that there is no universally-valid definition of a gene.[9] It has been shown that Mendelian genetics, molecular biology, genetic explanations of ontogeny processes and population genetics use all different concepts of genes based on different ontologies.[10] Ontogeny and phylogeny lead to different classifications of genes. There is the perception among biologists that attempting to formulate a clear definition of genes might be a fruitless enterprise. Some have instead chosen to substitute for genes the concept of the genome — the totality of DNA molecules transmitted from generation to generation — as the most fundamental entity of molecular biology. This makes a lot of sense, as contrary to what Dawkins and most of our non-biologist contemporaries believe,[11] there is growing evidence that in most cases, natural selection does not select genes, but rather, individuals and, therefore, genomes.[12] What is transmitted from

---

[8] See John Tooby and Lea Comides. *The Psychological Foundations of Culture* in Jerome Barkow, Lea Comides and John Tooby, *The Adapted Mind; Evolutionary Psychology and the Generation of Culture*. Oxford: Oxford University Press, 1992, pp. 20–136; Eliot Sober and David Sloan Wilson, *Unto Others; The Evolution and Psychology of Unselfish Behavior,* Cambridge Massachusetts: Harvard University, 1998; De Waal, *Our Inner Ape,* New York: Riverhead Books, 2005; Mark Hauser, *Moral Mind; How Nature Designed our Universal Sense of Rigt and Wrong,* New York: Harper and Collins, 2006; De Wall, Wright, Korsgaard, Kitcher and Singer, *Primates and Philosophers: How Morality Evolved*, Princeton: Princeton University Press, 2006, and, of course, many others.

[9] Morange, Michel. *The Misunderstood Gene*, Cambridge, MA: Harvard University Press, 2002, p. 27.

[10] Dupré. pp. 121–3.

[11] See Dawkins. *The Selfish Gene*, 2nd edition. New York: Oxford University Press, 1989.

[12] There is no consensus on this point among scientists. The debate concerning the level at which natural selection operates is far from being closed. A sympathetic view of the thesis that selection operates primary on genes can be found in Rosemberg and McShea, *Philosophy of Biology: A contemporary Introduction* (2008), pp. 158–169. Carmen Sapienza presents a defence of that view in her paper "Selection Does Operate Primarily on Genes," *In Defence of the Gene as the Unit of Selection* in Ayala and Arp Routledge, New York and London, 2010, pp. 127–140, while Richard Burian presents the opposite position in his paper "Selection Does not Operate Primarily on Genes" in the same book.

generation to generation is the genome, not the genes. However, substituting the genome for the genes can leave philosophers of science dissatisfied. The genome definition is purely descriptive and has no explanatory value because the molecular structure of the genome is too complex to be readily used. It is impossible to define what a genome mutation could be because mutations take place at the gene level, leaving again the neo-Darwinian Synthesis in disarray.

The problem of gene definition cannot be solved by science without resorting to ontological considerations simply because there can be many different ways of slicing reality. Two things must be taken into consideration. First, the genome cannot be isolated from its environment and, second, several levels of organization exist in the genome. Most attempts at defining the gene start from the assumption that the gene is either a 'primitive' object or that the gene organizational level is the most primitive level. These questions are questions more for philosophy of science and show that science, either theoretical or experimental, cannot be isolated from philosophy of science which is often introduced covertly. As we will see later, the notion of 'primitive object' is not part of Bahá'í philosophy of nature which is based on necessary relationships. In that case, it could be that relations between genes are a more fundamental level of explanation than the gene itself.

Many scientists acknowledge the existence of metaphysical or ontological issues in their disciplines but consider that these issues are no obstacle to scientific progress. This is because their

The confrontation between the two papers shows that since the 1980s there has been a considerable evolution that brings the two positions much closer. Additional literature on the subject includes R. Brandon and R. Burian, *Genes, Organism, Population: Controversies Over the Units of Selection*, Cambridge MA: MIT Press, 1984; R. Burian's 2005 paper 'Too Many Kinds of Genes? Some Problems Posed by Discontinuities in Gene Concepts and the Continuity of the Genetic Material" available at www.phil.vt.edu/Burian/GeneKindsCVP.pdf; S. Okasha's 2006 paper "The Level of Selection Debate: Philosophical issues" available at www.blackwellpublishing.com/pdf/compass/PHCO_ 001.pdf; E. Sober and D. Wilson's 1994 paper "A critical Review of Philosophical Work on the Units of Selection Problem" available at www.jstor.org/stable/188334.

understanding of science is inspired by instrumentalism and phenomenalism, which assigns to science the limited role of formulating theories enabling correct predictions or merely producing descriptions of experimental results and observations. From a Bahá'í perspective, the objective of science is not only to produce knowledge that will generate technologies capable of improving our life but also to bring about a closer understanding of our place within nature and its implication for our spiritual development.

A Holistic Approach to Reality

Another fundamental difference between philosophy of science and philosophy of nature is that the later takes a holistic approach to reality. Science is analytical in the sense that it understands a system by the working of its parts. This is a powerful method that has brought great success. However, under such an approach nature appears as highly fragmented. The result is not a unified model of nature but an entanglement of maps established at different scales and using different measurement units, different concepts and different methodologies and often at conflict with each other. By contrast, without neglecting the discontinuous aspect of nature, philosophy of nature looks more at the continuous aspects and at the interconnections between the different fields of knowledge.

This holistic approach to reality cannot be achieved by connecting together the various maps of nature's sub-systems produced by science. The heterogeneity of these maps is irreducible and any attempt to reduce them to the same language would deprive them of any useful meaning. This is the reason for which philosophy of nature cannot replace the various philosophies of science such as the philosophy of physics or philosophy of biology.

Our holistic approach cannot either be reached by ontology, because ontology operates in a way that is very similar to science by trying to identify the smallest logical constituent of reality and suggest reduction to a unique scale or dimension of reality. Rather this holistic approach is based on identifying the logical structure of reality that can produce concepts independent from any scale of reality or from any field of science. We will see that in this approach the concept of necessary/non-necessary relationship, developed by 'Abdu'l-Bahá, plays an eminent role. This holistic approach leads to a complementary view of reality, also called in the past *conjunctio oppositorum*, in which a representation of reality is reached from the superposition of different perspectives, which helps to solve apparent contradictions between various aspects of reality.

PHILOSOPHY OF NATURE AND SUBJECTIVITY

While philosophy of science pretends to be anthropologically neutral, philosophy of nature considers that the existence of conscious beings is central to any explanation of nature. The first mystery of nature is the existence of something rather than nothing. The second mystery is our own existence which, as Brandon Carter demonstrated through his anthropic principle, constrains the conditions prevailing at the time of the Big Bang and the selection of laws of nature and universal constants.[13] The fact that we live in the only universe compatible with our existence is something hard to deny. We will see that Bahá'í metaphysics considers consciousness as an emergent property that owes its existence to specific characteristics of the universe we are living in. This means that our existence as conscious beings cannot be dissociated from the structure of nature and therefore nature is conveying to us meaningful message about who we are and how to understand our place in the natural order.

PHILOSOPHY OF NATURE AND THE THEORY OF INTELLIGIBILITY

In the same way that philosophy of science requires an epistemology, a philosophy of nature requires a theory of intelligibility. We cannot make significant progress in our understanding of the metaphysical framework of Bahá'í philosophy of nature unless we address the issue of intelligibility.

---

[13] Barrow and Tipler. *The Anthropic Principle*. Oxford: Oxford University Press, 1998.

There is a major difference between a theory of intelligibility and epistemology. While epistemology answers the question: "How do we know what is in the world?" intelligibility answers the question "What is there in the world that we can know?" Whereas epistemology is limited in scope by its naturalist paradigm, a theory of intelligibility must be grounded in ontology and metaphysics. Such a theory must address the following key questions: (i) what is the relationship between reality and the human mind; (ii) what is human capability to understand reality and what could be the limit of that capability if any; (iii) what makes nature intelligible and what are the conditions of that intelligibility, (iv) what is the relationship between intelligibility and spirituality, or between rationality, intuition and other forms of knowledge.

When discussing the question of intelligibility, the Bahá'í writings raise different issues. The first issue, related principally to epistemology, is the absence of a sure foundation for human knowledge. A second issue is the limits of intelligibility. A third issue is the relationship between rationality, language and intelligibility. A fourth issue is the relationship between an individual's knowledge and their spiritual development.

In *Some Answered Questions,* 'Abdu'l-Bahá states that there are four sources of knowledge: sensory data, rational reasoning, the authority of tradition and of Holy Scriptures, and intuition.[14] He demonstrates that none of these sources can lead to any certainty: "*They are all faulty and unreliable.*"[15] The only hope of achieving an understanding of reality is by combining these four sources of knowledge. This is what I call the *epistemological agreement* that represents the ideal of Bahá'í philosophy. Sensory data is notably unreliable. Philosophers who follow the path of reason can scarcely agree on anything. Even supposedly well-established scientific theories can be rapidly displaced by a competing theory, and each theory is subject to various interpretations. The history

---

[14] 'Abdu'l-Bahá. *Some Answered Questions* (latter abbreviated as SAQ), Wilmette, IL: Bahá'í Publishing Trust, 1981, pp. 297–8.

[15] *Promulgation of Universal Peace* (latter abbreviated as PUP), Wilmette, IL: Bahá'í Publishing Trust, 1982, pp. 22, 255.

of philosophy shows that theologians who view themselves as the guardians of exegesis have greatly erred through the centuries. As for inspiration, it is difficult to distinguish genuine spiritual inspiration from the prompting of the Self. It is only by combining these four sources of knowledge that we can hope reaching a better understanding of reality. However, 'Abdu'l-Bahá warns us that reaching an agreement between the four sources of knowledge cannot be a purely intellectual process because human intellect is faulty: *"...there is no standard in the hand of people upon which we can rely."* By his own effort no human being can reach true understanding of reality. Such an understanding can only be reached through the assistance of the Holy Spirit: *"But the bounty of the Holy Spirit gives us the true method of comprehension which is infallible and indubitable. This is through the help of the Holy Spirit which comes to man, and this is the condition in which certainty can alone be attained."* [16] Elsewhere, 'Abdu'l-Bahá says *"How shall we attain the reality of knowledge? By the breaths and promptings of the Holy Spirit, which is light and knowledge itself. Through it the human mind is quickened and fortified into true conclusion and perfect knowledge."* [17] The process of obtaining the assistance of the Holy Spirit requires some form of "openness" which is directly linked with personal and collective spiritual development. Clearly no sure method exists to reach this epistemological agreement, if by method we intend a purely intellectual process. Accepting this position means that intellectual and scientific knowledge is limited and cannot give us a full understanding of reality. From a scientific perspective human knowledge must therefore remain without firm foundation.

The second issue we have to deal with is the intelligibility of nature. The basic idea behind Bahá'í philosophy of nature is that nature is the manifestation of a more fundamental reality. Nature by itself is intelligible in most of its manifestations, but a deeper analysis of nature requires not just science but ontology and intu-

---

[16] SAQ, p. 299.
[17] PUP, p. 22.

ition in order to include our subjectivity and the fact that we are ourselves part of nature.

The human existential *situs* limits our perception to a certain ontological horizon. What is behind that horizon can only be guessed. This situation creates the illusion of duality between a spiritual and a material world while, in fact, there is only one world. The spiritual world has an influence on the material world that cannot be explained in scientific terms. Man is caught in a *hermeneutical circle*: to know himself, he needs to know God and the world; to know the world, he needs to know himself and God; and, of course, he cannot know God unless he understands himself and the world. The circularity of human knowledge is another reason for the limits of intelligibility and for the absence of a sure foundation of human knowledge. Knowledge can never be fully objective. The reason that there is so much disagreement in contemporary metaphysics is that all systems have hidden assumptions about our place in the universe and its meaning. As long as we do not have a consensus on this question, it is difficult to reach a consensus on anything else.

A comprehensive theory of intelligibility cannot be developed in isolation but instead requires linkage with a theory of rationality and a theory of language. In the Bahá'í writings, rationality includes spirituality because rationality is the capacity to see beyond appearance. Rationality is a manifestation of the Logos, the Word of God, and we can expect that everything created follows the same rationality, even if this rationality might not be fully intelligible to us. Language is what links us to the universal rationality and makes it intelligible to us. Language is the incarnation of rationality and the instrument of spirituality. We are rational beings, and, therefore, spiritual beings too, because we are beings endowed with linguistic capability.

'Abdu'l-Bahá says that man can understand the abstract only through the concrete.[18] Lakoff and Johnson demonstrated that all

---

[18] "Tablet to Professor Forel" also quoted in *Bahá'í World Faith,* 6th printing of the 1956 edition, Wilmette, IL: Bahá'í Publishing Trust, 1976, p.

abstract ideas, but not only abstract ideas, are metaphors or metaphors of metaphors. "Time passes" or "flows", "problems are burden", "we grasp an issue", "life is a journey", "affection is warmth," "prices rise," and "markets plummet" are all metaphors which have been developed using rules that have shaped our mental life. All expansion of our knowledge and experience requires the spinning of new metaphors.[19] Metaphors not only shape our ordinary language, but as Theodor Brown has shown, metaphorical thinking has also produced some of the best science.[20] Metaphors reveal the underlying common rationality of all phenomena. Metaphors generate meaning, and meaning is what links rationality to spirituality. But the Bahá'í writings go one step further: metaphors are part of nature. Not only are metaphors part of nature but we can see God's creation as a nexus of metaphors.[21] If nature uses fractal geometry like a "copy and paste" function (another metaphor), there is no surprise that it could use also transposition of one principle from one domain to another domain, from one level of reality to another level. Laws of nature could be the manifestations of such a process. This is the reason that nature in particular and God's creation in general are endowed with meaning for humans. Metaphors reveal the common rational structure that links all the different ontological levels of the universe.[22]

336: "The mind comprehendeth the abstract by the help of the concrete, but the soul has limitless manifestation." A revised translation can be found in *The Bahá'í World*, vol. XV (1968–1973) Bahá'í World Centre, Haifa, 1976, pp. 37–43 or at http://www.gutember.org/files/19292/19292-h/19292-h.html. In the online version the quotation appears on pp. 6–10, paragraph 6.

[19] See Lakoff and Johnson, *Metaphors We Live By*, Chicago, IL: University of Chicago, 1980, and *Philosophy in the Flesh: The embodied Mind and its Challenge to the Western Thought*, New York: Basic Book, 1999.

[20] Brown, Theodore. *Truth Making: Metaphors in Science*, Champaign IL: University of Illinois Press, 2008.

[21] Lepain, Jean-Marc. *Archéologie du Royaume de Dieu* ; Ontologie des Mondes Divins dans les Ecrits de Baha'u'llah, Librairie Bahá'íe, Paris, 1993, pp. 64–5; Le Principe Anthropique ; Le Problème de l'Intelligibilité et de la Rationalité du Monde dans la Pensée de Baha'u'llah, Librairie Bahá'íe, Paris 1995, p. 52, available at www.bahai-biblio.org.

[22] Lepain, Jean-Marc, 1993 and 1995.

Last but not least, even if science can readily understand natural phenomena, it cannot grasp the universe in its totality and it cannot understand its relationship with what

Bahá'u'lláh describes as other "worlds." However, it appears clear that these worlds interact with each other and that certain fundamental aspects of our universe depend on these interactions. For that reason, some natural phenomena will always appear mysterious. This is the case concerning the origin of the universe itself, but also regarding the appearance of life, the existence of consciousness, free will and the nature of the human soul, all of which cannot be explained in purely naturalistic terms. Some aspects of God's creation are fully intelligible and accessible to human rationality, while other aspects are mysterious. There are countless passages in the Bahá'í writings about the mysterious aspects of the world we live in. Here are some similarities with the position of a group of philosophers called the Mysterians. Collin McGinn coined the expression 'transcendental Naturalism' to describe this position. He writes: "... *we are programmed to employ concepts that are mysteries to us at a logical level. We can solve problems by using these concepts, but we cannot solve the problems they themselves raise..."* [23] This situation is due to the cognitive architecture of our mind: *"Philosophy is an attempt to get outside the constructive structure of our mind. Reality itself is everywhere flatly natural, but because of our cognitive limits we are unable to make good on this general ontological principle. Our epistemic architecture obstructs knowledge of the real nature of the objective world."* [24] Consequently, *"we are trying to force our cognitive faculties to deliver knowledge of phenomena whose nature those faculties are not cut out to comprehend."* [25] While McGinn thinks that the reasons for human cognitive limitation are essentially biological, the Bahá'í writings give a more metaphysical interpretation. Those limitations are due to our position in

---

[23] McGinn, Collin. *Problems in Philosophy: The Limits of Enquiry*, Oxford: Blackwell, 1993, p. 21.

[24] Ibid, p. 2

[25] Ibid, p. 150.

the chain of being and to discontinuous aspects of reality. John Carroll holds similar views, but instead of concluding that philosophy is doomed, he concludes that science will remain always incomplete.[26] This incompleteness is the result of the nature of the "*inanimate*" world. After reviewing the relationship between necessity, the laws of nature and causation, Carroll concludes: "*The various examples discussed... show that we may not be intelligent enough to discover every fact, that we may not have the requisite sensory ability to discover every fact, and that events in the external world may occur in such a way as to prevent us from discovering every fact.*"[27] This thesis of the incompleteness of philosophy and science is fully supported by the Bahá'í writings.

METAPHYSICS AND PHILOSOPHY OF NATURE

Bahá'í metaphysics is premised on the notion that the physical reality is not the entire reality of the existing universe. It might even be difficult to distinguish clearly between a so called physical reality and a broader understanding of reality that includes non-physical elements. The universe is made not only of physical elements but possesses an ontological structure that is distinct from its physical structure. This ontological structure is believed to have causal powers that put constraints on the manner in which the physical reality unfolds.

To understand the place of metaphysics in Bahá'í philosophy generally, and in Bahá'í philosophy of nature in particular, it is necessary (i) to understand the relationship between metaphysics and the Bahá'í theory of intelligibility; (ii) to define the metaphysical framework existing in the Bahá'í writings and its implications for the ontological structure of reality, and finally (iii) to understand the relationship between metaphysics, science and other fields of knowledge such as sensory experience, intuition, faith and the like.

---

[26] Carrol, John W. *Laws of Nature*. Cambridge: Cambridge University Press, 1994, p. 153.

[27] Ibid, p. 157.

The place occupied by metaphysics in Bahá'í philosophy flows directly from the theory of intelligibility. Metaphysics cannot rely only on the use of logic as a methodology. It must be part of *the epistemological agreement* described earlier. In the nineteenthcentury, metaphysics came to be criticised as being purely speculative. Bahá'u'lláh also strongly condemns scholastic or speculative metaphysics, which he describes as *"sciences that begin with words and end with words."*[28] Metaphysics, like science and religion, is a means of investigating reality. It can start only from the observation of nature and for this reason, ontology should be considered as part of the philosophy of nature. Ontology tells us what exists, and this question is one of the most fundamental questions of science and of philosophy of nature. Indeed, it is precisely where science and metaphysics meet. Metaphysics itself should not be seen as a distinct branch of philosophy of nature but rather as a component of all the main three branches of Bahá'í philosophy.

Bahá'í philosophy must of course remain based on the Bahá'í writings, which contain a significant amount of material about the nature of reality. This is what I call *the metaphysical framework* of Bahá'í philosophy — elements of which will be described in the next section of this paper. Because there is no definite foundation of human knowledge and because not everything is knowable or can be described in scientific terms, there are in all philosophies a number of propositions that are called primitive (in the sense that they cannot be demonstrated). The existence or non-existence of God and the naturalistic assertion that nothing exists outside of nature are typical examples of primitive propositions. Following these primitive propositions, there are a number of other propositions that are not primitive but which cannot be demonstrated without recourse to primitive propositions. We also find in the Bahá'í writings other statements about the nature of reality that may be viewed as 'metaphysical' but which are strongly correlated

---

[28] Baha'u'llah, 'Tajallíyyât (3rd)," in *Writings of Baha'u'llah*, 3rd expanded edition, New Delhi, India: BPT, 2006.

to scientific propositions (in the sense that a scientific interpretation of these statements might be possible). The discontinuity of reality and the organization of nature within hierarchical levels of complexity is a good example of a thesis found in the Bahá'í writings, which is susceptible to scientific refutation or justification. In so doing, we must remember that the Bahá'í writings are not considered authoritative with regards to scientific questions and when statements about the nature of physical reality are found they should be interpreted in the light of the best science available, knowing that our knowledge is not definitive. The purpose of the Bahá'í writings is not to inform us about the nature of the physical reality but to provide guidance for our spiritual development. In similar terms, although ontology should be seen as part of the philosophy of nature, the primary purpose of metaphysics is not to inform us about the nature of reality but to inform us about human nature. However, we cannot understand the concept of human nature unless we understand our relationship to the universe and our relationship to God. This is what I called in a previous work *the hermeneutic circle*.[29]

This naturally raises the question of the relationship between science and metaphysics. When the aim of eradicating entirely metaphysics from philosophy was proved illusory, analytical philosophers like Quine have proclaimed that metaphysics is '*continuous to science*'. Since then, we have seen the flourishing of various proposals for the complete 'naturalization' of metaphysics — i.e. the idea that metaphysics does not need metaphysical concepts but can be developed using only concepts of physics, or proposals for the reduction of metaphysics to scientific realism or the idea that the role of metaphysics can be reduced to providing science with criteria allowing it to distinguish between real physical objects from intellectual devices created by the mathematical formalism of physics. It is not difficult to refute such theories for many reasons; one of them being that they imply a reduction of all sciences to physics; something that only die-hard naturalists

---

[29] Lepain, 1993, pp. 220–1.

are ready to believe and other reason being, as we have seen, that there is no epistemological agreements among physicists about the exact meaning of the physical concepts they use. Last but not least, such explanations invariably lead one to posit some kind of physical entities as 'primitive' and beyond any explanation. For example, Tim Maudlin writes: "*The laws of nature stand in no need of 'philosophical analysis'; they ought to be posited as ontological bedrock.*"[30] He also takes space-time as being primitive. Such attempts at the naturalization of metaphysics always end up in constricting dramatically the field of metaphysics and putting a number of disturbing questions 'off limits'. Although these theories might appeal to some physicists, they are not widely supported by most biologists and scientists from other branches of science. All ontological questions are not amenable to the methods of empirical science. Physics remains an incomplete science, and an incomplete science cannot provide ontology capable of explaining all natural phenomena as well as the logical structure of reality. We still do not know if the ultimate building blocks of physical reality are strings, branes or something else. We cannot explain the expansion of the universe unless we assume the existence of very mysterious entities such as a cosmological constant, singularities, dark matter and dark energy. The fact that 96 percent of the universe's mass remains undetected is not very reassuring as to the completeness of our physical theories. We do not know how general relativity applies at a low-energy limit. We do not know what happens under the Planck length (10^{-33} cm). We are unable to choose between string theories and quantum gravity theories, which in turn exist in multiple variants. Considering physics' lack of knowledge about the most fundamental layer of reality, one can doubt that metaphysics can be naturalized or that physics can

---

[30] Maudlin. *The Metaphysics within Physics*, Oxford: Oxford University Press, 2007, p 1. See also John Carroll. *Laws of Nature*, Cambridge: Cambridge University Press, 1994, who follows the same path. John Lowe, *A Survey of Metaphysics*, Oxford: Oxford University Press, 2002, has presented a number of important arguments against the naturalization of metaphysics.

sort out the true nature of physical entities using its mathematical formalism. On the other hand, metaphysics can provide critical tools for resolving some of physics' ontological issues. Obviously, there are some elements of continuity between science and metaphysics as there are elements of continuity between metaphysics and theology, hermeneutics, philology, linguistics and almost any form of human knowledge. But to say that metaphysics *must be* 'continuous' to or coextensive with science is certainly wrong. Even a logical positivist like Russell opposed that view.[31] Bahá'í philosophy does not see metaphysics as continuous to science but as the result of an epistemological agreement between all sources of knowledge. This means that metaphysics (or religion as often mentioned by 'Abdu'l-Bahá) should not enter into contradiction with science. As a consequence, one of the responsibilities of Bahá'í metaphysics is proposed interpretation of Bahá'í writings regarding the nature of reality in the light of the latest progress in science. In this task, two levels must be considered. The first level considers our understanding of the world. While science is more concerned with the explanation of discrete phenomena, metaphysics is more concerned with our understanding of the universe as a whole through the development of macro-concepts such as interconnectedness, continuity and discontinuity, complexity, order, laws of nature, causality, evolution, diversity, adaptation, entropy, chance, stochasticity and determinism. A second level of metaphysics considers what sort of ontology can explain the macro-concepts developed at the first level.

SCIENCE, PHILOSOPHY AND RELIGION

We have already asserted the view that the Bahá'í Faith sees philosophy as the interface or the mediator between science and religion. As a religion, the Bahá'í Faith is unique in the fact that it places as much authority in science as in its own writings, to the point of making the agreement between science and religion

---

[31] Glock, Hans-Johan. *What is Analytical Philosophy?* Cambridge: Cambridge University Press, 2008, p. 135.

mandatory: "*Religion and science must conform and agree. If a question of religion violates reason and does not agree with science, it is imagination and not worthy of credence.*"[32]

If much has been written on the ways and means of reaching that agreement, very little attention has been given to the metaphysical principles that render this agreement necessary. This can be summarized as follows: science and religion, and by extension philosophy, have the same purpose — namely the understanding of reality. However, they operate on different levels of that reality. For that reason, their views are complementary, and conflict between the two should be impossible in principle, although there are a few areas where science and religion tend to overlap such as in the discussion concerning Darwinian evolution. If conflicts occur it is because there has been some confusion between the two levels of intelligibility.

'Abdu'l-Bahá appears to accord science, nature and religion identical definitions. In *Some Answered Questions* he writes: "*Religion, then, is **the necessary connection** which emanates from the reality of things.*"[33] In the "Tablet to August Forel," he gives a similar definition of nature: "*By nature is meant those **inherent properties** and **necessary relations** derived from the realities of things.*"[34] As science is also the study of '*necessary relations*' existing between things, the consequence is that "*Religion and science are the same; they cannot be separated from each other*"[35] because "*The basis of religion is reality itself.*"[36] Soon we will see that this '*neces-*

---

[32] PRP, p. 169.

[33] SAQ, p. 159

[34] "Tablet to Professor Forel" (later abbreviated as Forel), revised translation published in The Bahá'í World, vol. XV, Bahá'í World Centre, Haifa, 1976, p. 38 and can be found at http://www.gutenberg.org/files/19292/19292-pdf.pdf. The quotation can be found on p. 16, paragraph 3 and remains unchanged from previous translation.

[35] From a Tablet of 'Abdu'l-Bahá quoted in a memorandum of Research Department of the Universal House of Justice dated 14 January 1991.

[36] 'Abdu'l-Bahá on Divine Philosophy (latter abbreviated as ADP), Compiled by Elisatheth Frazer Chamberlain. Boston, MA: Tudor Press, 1918, p. 186, online at http://bahai-library.com/abdulbaha_divine_philosophy&chapter=-1918.

sary connection' is a key concept underpinning the Bahá'í philosophy of nature and its ontology.

However, if science and religion have the same purpose (namely the study of necessary relations existing between things), they do not operate on the same level of reality and do not have the *same modus operandi*. While science deals with the physical world, religion is primarily concerned with the spiritual development of humankind. This spiritual development can be understood in terms of *'necessary relations'* existing between the body and the soul on one hand and the soul and the spiritual worlds on the other. Physical reality is viewed as an instrument of spiritual development. Religion is interested in science because we need a better understanding of how physical reality can contribute to our spiritual development, because science can contribute to the well-being of humanity and to the advancement of civilization, and because understanding the mysteries of the universe helps us understand ourselves and our relationship to God's creation.

THE BAHÁ'Í CONCEPT OF NATURE

It seems possible to identify in the Bahá'í writings five different views of nature, which can be seen as complementary: (i) nature is the expression of God's will; (ii) nature is a modality of reality; (iii) nature is an intelligible reality, (iv) nature is the expression of the necessary relations existing between the realities of things, and (v) nature is a unifying agency. Once these perspectives are woven together, a compelling and deeply philosophical representation of nature emerges.

NATURE AS THE WILL OF GOD
Bahá'u'lláh defines nature as the expression of God's Will in his creation:

> Nature in its essence is the embodiment of My Name, the Maker, the Creator. Its manifestations are diversified by various causes, and in this diversity, there are signs for

> men of discernment. Nature is God's will and its expression in and through the contingent world. It is a dispensation of Providence ordained by the Ordainer, the All-Wise. Were anyone to affirm that it is the Will of God as manifested in the world of being, no one should question this assertion. It is endowed with a power whose reality men of learning fail to grasp.[37]

There are a number of important ideas expressed in this quotation. Nature is the instrument of God and manifests His purpose. Nature has a spiritual dimension, and humanity can learn important lessons from it. From a spiritual perspective, understanding nature is tantamount to understanding the purpose of God in creating the physical reality. Laws of nature express the will of God and as a consequence, God does not need to interfere with the working of nature. Experience shows that the laws of nature are sufficient to accomplish God's purpose: there is no need for divine intervention in nature, and science need not be concerned by questions such as the existence of God.

NATURE AS A MODALITY OF REALITY AND AS AN INTELLIGIBLE REALITY

'Abdu'l-Bahá's book *Some Answered Questions* opens with a chapter on nature. The first paragraph of that chapter provides a sort of definition of nature which is neither easy to translate nor to understand. The first sentence is very elliptical and may be translated literally as follows: "*Nature (tabîyyat) is a modality (kayfîyyat-i) or a reality (haqîqat-i)*." There is no doubt that much ink will be spent in attempting to explain this first sentence. I believe that it could be paraphrased as: "Nature is a modality of existing things that is an intelligible reality".

Kayfîyyat is a word that translates Aristotle's category of '*modality*' or '*quality*'. The word comes from the Arabic '*kayf* (how) and in response to the question of 'How is that thing?' It denotes a mode of being. It stands in contrast to the question 'What is

---

[37] Baha'u'llah. *Tablets of Wisdom,* in WOB, p. 447.

that thing?' which instead denotes its quiddity. The origin of the term dates back to Aristotle's *Categories,* which enumerates all possible kinds of thing that can be the subject or the predicate of a proposition. The third category is 'Quality' (*poion*) which characterizes the nature of an object by identifying its essential properties. In Islamic philosophy, the term came to denote the mode of existence of an essence. There might be two ways to translate the word *kayfiyyat* within this context. The first is to consider the sentence "*tabiyyat kayfiyyat-î'st*" to mean "Nature is a set of properties or qualities". In this sense, this definition of nature is indistinguishable from the definition of nature as a set of necessary relations between things. However, a second interpretation is possible as the word *Kayfiyyat-î* is used with the definite article, and hence the sentence can also be paraphrased as "*Nature is one of the modalities of reality among other modalities.*" This means that nature is one aspect among many aspects of reality. In my view, both meanings are intended. It follows that nature, when considered as a set of properties (as it is considered by science) is only one modality through which reality, including the physical universe, is perceived by us. Other modalities, or other ways to consider the universe, exist. When we see reality as nature, we do not see reality in all its aspects. Put another way, there is more to reality than simply nature. This definition of nature carries significant philosophical implications.

The second term of the definition, *haqîqat,* is usually translated as 'reality'. 'Reality' is a vague term that can mean either 'essence' or an 'intelligible reality'; an entity that exists on a metaphysical level, an abstraction, but an abstraction existing independently from the human mind. In the same book, 'Abdu'l-Bahá adds this comment: "*In the same way, nature, also, in its essence, is an intellectual (*intelligible*) reality and is not sensible...*"[38] It clearly follows that nature is not something that can be perceived through the senses but only through the intellect. Nature is, therefore, defined as a metaphysical category. When read together, the two el-

---

[38] SAQ, p. 83.

ements of 'Abdu'l-Bahá's definitions mean that nature should not be seen as an assembly of things but as an organic whole whose existence transcends the existence of its components.

NATURE AS NECESSARY RELATIONS BETWEEN THE REALITIES OF THINGS AND AS UNIFYING AGENCY

As we have already seen, 'Abdu'l-Bahá in the "Tablet to Professor August Forel" provides another definition of nature:

> By nature is meant those inherent properties and necessary relations derived from the realities (essence) of things. And these realities of things, though in the utmost diversity, are yet intimately connected one with the other.[39]

From a metaphysical vantage-point, this definition, which does not contradict the one given in *Some Answered Questions*, is highly important, as it introduces the concepts of "*inherent properties*", "*necessary relations*" and "*essence*" which are, we believe, the key elements of Bahá'í ontology. We will consider them in greater detail in the last section of this paper. The general idea is that nature is a nexus of necessary relations existing between things. Through them everything is linked to everything. The universe is made of things, but nature is made of processes and necessary relations stemming from their inherent properties manifested by things according to their essence. These processes and necessary relations constitute this modality of reality that we have just discussed.

Because nature is a nexus of processes and necessary relations, it is more than the sum of its parts. Although nature might appear to be discontinuous and made not only of objects but of different subsystems, it contains properties and potentialities which are not possessed by its components. Through the universality of a natural order, and as a manifestation of a more fundamental law,

---

[39] "Tablet to Professor Forel," p. 16, paragraph 3 at http://www.gutenberg.org/files/19292/19292-pdf.pdf

it forms one single body endowed with an existence of its own. This is probably what 'Abdu'l-Bahá means when he calls nature a unifying agency, as is shown in this quotation:

> For these diverse realities an all-unifying agency is needed that shall link them all one to the other. For instance, the various organs and members, the parts and elements, that constitute the body of man, though at variance, are yet all connected one with the other through that all-unifying agency known as the human soul that causeth them to function in perfect harmony and with absolute regularity...[40]

Nature is, therefore, not merely the collection of all existing things. It is a repository of information, including properties and relations. Nature is more than the sum of all the particulars and relations that constitute it.[41] It has properties and dispositions of its own which cannot be found in the particulars.

CONTINUITY AND DISCONTINUITY IN NATURE

The Bahá'í writings appear to uphold two contradictory views: the first is the unity of the world of existence, the second

---

[40] Tablet to Professor Forel. Ibid. pp. 11–20, paragraph 4.

[41] It might be useful at this stage to clarify the concept of 'particular'. Based on standard definitions found in various dictionaries of philosophy, a particular is member of a class as opposed to the property which defines that class or a particular can be an individual as opposed to a universal. Particulars are often opposed to universals because universals need particulars to be exemplified; but particulars can be different from individuals and can be changing (Abelard gives the example of a flame as a changing particular; Strawson gives the example of mental states). Particulars can also be abstract. They include not only physical objects, but concepts, consciousness, mental states or events. Particulars do not need to have individuality but they need a quiddity and here we are on solid ground because 'Abdu'l-Bahá attributes quiddity to the constituents of nature. As the concept of particular has a very broad meaning, I will use it every time that the nature of objects cannot be specified or to reflect the heterogeneity of natural objects. While rocks and birds are tangible realities, this is not the case of elementary particles that do not have locality and do not seem to have independent individuality either.

the discontinuity of reality. These conflicting views of reality are due to our limited cognitive capacity, as explained in the theory of intelligibility. What we perceive is discontinuity, while what actually exists is continuity. However, discontinuity is not a mere illusion: it is just that we do not have the cognitive tools to reconcile and articulate logically the two aspects of reality. Science will be more concerned by discontinuity while metaphysics will be more concerned with establishing the principles of continuity. However, neither can ignore these two complementary aspects of reality. Continuity and discontinuity in nature are the two faces of the same coin.

'Abdu'l-Bahá writes: *"Reality is one; it does not admit plurality."*[42] This means that the distinction that we make between a spiritual world and a material world is not real. This distinction appears to us only because of our cognitive limitations. Fundamentally, there is only one reality and that reality has spiritual and material manifestations. Because the material world exists inside the spiritual world, physical realities also have a spiritual dimension. In this regard, a sharp distinction between the material and the spiritual is sometimes difficult. Because the two worlds are not separated, they interact with each other. Some necessary relations operate across the two worlds and bind spiritual and material things together.

On the other hand, the way we perceive reality is discontinuous. Nature is made of subsystems organized hierarchically and operating through different sets of principles. The most obvious discontinuity in reality is the distinction we made between minerals, plants and animals, but we can also find elements of discontinuity inside each kingdom and even between closely related species. Based on Aristotle, 'Abdu'l-Bahá uses a classification that divides reality into five kingdoms: the mineral kingdom, the vegetable kingdom, the animal kingdom, the human kingdom and the spiritual kingdom. It would be mistaken to give biological

---

[42] PRP, p. 297; Makátib-i-'Abdu'l-Bahá published by Faraju'lláh Zakí al-Kurdí. Cairo. 1921. Vol. I, p. 341.

taxonomic value to such classification which is not concerned
with biological taxonomy but with metaphysical relations. Its
only purpose is to establish that the human soul does not originate from nature but rather from the spiritual world. However, it
clearly demonstrates the principle of the discontinuity of reality.
The same principle exists in Bahá'u'lláh 's writings where he distinguishes various worlds, designated by Aramaic names such as
Nâsût (the human world), *Malakût* (the spiritual world), *Jabarût*
(the world of the divine will), *Lâhût* (the world of the divinity)
and *Hâhût* (the world of the unmanifested).[43] However, he uses
many other phrases such as *'the world of the divine essence', 'the
world of existence', 'the world of being'*,[44] *'the world of the visible
and invisible'*,[45] *'the world of contingency'*,[46] *'the world of the divine
command'*,[47] *"the realm of revelation and creation"*,[48] and *'the kingdom of names'*.[49] I have already demonstrated elsewhere that the
notions of *'world'* or *'kingdom'* represent hermeneutical or epistemological concepts rather than ontological domains. A world
is a category of intelligibility. On one hand, reality is discontin-

---

[43] For a more detailed analysis see my article 'The Tablet of All Food: The
Hierarchy of the Spiritual World and the Metaphoric Nature of Reality"
in *Bahá'í Study Review*. Vol. 16, pp. 43–60, and my book *Archéologie
du Royaume de Dieu*. http://www.bahai-biblio.org/centre-doc/ouvrage/
archeologie-royaume-dieu/archeologie-royaume-dieu-sommaire.htm,
Ch 1, 2, and 5.

[44] The *'world of existence'* and the *'world of being'* are two different translations of the same Persian expression (*'âlam-i-wujûd*). Examples of the
use of this expression can be found in 'Epistle to the Son of the Wolf'
in *Writings of Baha'u'llah*, 3rd expanded edition BPT, New Delhi, India,
hereafter abbreviated in WoB p. 594 and 597.

[45] See *Prayers and Meditations by Baha'u'llah*, XIII, in WoB p.799, XXXI,
p. XLIV, p. 821, LXXII, CLXXVIII, or *Munajât* (*Prayers and Meditations
in Arabic*), n° 38, Editora Bahá'í-Brazil. Rio de Janero, 198.1 p. 41 for an
example in Arabic.

[46] See, for example, SAQ. Ch. 38, p. 152, and Ch. 80, p. 281.

[47] In Persian *'âlam-i-Amr*. Shoghi Effendi often translates this expression
by *Kingdom of thy Cause*. See "Gleanings of Baha'u'llah," CLV. in WoB p.
777. See also *Munajât*. n° 75, Rio de Janero.Editora Bahá'í-Brazil.p. 86,
and n° 80, p. 92.

[48] See *Prayers and Meditation by Baha'u'llah*. XXXI, in WoB p. 808

[49] See *Prayers and Meditations*, LVI. in WoB p. 830, and *Munajât*, p. 83.

uous because each world, or kingdom, requires a separate mode of intelligibility and, therefore, different ontology. On the other hand, not every world is part of a hierarchical order. Many names of worlds simply try to capture various aspects of reality. A better understanding of reality requires a juxtaposition of different perspectives, different hermeneutic categories. This idea of discontinuity of reality, or of nature, has far-reaching consequences. It explains why unity of science is impossible. Each natural kingdom, having a different ontology, requires a different scientific methodology. Reduction of one level of nature to another is impossible and, as a consequence, so too is the completeness of science. Although biology includes physics and chemistry, it cannot be reduced to physics or chemistry and chemistry cannot be reduced to physics.[50] Another idea is that discontinuity of nature is possible only under a common source of order. Order and complexity are linked to discontinuity. Last but not least, nature, as we have seen is a unifying agency. Discontinuity does not mean separateness. The complementarity and harmony that we see in nature shows that there must be some unifying principles and those unifying principles are metaphysical principles. This view of nature is fundamentally opposed to the Humean view of nature as a mosaic of discrete phenomena or logical atoms that, since Russell, has become one of the fundamental tenets of many contemporary philosophers.

The conclusion of this section should be that nature remains a mysterious reality that cannot be fully grasped by the human mind. To combine the five aspects or functions of nature identified in the Bahá'í writings and to understand their implications is already a significant challenge. However, even if we were to succeed in this task, something would remain elusive. There are two reasons for that. The first reason is that nature cannot be defined as an objective reality because we are part of it. As a part

---

[50] On the debate about the question of a possible reduction of biology to physics, see Rosemberg and McShea. *Philosophy of Biology: A Contemporary Introduction.* London: Routledge, 2007, pp. 96–126.

of nature, we can see easily its objective manifestations, but other aspects can only be grasped through our subjectivity and our intuition. The second reason is that because nature is not just a physical reality but also an intelligible concept, the very idea of nature is deeply metaphysical, and relates directly to human spirituality. Because nature has meaning for us it has also a spiritual dimension. The understanding of this spiritual dimension depends deeply on the spiritual progress of humankind and, therefore, is likely to change with time. Nature cannot be captured by any definition. As Bahá'u'lláh said: "*It is endowed with a power whose reality men of learning fail to grasp.*"[51]

ELEMENTS OF THE BAHÁ'Í METAPHYSICS OF NATURE

Metaphysics of nature operates at two levels. On one level, we find the general principles of Bahá'í metaphysics and how they relate or apply to metaphysics of nature. On another level, we find concepts that apply specifically to the metaphysics of nature such as interconnectedness, continuity and discontinuity, complexity, order, laws of nature, evolution, emergence, diversity, adaptation, entropy, chance, stochasticity or determinism. In the present section, after reviewing some of the key principles, we will deal mostly with interconnectedness, emergence and change.[52]

ORIGIN OF THE UNIVERSE

In the history of Western intellectual tradition, the question of the origin of our universe has been an important point of contention and a source of conflict between science and religion. The Bahá'í understanding of the origin of the universe is fundamentally different from Christian and Islamic theology. Four points deserve attention. Firstly, the Bahá'í writings draw a sharp distinction between the origin of our universe, which

---

[51] TOB, p. 141.
[52] Evolution is discussed in the longer version of this paper.

might have a beginning in time, and God's creation, which is eternal. Secondly, God is considered as creator, but as his creation is eternal, the existence of God cannot be separated from the existence of his creation. Thirdly, God's act of creation is indirect as he uses the Spirit as his creative agent. Fourthly, our physical universe is an emanation from the spiritual world and, therefore, direct intervention of God in the genesis of our universe is not necessary.

The Bahá'í writings give two different accounts of the origin of the universe: one in which the universe has an origin in time and one in which it is eternal. Bahá'u'lláh says explicitly that both accounts are true and should be considered as complementary views of reality under the theory of intelligibility that we have already presented. The first account is purely naturalistic and fits well with the Big-bang scenario. In "The Tablet of Wisdom," Bahá'u'lláh writes:

> The world of existence came into being through the heat generated from the interaction between the active force and that which is its recipient.[53]

In other words, a force has interacted with itself to create the energy[54] that set everything into motion. In that account, the universe has a beginning. However, even if our universe has a beginning, the process of creation is eternal. In the same tablet Bahá'u'lláh writes:

> As regard thine assertions about the beginning of creation, this is a matter on which conceptions vary by reason of divergences in men's thoughts and opinions. Wert thou to assert that it has ever existed, and shall continue

---

[53] "Tablet of Wisdom," in *Writings of Baha'u'llah.* p. 139. In my view, the translation of this passage, allows for various interpretations. Baha'u'llah may have meant here that the universe has been created by one single force that has interacted with itself.

[54] In the nineteenth century, the Arabic word for "heat" had a very broad meaning that covers the modern concept of "force" or "energy."

to exist, it would be true; or wert thou to affirm the same concept as is mentioned in the sacred Scripture, no doubt would there be about it, for it hath been revealed by God, the Lord of the worlds.[55]

This was clarified by 'Abdu'l-Bahá when he said:

The universe never had a beginning. From the point of view of essence, it transforms itself.[56] God is eternal in essence and in time. He is his own existence and cause. This is why the material world is eternal in essence, for the power of God is eternal.[57]

The question of creation having a beginning or no beginning is treated by Bahá'u'lláh as two complementary views in an example typical of the theory of intelligibility, which says that the apprehension of reality requires the juxtaposition of different complementary views. Another important point is that the material world, but not necessarily this universe, is also eternal like the spiritual world. Materiality and spirituality are associated in eternity. Matter is an attribute of creation without which creation would not be complete and would not be able to attain its fundamental purpose. This makes the question of *ex nihilo* creation irrelevant.[58] This also has profound consequences for the concept of God as creator. God is a not the great architect who has pondered on the blueprint of His creation and reviewed minute details before launching the project. Creation is a manifestation of God in which nature is a very small component of a much larger structure. Although this small component throws some light on the larger structure, it does not allow us to grasp its scale and finality. God is creator in the sense of being ontologically anterior to the creation and non-contingent,

---

[55] Ibid, p. 139.

[56] It is interesting to note that 'Abdu'l-Bahá defines the universe as an eternal self-transforming essence.

[57] ADP, p. 106.

[58] See Gerhard May (translated by A. S. Worrall), *Creatio Ex Nihilo: The Doctrine of 'Creation out of Nothing' in Early Christian Thought.* London: T&T Clark International, 1994.

whereas creation is contingent and dependent on a first cause. Once again, God is not the creator in the sense that one day He commenced the process of matter and space-time generation. He is the creator in the sense that we can say that we are the creators of our mind and of our thoughts. As we all know, we cannot stop thinking, and our thoughts tell us something about ourselves, but our thoughts are not us and are contingent in relation to us. The rationality that we see in the universe is a reflection of God's rationality. Science tells us how to read the mind of God.

THE AGENCY OF THE SPIRIT

The distance that the Bahá'í writings put between God and His creation is reinforced by the fact that God is only indirectly the creator, as He acts through an agent: the Spirit. The Spirit is described in the Bahá'í writings as the *First Emanation,* the *Primal Will,* the *Word of God* or Logos or simply Love. The Spirit links God to His creation like the rays of the sun emanate from the sun and can be reflected into a mirror. Bahá'u'lláh writes:

> Thus does the Great Announcement[59] inform thee about this glorious structure.[60] Such as communicate the generating influence[61] and such as receive its impact are indeed created through the irresistible Word of God which is the Cause of the entire creation, while all else besides His Word are but the creatures and the effects thereof.[62]

And 'Abdu'l-Bahá comments:

> The first emanation from God is the bounty[63] of the Kingdom, which emanates and is reflected in the reality of the creatures, like the light which emanates from

---

[59] By "Great Announcement" we understand Bahá'u'lláh himself.
[60] By "glorious structure" we understand the universe.
[61] "Generating influence" refers to the active force mentioned by Bahá'u'lláh.
[62] TOB, p. 140.
[63] The Arabic word *'fadl'* can be translated alternatively by 'bounty', 'grace' or 'emanation'.

the sun and is resplendent in creatures; and this bounty [emanation] which is the light, is reflected in infinite forms in the reality of all things, and specifies and individualizes itself according to the capacity, the worthiness, and the intrinsic value of things...[64]

But even if the Spirit is the agent of creation, God remains the creator: "*It is He Who hath called into being the whole of creation, Who hath caused every created thing to spring forth at his behest.*"[65]

The nature of the Spirit is of course something that is as mysterious as the nature of God. This cannot be explained in philosophical language but only in metaphorical terms. However, if the nature of the Spirit cannot be comprehended by the human mind, its manifestation can be and the Bahá'í writings teach that the manifestations of Spirit are as diverse as the various domains of God's creation and are responsible for the unity/discontinuity dialectic that we see in reality.

THE TWO PROCESSES OF EMANATION AND MANIFESTATION

This agency of the Spirit cannot be understood without introducing two fundamental concepts of Bahá'í metaphysics: the concepts of emanation and manifestation. Whereas emanation has been used a great deal in Christian and Islamic philosophy (inspired by Neo-Platonism), the Bahá'í writings hold that the process of emanation alone cannot explain the relationship between God and His creation and must be completed by the process of manifestation. Emanation is what confers existence upon things. The physical world is an emanation of the spiritual world.[66] Essences are created by emanation. However, everything that exists manifests the Spirit. While emanation is a one-to-one relationship, manifestation can be a one-to-many relationship.[67]

---

[64] SAQ, p. 295.
[65] *Gleaning from the Writings of Baha'u'llah*. Wilmette, IL: Bahá'í Publishing Trust, 1983, p. 193
[66] SAQ, p. 202.
[67] SAQ, p. 295.

One property or entity can be manifested in many things, i.e. in contemporary philosophical parlance, we can have many instantiations of the same universal and these instantiations can have diverse forms, depending on the *locus* of manifestation. Without this process of manifestation, creation would be stillborn due to the impossibility of change or evolution. Things are endowed with potentialities and manifestation is the process by which these potentialities can be expressed.

Many allusions in the Bahá'í writings suggest that the processes of emanation and manifestation are two complementary aspects of reality which, due to the cognitive limitations of the human mind, cannot be perceived in their unicity. The process of emanation is responsible for the continuity aspect of reality, while manifestation is responsible for its discontinuity aspect.

MANIFESTATIONS OF THE SPIRIT AND DISCONTINUITY IN REALITY

Everything that exists is a mirror capable of reflecting the Spirit according to the capacity of its own essence. In each natural kingdom, the Spirit has its own manifestations according to the capacity and potentialities of that kingdom. This is the reason that 'Abdu'l-Bahá speaks of a mineral spirit, a vegetable spirit or an animal spirit. They are different manifestations of the same Spirit: the universal spirit, the Logos or Word of God.

Each manifestation of the spirit is responsible for the fundamental properties of that kingdom. For example, the mineral spirit is responsible for the force of cohesion that exists in matter and holds it together: the electro-magnetic force, the strong atomic force, the weak atomic force and gravity in modern parlance. Or rather, we can say that these four forces of the universe are the manifestation of a more fundamental spiritual force that embraces all aspects of God's creation and that 'Abdu'l-Bahá calls Love, i.e. the force that binds everything together, including God to His creation. In the vegetable kingdom, the Spirit manifests itself through the vegetable spirit, which confers biological life and vegetative functions, including the capacity of growth. Then, comes the animal spirit, which brings to life different potentialities, including powers of sensory perception. The human spirit confers to humanity rational and spiritual powers that allow individuals to free themselves from the prison of phenomenal appearances. 'Abdu'l-Bahá speaks even of a Spirit of Faith that allows humans to bind with their creator.

It is clear that when 'Abdu'l-Bahá makes these distinctions between the four kingdoms and the five sorts of spirit, his aim is not to give a taxonomic description of nature but rather to identify spiritual principles that will help us to understand human nature and our relationship with the spiritual dimension of reality. As usual, in order to understand the spiritual realm, he starts from observation of nature, and because the observation of natural realities helps us to understand spiritual realities, it cannot be completely dismissed as scientifically irrelevant. However, what is important here is the metaphysics beyond the science. It does not matter if there are four, five or six natural kingdoms. What is important is the type of relationships that exists between these different domains of reality. For example, a higher kingdom remains always dependent on a lower kingdom for its existence, or a higher kingdom always exemplifies a higher degree of cooperation between its various components.[68] The metaphysical connotation of 'Abdu'l-Bahá's typology has also been remarked by Kitzing who writes: *"In modern biology the kingdoms, originally introduced by Aristotle, are today used in a taxonomic sense; they designate distinct classes of organisms. 'Abdu'l-Bahá is obviously not concerned with a taxonomic distinction of biological classes, but with a hierarchy of increasingly complex faculties ... Thus in this context, the "kingdoms" do not designate taxonomically distinct classes but hierarchical levels."*[69] This does not mean that a theory

---

[68] See *'Abdu'l-Bahá in Compilation on Huqúqu'lláh*, in Compilation of Compilations, No 61, New Delhi, BPT, p. 504: "The higher a kingdom of creation on the arc of ascent, the more conspicuous are the signs and evidences of the truth that cooperation and reciprocity at the level of a higher order are greater than those that exist at the level of a lower order."

[69] Kitzing in *Brown Evolution and Bahá'í Belief*. Los Angeles: Kalimat Press, 2001, pp. 198–9.

of discontinuity of nature cannot be developed on these bases. However, such a theory would probably need more than four levels or kingdoms. A distinction would have to be made between the molecular level and the atomic level and below the atomic level it is not yet clear how many additional levels would be required. Each level would require a distinct and specific ontology to be harmonized and reconciled into a more general theory of ontology. Each level would also require a specific form of scientific and metaphysical realism to understand its relational structure and its interconnection with the whole reality of the universe.

INTERCONNECTEDNESS

Although nature manifests itself in a discontinuous manner, we have seen also that nature is a unifying agency. The principle of oneness of reality already mentioned cannot by itself explain the unifying role of nature. That requires principles that transcend the different sets of laws of nature operating at different levels of reality. The unifying role of nature is possible because everything in the universe, material and spiritual, is interconnected through a web of necessary relationships that play a major role in the working of reality. In fact, nature is made of two things: particulars or things in themselves and relationships that link particulars through their properties. 'Abdu'l-Bahá writes:

> Reflect upon the inner realities of the universe, the secret wisdom involved, the enigmas, the inter-relationships, the rules that govern all. For every part is interconnected with every part by ties that are powerful and admit no imbalance, nor any slackening whatever.[70]

Everything in this universe is interconnected, and everything in the spiritual world is also interconnected. 'Abdu'l-Bahá writes:

> All phenomena are involved in all phenomena. Consider what a transcendent unity exists, that, from this stand-

---

[70] *Selection from the Writings of 'Abdu'l-Bahá.* Haifa, Israel: Bahá'í World Center, 1978, p. 157.

point, every monad is the expression of the whole creation; this is the law and order of the world of existence.[71]

Explaining the interconnectedness of things in nature is another important task of the Bahá'í philosophy of nature. The affirmation of the interconnectedness of everything in the universe has far-reaching metaphysical and ontological implications. It is incompatible with a Humean view of the world in which the universe is made of discrete self-contained events and passive particulars and in which regularities are the expression of contingent laws. Interconnectedness implies a world in which connections play a prominent role. This sort of connectedness implies that properties have active powers that bond particulars together in a non-contingent manner. This implies also a holistic view of nature: a view that sees nature as a web of necessary relations which has a natural as well as a metaphysical dimension (in opposition to a worldview of discrete events and a metaphysics of discreta). It implies a world, as Munford writes that "comes *with a whole, connected system of properties.*"[72] In such a system the understanding of relations is what gives us an understanding of the world. Particulars cannot be understood in abstraction from the web of relations in which they exist.

EMERGENCE

If we look carefully at what 'Abdu'l-Bahá calls 'spirits', he is describing a set of properties that are specific to an ontological domain that he calls 'kingdom.' He explains that these properties cannot be the result of properties and laws existing at a lower level of reality; in other words, they are non-reducible. The vegetable kingdom is identified by a form of life that includes a metabolism, the capacity for growth and a form of reproduction. All these properties of the vegetable kingdom are absent from the mineral kingdom. Each level of nature is characterized by new

---

[71] PRP, p. 168.
[72] Stephen Munford. *Laws in Nature*. London: Routledge, 2004, p. 182.

properties: the cohesion of matter, vegetative life, faculties of perception, reflexive consciousness, and the like. This is exactly the concept of emergence that is now assuming paramount importance within our modern understanding of complex systems.

At the time of 'Abdu'l-Bahá, Persian or Arabic did not have a word for '*emergence*', but as we have seen, it does not mean that the idea did not exist. In fact, Bahá'u'lláh and 'Abdu'l-Bahá use another word; a word so obvious and so ubiquitous that its fundamental meaning escapes most readers. That word is '*manifestation*'. It is true that the word '*manifestation*' has broader scope than '*emergence*'. '*Manifestation*' can apply to God Himself, or to His representative on earth, or to the human soul. However, when '*manifestation*' applies to natural phenomena, it describes exactly what modern science and philosophy call '*emergence*'. Another good example of this can be found in 'Abdu'l-Bahá's writings, when he says that '*intelligence*' (meaning the mind) is "manifested" gradually in the body and that the body must grow to a certain level of complexity and maturity to manifest fully the potential of intelligence, as we can see with young children who grow in intelligence when they are bodily developed and mature.[73] The important point is that both Bahá'u'lláh and 'Abdu'l-Bahá link the concept of emergence with the idea of complexity. When a threshold of complexity is passed, new properties naturally emerge, not as the result of the interaction of particulars but because they already exist potentially in the universe. Other examples of other forms of emergence can be found in 'Abdu'l-Bahá's writings when he says:

> ...for example, the seed, which is a single thing possessing the vegetative perfection, which it manifests in infinite forms, resolving itself into branches, leaves, flowers and fruits: this is called appearance in manifestation...[74]

---

[73] *Selection from the Writings of 'Abdu'l-Bahá*, Haifa: Bahá'í World Centre, 1978 p. 285.
[74] SAQ, p. 295.

In fact, a careful examination of the Bahá'í writings shows that they refer to two types of emergence: (a) emergence that occurs between different levels of reality (kingdoms) such as, for example, the emergence of life out of the mineral kingdom; and (b) emergence between different levels of complexity within the same level of organization of nature, as we have seen with the example of the branches and leaves manifested out of the seed. I will call the first type of emergence *ontological emergence* and the second type *systemic emergence*. The difference between ontological and systemic emergence is that while each level of ontological emergence requires new sets of laws of nature in addition to the existing ones, systemic emergence operates under the same set of laws.

Since the late 1960s and 1970s, various new mathematical theories permit the study of nonlinear systems as well as the understanding of their evolution and of the conditions of their dynamic stability. These new investigative techniques include chaos theories, catastrophe theory, genetic algorithms, cellular automata, and others. They show that, as the Bahá'í writings predicted, complexity is not something added to our universe but something inbuilt in it from its very beginning and one of its key characteristics. Understanding how complexity and order appear in a chaotic system involves almost immediately the idea of emergence. Significant progress has been made in understanding systemic emergence but little in understanding ontological emergence. The emergence of life and of consciousness remains a mystery despite all the research in artificial life and artificial intelligence based on computational emergence.

There is a growing consensus among theoreticians of emergence that for an emergent phenomenon to be recognized as such, it must at least display five characteristics: complexity, irreducibility, unpredictability, conceptual novelty and holism. Complexity means that emergence occurs only in systems having a certain degree of complexity and that emergence is directional, always going from one level of complexity to a higher degree of complexity. Irreducibility and unpredictability mean that new emergent properties cannot be explained by the properties of the level from which they emerge and that their appearance cannot be predicted by the properties of that level. Novelty means that new emerging structures display new features and properties that bear limited resemblance with lower structures and that require different conceptual tools for their analysis (conceptual novelty). Holism means that properties are the properties of the system, not properties of its components. Natural structures are not determined by the structure of the system components but by their level of complexity which implies new information not existing at a lower level. This means that nature (if we consider the universe as a system) has properties distinct from its components or subsystems.

This does not mean that every scientist or philosopher is ready to embrace emergentism. The concept of emergence is still so much in need of clarification that its epistemological status remains in question. Once again, we believe that this lack of clarity is due to the lack of a supportive ontology that is integrated with the metaphysical framework of philosophy of nature. A first conceptual difficulty is to find a definition of emergence. This task has proved incredibly difficult. Workable definitions of emergence are rare phenomena, whilst weak definitions are ubiquitous. Then, there comes the difficulty of defining the different organizational levels of nature. Life seems easy to distinguish from nonorganic matter, but what about viruses and prions? Do prokaryotes and eukaryotes represent different levels of organization of life? Do fungi and plants belong to the same level of complexity? How does scale in nature relate to complexity? Subatomic physics is different from atomic physics such as chemistry partially because they operate on different scales.

Here we should remember that we are looking for a metaphysical theory of emergence and metaphysics cannot solve scientific problems; it can only provide a better ontology that will bring greater clarity to the interpretation of scientific theories. But it cannot remedy the deficiency of such theories. Finding valid examples of emergence in natural processes that can be analysed in a scientific manner is the task of science, but the validity of a metaphysical theory would not rest on such examples. A metaphysical theory would be only remotely concerned by the problem of emergence of new properties between different levels of complexity within the same system of nature. A metaphysical theory is more about emergence of a higher ontological level out of a lower ontological level. Although many scientists entertain the hope, or the fancy, that one day they will be able to explain the emergence of life or consciousness in purely naturalist terms, we think that this is impossible. Only ontological emergence is of significance for Bahá'í metaphysics; systemic emergence does not play any role.

PROPERTIES AND NECESSARY RELATIONS

Finally, one of the most important concepts of Bahá'í metaphysics is the concept of necessary relation. Besides the fact that essences are vehicles for fundamental properties of things and, therefore, determine the logical and intelligible structure of reality, little can be known about essences. We know about essences through the properties of things. From a philosophical viewpoint, the study of these properties and the necessary relations that they determine are far more important than knowing what essences in themselves are. As already said, necessary relations should be viewed as the central concept of Bahá'í ontology.

Natural objects have properties and dispositions that determine what they are and what sort of bounds or relations, under the universal law of attraction and affinity, they can forge with other natural objects. It means that there can be two complementary views of nature. The first one is a description of nature as a structure made of natural objects in which each object is described precisely in terms of properties and behaviours. This view of nature is very powerful as long as natural objects are discrete, relatively simple and interacting with a limited number of other objects as it is the case in fundamental physics. This is the view of nature that we find in Western science. The second complementary view of nature is a view that takes a holistic approach and sees nature as a web of necessary and accidental relations between natural objects. This view is very powerful when applied to complex systems of natural objects such as the weather or an ecological system. This is the view that Bahá'í philosophy should try to promote while recognizing that the first view is complementary and should not be neglected.

The important point to grasp is that relations are relatively independent in their expression and causal powers from the properties that generate them. A natural object A has a property (a) and a natural object B has a property (b). The properties (a) and (b) determine a necessary relation 'x' between A and B. However, in many cases 'x' can be explained neither by (a) nor (b). The relation that binds things together is made of information different in nature from the information carried by the properties of A and B. In other words, relations cannot be reduced to properties. They are distinct from the causing power of any of the two natural objects because the causality that results from the relation is distinct from the causal powers of (a) and (b). Necessary relations must be studied for their own sake because they play a crucial role in the architecture of the system of nature and are the unifying agency of reality, as discussed earlier.

One of the great advantages of the concept of necessary relations is that it is a universal concept that applies to all fields of human knowledge and cognition. Necessary relations not only apply to all natural objects existing in the universe but encompass all metaphysical and spiritual worlds. They apply to inanimate objects as well as to living beings. While science is not a unified activity because the ontological discontinuity of nature prevents the existence of a single scientific methodology, on a philosophical level, necessary relations provide a unifying concept that can give a unifying view of all scientific activities and knowledge. It also helps to understand the origin of order in the universe and to understand that laws of nature are simply the mathematical formulation of some of these necessary relations. As a consequence, necessary relations also explain complexity. Physics and chemistry can be based on a relatively limited number of 'laws' because the relations existing between physical objects are relatively few. On the other hand, it is far more difficult to formulate biological laws because biological phenomena are far more complex than physical or chemical phenomena. When we come to the study of animals, this study must be put in the perspective of the vast web of relations that link and interconnect all living beings in a community that itself extends not only to plants but also to geological and meteorological systems that form the biosphere.

Because necessary relations are not limited to the physical world, they also apply to human activities. Human societies are based on necessary relations that we try to formulate through psychology, anthropology, sociology and political science. Economics, with its theory of markets and price formation, is a good example of necessary relations applied to human activities. Ethics itself could not exist without the deep belief in the existence of a number of fundamental relations in human society determined by human nature. Because human nature is not just physical but also spiritual, human 'properties', or rather attributes, are not just biological but also spiritual. Spiritual laws that govern our spiritual existence are born from the necessary relations existing between this universe and the spiritual world. Finally, as 'Abdu'l-Bahá seems to show, the concept of necessary relations is what unifies science, philosophy and religion.

Necessary relations are not only a universal concept that integrates all areas of human knowledge and cognition but is also a concept that provides a tool that can help formulating in a coherent manner philosophical or ontological theories, addressing some of the mysteries of our universe. For example, the origin of numbers can be explained in terms of relations between sets. The existence of physical constants in the universe can also be explained the same way. This is also true for the existence of the forces of physics or non-local connectedness as demonstrated in Aspect's experiment. The space-time continuum can be seen as being generated by necessary relationships existing between natural objects or simply as the sum of all these relations. Necessary relations probably play a great role in all emergent phenomena.

They explain why the different kingdoms of nature seem to unfold with a ready-made architecture that makes everything fit in its place. Necessary relations certainly play a role in the explanation of biological evolution, and particularly in the explanation of biological convergence between species. The dolphin, a mammal that shares the same environment as fishes, and looks like a fish, is a good example. We are discovering that forms in nature play a great role also in evolution.[75] Nature knows how to design complex geometrical forms such as Fibonacci spirals, Bénard cells, spiral wave patterns and uses repetitive fractal geometry in very effective ways. Forms play a great role in determining the properties of molecules, and they probably play an important role in determining the evolutionary path of living beings. The emergence of regular and repetitive patterns seems to be a fundamental characteristic of nature and can be explained by the concept of necessary relations.

---

[75] On the role of forms in biology see D'Arcy Wentworth Thompson and John Tyler Bonner *On Growth and Forms.* New York: Dover Publications, 1994 (originally published in 1917 by Cambridge University Press); Philip Ball. *The Self-Made Tapestry: Pattern Formation in Nature*, Oxford: Oxford University Press, 2001; Yves Bouligand (editor). *Les Sciences de la Forme Aujourd'hui,* Paris: Seuil, 1994; and Paul Bourgine and Annick Lesne. *Morphogénèse: L'Origine des Formes*, Paris: Belin, 2006.

The Criteria of Knowledge: Beyond Inspiration

JULIO SAVI
Wilmette Institute

'Abdu'l-Bahá specifies four criteria of human knowledge: sense perception, intellect, tradition or Scripture and inspiration.[1] He explained this concept in two of the talks he delivered in the United States, specifically in Hotel Ansonia on 17 April 1912[2] and

---

[1] See "Tablet to Dr Auguste Henri Forel," in *The Bahá'í World*, vol.15, 1968–1973 (Haifa: The Universal House of Justice, 1976) 37–43; 'Abdu'l-Bahá. *Some Answered Questions,* trans. Laura Clifford-Barney, (Wilmette, IL: Bahá'í Publishing Trust, 1957) 297–9, sec. 83; Persian edition: *An Núr al-Abhá fi Mufávaḍát-i 'Abdu'l-Bahá. Table Talks,* collected by Laura Clifford Barney (New Delhi: Bahá'í Publishing Trust, 1983) 207–8, from now on *Mufávaḍát; The Promulgation of Universal Peace. Talks delivered by 'Abdu'l-Bahá during His visit to the United States and Canada in 1912,* comp. Howard MacNutt (Wilmette, IL: Bahá'í Publishing Trust, 1982) 20–2, 253–5, 355–7, from now on Promulgation; *'Abdu'l-Bahá on Divine Philosophy* (Boston: Tudor Press, 1918) 88–90 (from now on *Divine Philosophy*). See also Udo Schaefer. *Bahá'í Ethics in Light of Scripture. An Introduction. Volume 1. Doctrinal Fundamentals.* Translated from the German by Dr Geraldine Schuckelt (Oxford: George Ronald, 2007) 273, Julio Savi. "Methods and Qualities of the Seeker of Reality," *Lights of 'Irfán*, vol. 10 (Papers presented at the 'Irfán Colloquia and Seminars. Evanston, IL: Haj Mehdi Arjmand Memorial Fund, 2009) 311–25, from now on "Methods," and Peter Terry. "Bahá'í Epistemology," (http://bahai-library.com/pdf/t/terry_abdulbaha_epistemology.pdf, retrieved on 3 July 2018).

[2] *Promulgation* 20–2.

at the Green Acre Bahá'í School on 16 August 1912,[3] as well as in a talk he delivered on the occasion of his second visit to Europe, in 1913.[4] He also explained the same concept in one of his table-talks with Mrs. Laura Clifford Barney[5] (1879–1974), an early American Bahá'í. He said in this talk:

There are only four accepted methods (*mízán*) of comprehension — that is to say, the realities of things are understood by these four methods.[6]

Similar words are written in one of his Arabic Tablets,[7] sometimes entitled Lawḥ-i-Fu'ad (Tablet of the Inmost Heart), provisionally translated into English by Steven Phelps and William McCants in March 2000: "...know that all the peoples and kindreds possess four balances with which they weigh the realities, the significances, and the divine questions."[8]

This list of criteria of knowledge is reminiscent of the following words ascribed to the Greek philosopher Plotinus (203–269/270 CE), the founder of Neoplatonism, by Robert Alfred Vaughan (1823–1857), Protestant minister and writer, in his book *Hours with the mystics; a contribution to the history of religious opinion* published in 1860:[9] "Knowledge has three degrees: opinion, science, illumination. The means or instrument of the first is sense; of the second dialectic; of the third, intuition."[10]

'Abdu'l-Bahá examines each of these four criteria and concludes that all of them are limited in their possibilities and fallible

---

[3] *Promulgation* 252–5.
[4] *Divine Philosophy*, 88–90.
[5] She is also known as Laura Dreyfus Barney.
[6] Some Answered Questions (trans. 296, sec. 83; Mufávaḍát 207).
[7] Letters or short writings.
[8] *Makátíb-i-Ḥaḍrat-i-'Abdu'l-Bahá*, vol. 1. (Bahá'í Publishing Trust, Iran, n.d.) 109, from now on Lawḥ-i-Fu'ad; English provisional translation: http://bahai-library.com/pdf/t/terry_abdulbaha_epistemology.pdf, retrieved on 3 July 2018.
[9] Its third edition, 1893, may be found at http://archive.org/stream/hourswithmystics1893vaug#page/n35/mode/2up, retrieved on 3 July 2018.
[10] Plotinus. "Letter to Flaccus," quoted in Vaughan, in his book *Hours with the mystics* 80, http://archive.org/stream/hourswithmystics1893vaug#page/n123/mode/2up/search/dialectic, retrieved on 3 July 2018..

in their results. For example, he said: "Briefly, the point is that in the human material world of phenomena these four are the only existing criteria or avenues of knowledge, and all of them are faulty and unreliable."[11]

The same concept is explained in his Tablet of the Inmost Heart:

> ...know that all the peoples and kindreds possess four balances with which they weigh the realities, the significances, and the divine questions. All of them are imperfect, unable to quench the burning thirst or heal the sick. We shall therefore make mention of each one and demonstrate its limitation and inaccuracy.[12]

In this paper we will only examine one of these four criteria of knowledge mentioned by 'Abdu'l-Bahá, inspiration.

INSPIRATION[13]

'Abdu'l-Bahá describes inspiration (*ilhám*) as "the suggestions of the heart (*khuṭúrátin qalbiyyatin*),"[14] "the influxes of the heart (*wáridátu'l-qalbíyyan*),"[15] "the influx of the human heart,"[16] "the promptings or susceptibilities of the human heart."[17] The meanings of these definitions may be more easily understood, in the light of the meanings of the words *qalb*, *khuṭúrát* and *wáridát* in Islamic literature. The Italian Islamicist Alessandro Bausani

---

[11] *Promulgation* 22.

[12] Lawḥ-i-Fu'ad 109.

[13] See 'Abdu'l-Bahá. *Selections from the Writings of 'Abdu'l-Baha*, trans. Marzieh Gail (Haifa: Bahá'í World Centre, 1978) 37–8, sec. 18; *Some Answered Questions* 157, sec. 40, para. 4; *Paris Talks: Addresses Given by 'Abdu'l-Bahá in 1911*. (London: Bahá'í Publishing Trust, 1995) 83–4, sec. 28, para.14, 185–8, sec. 54, paras.1–19; *Divine Philosophy* 122. See also Savi, "Methods" 316–21.

[14] Lawḥ-i-Fu'ád 112.

[15] *Makátíb-i-Ḥaḍrat-i-'Abdu'l-Bahá*. vol. 1 (Bahá'í Publishing Trust, Iran, n.d.) 153 and 397, from now on *Makátíb*.

[16] *Promulgation* 22.

[17] *Promulgation* 254.

(1921–1988) remarks in this regard that the Persian word *dil* (corresponding to the Arabic *qalb*) is "generally translated as 'heart,' but 'brain' or 'intuition' would be better."[18] As to the definition "the suggestions of the heart (*khutúrátin qalbiyyatin*)," it could mean the "'incoming thoughts (*khawátir*)'[19] which reach the heart," mentioned by the Andalusian philosopher Muhíyi'd-Dín Ibn al-'Arabí (1165–1240), sometimes considered the greatest Sufi philosopher.[20] And as to the definition "the influxes of the heart (*wáridátu'l-qalbíyyan*)," it could mean an "'inrush (*wárid*)... which arrived at the heart without self-exertion,"[21] mentioned by the same philosopher.

In his explanation of inspiration (*ilhám*) as the fourth criterion of knowledge, 'Abdu'l-Bahá mentions the categories of people that usually uphold it. He said: "There is still another, a fourth criterion, upheld by religionists and metaphysicians who say that the source and channel of all human penetration into the unknown is through inspiration."[22]

He said moreover:

> The fourth standard is that of inspiration. In past centuries many philosophers have claimed illumination or revelation, prefacing their statements by the announcement that "this subject has been revealed through me"

---

[18] Alessandro Bausani. *Religion in Iran* (Translated by J. M. Marchesi. New York: Bibliotheca Persica Press, 2000) 263.

[19] *Khawátir e khutúrát* are two plural forms of *khátir,* "An opinion, or an idea, or object of thought, bestirring itself in the mind... a thing coming at random into the mind: or a cogitation which bestirs itself, or occurs, in the mind, with a view to the end, issue, or result, of a thing: [whence the phrase,]... *khatarátu ash-Sháyátín* the vain suggestions of the devil" (E. W. Lane. *An Arabic-English Lexicon* (London and Edinburgh: Williams and Norgate, 1863–93. CD-Rom edition published by Thesaurus Islamicus Foundation. Cairo: Tradigital, 2003) vol. 3, p. 401).

[20] See William C. Chittick. *The Sufi Path of Knowledge: Ibn al-'Arabí's Metaphysics of Imagination* (Albany, NY: State University of New York Press, 1989) xiii, from now on *Sufi Path.*

[21] Chittick. *Sufi Path* 266.

[22] *Promulgation* 20–21.

or "thus do I speak by inspiration." Of this class were the philosophers of the Illuminati.[23]

In another circumstance, he explained: "Inspiration is the fourth criterion. Occultists say, "I have had a revelation. This truth has been revealed to me." For them everything outside direct revelation is viewed with doubt.[24]

And thus, the categories of people who use inspiration as their preferred criterion of knowledge are, in 'Abdu'l-Bahá's words, "religionists and metaphysicians," "the Illuminati," whom he also calls "followers of the inner light,"[25] and "occultists."

As to "religionists," they could be those people whom the Islamic world calls "*ummat.*"[26] They are "the community of the believers... the mass of the believers."[27]

As to "metaphysicians," they could be philosophers who believe in God and deal with metaphysics intended as "something that deals with what is beyond the physical or the experiential,"[28] or "those informed with divine philosophy."[29]

As to "the Illuminati," they could be the *Ishráqiyyún*, who follow the philosophy of the Muslim mystic Shihábu'd-Dín Suhravardí (1154–1191). Their school of thought holds that the origin of philosophy is divine revelation and that this wisdom was

---

[23] *Promulgation* 254.
[24] *Divine Philosophy* 93–4.
[25] *Paris Talks* 186, sec. 54, para. 2.
[26] See 'Abdu'l-Bahá *Selections* 229, sec. 193, Persian text: *Muntakhabátí az Makátíb-i Ḥaḍrat-i 'Abdu'l-Bahá* (Wilmette, IL: Bahá'í Publishing Trust, 1979) 222.
[27] Marcello Perego. *Le parole del sufismo: Dizionario della spiritualità islamica* (Milan: Mimesis, 1998) 248.
[28] Webster's (1986) 1420–1.
[29] *Divine Philosophy* 100. 'Abdu'l-Bahá explains that divine philosophy studies and realizes "spiritual verities" (*Promulgation* 138), "spiritual realities" (ibid.), "the mysteries of God... the wisdom of God, inner significances of the heavenly religions and foundation of the law" (ibid.), that is the "phenomena of the spirit" (*Promulgation* 326). The Persian notes of the talk recorded in English in *Promulgation* 138–9 may be found in *Majmú'iy-i-Khaṭábát-i-Ḥaḍrat-i-'Abdu'l-Bahá* (Langenhain: Bahá'í-Verlag, 1984) 386–9, from now on *Majmú'ih*.

handed down in ancient times to the Persians and the Greeks, creating two traditions that met again in Suhrawardi, who spoke explicitly of eternal wisdom or the perennial philosophy. This school believes that authentic philosophy must combine the training of the mind with the purification of the heart and that all authentic knowledge is ultimately an illumination. The ishraq-is always emphasized the unbreakable link between philosophy and spirituality and the salvific power of illuminative knowledge. They considered God to be the Light of lights and all degree of cosmic reality to be levels and grades of light.[30]

In other circumstances 'Abdu'l-Bahá mentions the Illuminati as "the Society of the Friends, who gathered together for silent communion with the Almighty."[31] Later he explained in a Tablet:

> This Society was founded in the city of Hamadan six hundred years ago and has nothing to do with this [Bahá'í] movement. It is almost disbanded, but under different names and forms one may come across them in Persia. They were called the Society of Sokoutyyoun, that is, the "Silent Ones."[32]

As to "occultists," occultism is "a belief in hidden or mysterious powers and the possibility of subjecting them to human control."[33] He mentioned "occultists" in a talk delivered in Europe in 1913 and registered in *Divine Philosophy* 93. During his Western travels (1911–1913) 'Abdu'l-Bahá was in touch with members of the Theosophical Society. The initial objective of the Theosophical Society, officially formed in New York, in November 1875 by

---

[30] "Ishraqi School," November 30, 2011, in *Islam Encyclopedia*, https://www.encyclopedia.com/religion/encyclopedias-almanacs-tran-scripts-and-maps/ishraqi-school, retrieved on 3 July 2018.

[31] *Paris Talks* 185, sec. 54, para. 1.

[32] "A question answered. [From a Tablet of 'Abdu'l-Baha to Ella G. Cooper, translated and mailed from Haifa, Syria, March 19, 1916]," *Star of the West* (The first Bahá'í magazine in the Western world, published from 1910 to 1935. Issues 1910 to 1924, RP 8 vols. Oxford: George Ronald, 1978), vol. 8, no. 14 (23 November 1917) 204.

[33] Webster's 1560.

Helena Blavatsky (1831–1891) and others, was the "study and elucidation of Occultism, the Cabala etc."[34] Therefore when he mentioned occultists, perhaps he also meant theosophists.

'Abdu'l-Bahá takes into consideration the effectiveness of inspiration as a criterion of knowledge. He writes for example in his Tablet of the Inmost Heart:

> And the whisperings (*wasáwis*) of Satan are also inclinations (*khuṭúrát*), which arrive successively upon the heart (*qalb*) by the agency of the soul (*nafs*). If there occureth to the heart a certain idea or question, how is it to be known whether it is an inspiration (*ilhámát*) of the All-Merciful or a whispering (*wasáwis*) of Satan?[35]

He writes in another Tablet:

> Verily, inspiration, as people understands it, consisteth of the insights (*wáridát*) of the heart and of the intimations (*khuṭúrátin*) and whispers (*wasavis*) of Satan. And when this occureth in the heart, how is it to be known whether it is a divine inspiration (*ilhámát*) or a whispering (*wasáwis*) of Satan?[36]

As to the whisperings of Satan, this locution has its origin in the Surih of Men, which says:

> In the Name of God, the Compassionate, the Merciful. Say: I betake me for refuge to the Lord of Men, The King of men, The God of men, Against the mischief of the stealthily withdrawing whisperer (*al-waswási*), Who whispereth in man's breast — Against djinn and men. (114:1–6)

This critique of inspiration also is expounded in two of 'Abdu'l-Bahá's talks:

---

[34] See http://hpb.narod.ru/EarlyDaysTheosophyAPS.htm, retrieved on 3 July 2018.

[35] Lawḥ-i-Fu'ád 112.

[36] *Makátíb* 153.

> But what are satanic promptings, which afflict man-
> kind? They are the influx of the heart also. How shall
> we differentiate between them? The question arises:
> How shall we know whether we are following inspiration
> from God or satanic promptings of the human soul?[37]

The promptings of the heart are sometimes satanic. How are
we to differentiate them? How are we to tell whether a given
statement is an inspiration and prompting of the heart through
the merciful assistance or through the satanic agency?[38]

These words by 'Abdu'l-Bahá reflect a specific vision of human beings, which is summarized in his following words:

> ...the spirit of man (rúḥ-i-insání) has two aspects: one di-
> vine (raḥmaní), one satanic (shayṭání)—that is to say, it is
> capable of the utmost perfection, or it is capable of the
> utmost imperfection. If it acquires virtues, it is the most
> noble of the existing beings; and if it acquires vices, it
> becomes the most degraded existence.[39]
> ...the evil spirit, Satan or whatever is interpreted as
> evil, refers to the lower nature in man. This baser na-
> ture is symbolized in various ways. In man there are two
> expressions: One is the expression of nature; the other,
> the expression of the spiritual realm.[40]
> Satan... [is meant as] the natural inclinations of the
> lower nature. This lower nature in man is symbolized as
> Satan — the evil ego within us, not an evil personality
> outside.[41]

Moreover, all these passages are reminiscent of the ancient
wisdom of Sufi philosophers and poets. The French Islamicist
Louis Gardet (1904–1986) writes that in Islamic thought the heart

---

[37] *Promulgation* 22.
[38] *Promulgation* 254.
[39] *Some Answered Questions* 144, sec. 36, para.4; *Mufávaḍát* 102
[40] *Promulgation* 294–5.
[41] *Promulgation* 286.

is not only the faculty of knowing, it is also the seat of all moral impulses, both evil desires and instincts and the struggle to be free of them and attentive to divine teaching... Salvation comes only from the heart's purified knowledge in its dual and inseparable aspects, speculative and actual. Thus, it is a complete education of the "heart" that spiritual teachers must constantly develop and enrich in themselves and their disciples.[42]

In this vein Ibn al-'Arabí distinguishes "'the incoming thoughts' which reach the heart[43] into four categories: divine (*ilāhī*), spiritual (*rūhānī*), ego-centric (*nafsānī*) and satanic" (*shaytānī*)."[44] He also distinguishes "the influxes of the heart (*wáridátu'l-qalbíyyan*)"[45] into "four species... Lordly (*Rabbānī*), angelic (*Malākī*), arising from the soul [ego-centric] (*Nafsī*), satanic (*Shaytānī*)]."[46] Moreover Jalálu'd-Dín Rúmí (1207–1273), the greatest poet in the Persian language, writes: "...both (Satanic) suggestion (*vasvasih*) and Divine inspiration are intelligible, and yet there is a (great) difference (between them)."[47]

He is echoed by the great Sufi poet Shamsu'd-d-Dín Háfiz (1315–1390): "In love's path, Ahriman's [the Zoroastrian God of evil] temptations (*vasvasih*) are many: Sense keep; and to Surush's [the Zoroastrian angel of obedience] message the ear of the heart put."[48]

---

[42] Louis Gardet. "Kalb. I. Mysticism," in *Encyclopaedia of Islam* (CD-ROM edition v. 1.0. Leiden: Koninklijke Brill NV, 1999).

[43] See "the suggestions of the heart (*khutúrátin qalbiyyatin*)" in Lawh-i-Fu'ád 112.

[44] Chittick. *Sufi Path* xiii.

[45] *Makátíb* 153 and 397.

[46] Ibn al-'Arabí, quoted in Perego, *Parole del sufismo* 255, s.v. Wāridāt.

[47] Rúmí. *The Mathnawí of Jalálu'Ddín Rúmí, edited from the oldest manuscripts available: with critical notes, translation and commentary by Reynold A. Nicholson. . .*, vol. 3 (Warminster, Wiltshire: Trustees of the E.J.W. Gibb Memorial Series, 1926) 3490; Persian text: *Mathnavíy-i-Ma'naví*. Available at http://www.masnavi.net/fa/2/, retrieved on 3 July 2018.

[48] *The Dīvān-i-Hāfiz*. Translated by H. Wilberforce Clarke (Bethesda, Maryland: Ibex Publishers, 1997) 744, n. 444, v. 6; Persian text: *The Divan of Hafiz* (Teheran: Aban Book Publication, 1387 [2008–2009]) 411, n. 398, v. 2.

In one of his talks delivered in London in 1913 'Abdu'l-Bahá suggested meditation as a path towards divine inspiration. He remarks that there is in man a faculty which "frees man from the animal nature, discerns the reality of things, puts man in touch with God,"[49] independently of the deductive or inductive processes of his mind. Through it "man attains to eternal life... he receives the breath of the Holy Spirit."[50] It is "the faculty of meditation."[51] While explaining the nature of this faculty. He quotes the school of "the Illuminati or followers of the inner light."[52] He said about them: "Meditating, and turning their faces to the Source of Light, from that central Light the mysteries of the Kingdom were reflected in the hearts of these people. All the Divine problems were solved by this power of illumination."[53]

Most people think that such a faculty can only be used in the mystic field. Yet it is well known that several great scientists have initially discovered physical laws through this "faculty of meditation" rather than reasoning and deduction: Newton, with his famous apple; Galileo, with the well-known episode of the swinging chandelier in the Cathedral of Pisa. The Bahá'í writings urge us to train ourselves in the use of divine inspiration by a daily practice of meditation and to use it in our endeavours to understand both physical and spiritual reality, for meditation — like a mirror — faithfully reflects whatever is placed in front of it. 'Abdu'l-Bahá says in this regard:

> The meditative faculty is akin to the mirror: if you put it before earthly objects it will reflect them. Therefore, if the spirit of man is contemplating earthly subjects he will be informed of these. But if you turn the mirror of your spirits heavenwards, the heavenly constellations and the rays of the Sun of Reality will be reflected in

---

[49] *Paris Talks* 187–8, sec. 54, para. 14.
[50] Ibid. 187, sec. 54, para. 11.
[51] Ibid.
[52] Ibid. 185, sec. 54, para. 2.
[53] Ibid.

your hearts, and the virtues of the Kingdom[54] will be obtained.[55]

'Abdu'l-Bahá explains that among the prerequisites to obtain the benefits of meditation are purification and detachment. He writes in an above-mentioned Tablet:

…if thy mind become empty and pure from every mention and thought and thy heart attracted wholly to the Kingdom of God, forget all else besides God and come in communion with the Spirit of God, then the Holy Spirit will assist thee with a power which will enable thee to penetrate all things, and a Dazzling Spark which enlightens all sides, a Brilliant Flame in the zenith of the heavens, will teach thee that which thou dost not know of the facts of the universe and of the divine doctrine.[56]

'Abdu'l-Bahá and, later on, Shoghi Effendi offered a number of suggestions for a better use of inspiration as a source of knowledge. Certainly, testing through the senses, the intellect and the Holy Scripture data received through inspiration and checking them against facts will help us to distinguish tinsel from gold. 'Abdu'l-Bahá wrote in this regard: "As to the difference between inspiration and imagination: inspiration is in conformity with the Divine Texts, but imaginations do not conform therewith.[57] And Shoghi Effendi said on the same issue: "The inspiration received through meditation is of a nature that one cannot measure or determine… We cannot clearly distinguish between personal

---

[54] The concept of "Kingdom" is very similar to the concept of "kingdom of heaven" in Matthews.
[55] *Paris Talk*I 188, sec. 54, paras.17–8. The locution "Sun of Reality" denotes the Holy Spirit.
[56] Tablets 706–7.
[57] Tablets 195. In this case inspiration could be interpreted as divine inspiration and imagination as the whisperings of our ego.

desire and guidance, but if the way opens, when we have sought guidance, then we may presume God is helping us."[58]

He also said:

> With regard to your question as to the value of intu-
> ition as a source of guidance for the individual; implic-
> it faith in our intuitive powers is unwise, but through
> daily prayer and sustained effort one can discover,
> though not always and fully, God's Will intuitively.
> Under no circumstances, however, can a person be
> absolutely certain that he is recognizing God's Will,
> through the exercise of his intuition. It often happens
> that the latter results in completely misrepresenting
> the truth, and thus becomes a source of error rather
> than of guidance.[59]

And thus, even the fourth criterion of knowledge, inspiration, is limited and fallible. 'Abdu'l-Bahá writes very clearly: "all the peoples and kindreds possess four balances with which they weigh the realities, the significances, and the divine questions. All of them are imperfect, unable to quench the burning thirst or heal the sick."[60]

And thus, one could think that human beings have no possibility of knowing any kind of truth. However, at the end of his talk on "the four methods of acquiring knowledge" in *Some Answered Questions*, 'Abdu'l-Bahá states: "But the bounty (*fayḍ*) of the Holy Spirit (*rúḥu'l-quds*) gives the true method of comprehension which is infallible and indubitable. This is through the help of the Holy Spirit (*rúḥu'l-quds*) which comes to man, and this is the condition in which certainty can alone be attained."[61]

---

[58] On behalf of Shoghi Effendi, 25 January 1943, quoted in Bahá'í Institutions. A Compilation (New Delhi: Bahá'í Publishing Trust, 1973) 111, see also ibid. 111–2.

[59] On behalf of Shoghi Effendi, 29 October 1938, quoted in Bahá'í Institutions 109.

[60] Lawh-i-Fu'ád 110.

[61] *Some Answered Questions* 296, sec. 83; Mufávidát 208.

The same statement is recorded in the talk he delivered in Hotel Ansonia on 17 April 1912:

> Briefly, the point is that in the human material world of phenomena these four are the only existing criteria or avenues of knowledge, and all of them are faulty and unreliable. What then remains? How shall we attain the reality of knowledge? By the breaths and promptings of the Holy Spirit, which is light and knowledge itself.[62]

THE INMOST HEART AS THE FIFTH CRITERION OF KNOWLEDGE

'Abdu'l-Bahá seems thus to suggest a fifth criterion of knowledge through which "certainty can alone be attained."[63] He specifically mentions this criterion in two of his Tablets. In one of them, the above-mentioned Tablet of the Inmost Heart or Lawḥ-i-Fu'ád, he quotes a Koranic verse: "His heart falsified not what he saw."[64] And he remarks that while explaining this verse he will

> unfold the details of the balances of discernment (*mawázíni'l-idrák*) that the people possess, and... explain and refute them, so that it will be evident and clearly proven that the divine balance (*al-mízani'l-iláhí*) is the inmost heart (*fu'ád*), the fountain-head of guidance (*ra-shad*).[65]

Then he adds in the same Tablet:

> ...it is evident that all of [the] balances current among the people are defective and their conclusions are unreliable. Nay, they are confused dreams, doubts, and idle fancies that neither allay the sore athirst nor satisfy

---

[62] *Promulgation* 22.
[63] *Some Answered Questions* 296, sec. 83; Mufáviḍát 208.
[64] *Koran* 53:11, Rodwell trans.
[65] Lawḥ-i-Fu'ád 110.

the seeker of knowledge (*'irfán*). As for the true, divine balance which never strayeth, and which ever apprehendeth the universal realities and the sublime inner meanings, it is the balance of the inmost heart (*mízánu'l-fu'ád*), of which God hath made mention in the blessed verse.[66]

The meaning of the criterion of the inmost heart (*mízánu'l-fu'ád*) will be better understood, if one remembers that in the Islamic world the inmost heart (*fu'ád*) is the abode of the light of gnosis (*ma'rifah*), which the ancient Sufi master Hakím al-Tirmidhí (820–932 CE circa) defines "a bounty which God gives to His servant."[67] It is the repository of the vision of reality, "for the inner heart (*fu'ád*) sees and the heart (*qalb*) knows."[68] Al-Tirmidhí writes, "as long as the inner heart does not see, the heart cannot make use of its knowledge."[69] Those whose hearts do not see "are veiled by their own selves from the subtleties of the truth because of their preoccupation with their own deeds."[70]

'Abdu'l-Bahá writes that the inmost heart:

...is an effulgence (*tajallíyát*) of the brilliant lights of the Divine Outpouring (*al-fayḍu'l-ilahí*), the secret of the All-Merciful, the manifestation of sincere faith, and the lordly sign. Verily it is an ancient Outpouring (*fayḍu qadím*), a manifest light and a mighty bounty. Should God favor with this gift one of His chosen ones, showering it upon one of His loved ones possessing certitude, verily he will draw nigh unto that station (*maqám*) of which

[66] Lawḥ-i-Fu'ád 112. The "blessed verse" is Koran 53:11, see above.
[67] Nicholas Heere. "A Ṣūfī Psychological Treatise," in The Muslim World (a quarterly journal dedicated to the promotion and dissemination of scholarly research on Islam and Muslim societies and on historical and current aspects of Christian-Muslim relations. Hartford, Connecticut: Wiley-Blackwell publishing, 1911-), vol.51, no.1 (January 1961) 31.
[68] Nicholas Heere. "A Ṣūfī Psychological Treatise," in The Muslim World, no.3 (July 1961) 163, from now on Heere.
[69] Heere 166.
[70] Ibid.

'Alí (upon him be peace) hath spoken, "If the veil be lift-ed, I would not increase in certitude!"[71]

These concepts re-echo in the above quoted words recorded in *Some Answered Questions*:

But the bounty (*fayḍ*) of the Holy Spirit (*rúḥu'l-quds*) gives the true method of comprehension which is infallible and indubitable. This is through the help of the Holy Spirit (*rúḥu'l-quds*) which comes to man, and this is the condition in which certainty can alone be attained.[72]

'Abdu'l-Bahá also mentions this fifth criterion of truth in an-other Tablet.[73] After having written that the four common criteria of knowledge are limited and fallible, he writes: "Therefore only unveiling (*al-mukáshifat*) and contemplation (*ash-shuhúd*) re-main..." These two words are very well known in the Sufi world, but deserve an explanation in the Western world, which is not usu-ally well versed in that tradition. The Italian essayist and expert in Sufism Paolo Urizzi explains in his Introduction to his transla-tion of the treatise *Maḥásin al-Majális*, translated into English by William Elliot and Adnan K. Abdulla as *The Attractions of Mystical Sessions*,[74] composed by the Sufi Andalusian philosopher Abú'l-Abbás Ibn al-'Aríf (1088–1141) that according to a number of Sufis the seeker obtains "a direct and real knowledge" of the spiritual verities "by virtue of an intuitive unveiling (*kashf*)[75] or of a theoph-anic radiation (*tajallî*) in the moment in which the individual in-tellect is wholly absorbed in a contemplative state (*mushâhada*)."[76]

---

[71] Lawḥ-i-Fu'ád 113. As to the quotation in the quotation, see 'Alí Ṣadrá'í Khu'í, "Mi'a kalima", in 'Alí-Akbar Rashád, ed., *Dánish-námah* (Tehran, 2001), vol.12, p. 472.

[72] Some Answered Questions 296, sec. 83; Mufáviḍát 208.

[73] See Makátíb 151–5.

[74] England: Avebury, 1980.

[75] The word kashf comes from the same root as the word mukáshifat.

[76] Ibn al-'arif, Sedute mistiche. Maḥásin al_majális traduzione dall'arabo, con introduzione e note a cura di Paolo Urizzi (Giarre, Catania: L'Ottava Edizioni, 1995) 53). The word mushâhada comes from the same root, from which also shuhúd derives.

Therefore, it seems that this fifth criterion implies two elements: on the one hand, a theophanic radiation (*tajallí* and *mukáshifa*), or divine illumination, on the other, a contemplative state (*shuhúd* or *musháhada*). As to the theophanic irradiation (or divine illumination), it is reminiscent of the description of the fifth criterion of knowledge as "inmost heart" given by 'Abdu'l-Bahá in his Tablet of the Inmost Heart: "an effulgence (*tajallíyát*) of the brilliant lights of the Divine Outpouring (*al-faiḍu'l-ilahí*)... an ancient outpouring (*fayḍu qadím*), a manifest light (*núru mubínu*) and a mighty bounty."[77] 'Abdu'l-Bahá said in this regard:

> But the human spirit, unless assisted by the spirit of faith (*rúḥ-i-ímání*), does not become acquainted with the divine secrets and the heavenly realities. It is like a mirror which, although clear, polished and brilliant, is still in need of light. Until a ray of the sun reflects upon it, it cannot discover the heavenly secrets.[78]

As to the spirit of faith, 'Abdu'l-Bahá explains that

> ...the spirit of faith (*rúḥ-i-ímání*)... comes from the breath of the Holy Spirit (*rúḥu'l-quds*), and by the divine power it becomes the cause of eternal life. It is the power which makes the earthly man heavenly, and the imperfect man perfect. It makes the impure to be pure, the silent eloquent; it purifies and sanctifies those made captive by carnal desires; it makes the ignorant wise.[79]

Shoghi Effendi compares the spirit of faith to a seed planted in the heart of the seeker, when he comes to recognize the Manifestation of God.[80] He explains:

---

[77] Lawḥ-i-Fu'ád 113. As to the quotation in the quotation, see 'Alí Ṣadrá'í Khu'í, "Mi'a kalima", in 'Alí-Akbar Rashád, ed., *Dánish-námah* (Tehran, 2001), vol.12, p. 472.

[78] *Some Answered Questions* 208–9, sec. 55; Mufáviḍát 148.

[79] *Some Answered Questions* 144–45; Mufáviḍát 102.

[80] The Manifestations of God are, according to the Bahá'í teachings, the Prophets-Founders of the revealed world religions: Hindu religions,

This seed must be watered by the outpourings of the Holy Spirit. These gifts of the spirit are received through prayer, meditation, study of the Holy Utterances and service to the Cause of God. The fact of the matter is that service in the Cause is like the plough which ploughs the physical soil when seeds are sown. It is necessary that the soil be ploughed up, so that it can be enriched, and thus cause a stronger growth of the seed. In exactly the same way the evolution of the spirit takes place through ploughing up the soil of the heart so that it is a constant reflection of the Holy Spirit. In this way the human spirit grows and develops by leaps and bounds.[81]

As to the contemplative state, 'Abdu'l-Bahá seems to describe it in this passage:

I now assure thee, O servant of God, that, if thy mind become empty and pure from every mention and thought and thy heart attracted wholly to the Kingdom of God, forget all else besides God and come in communion with the Spirit of God, then the Holy Spirit will assist thee with a power which will enable thee to penetrate all things, and a Dazzling Spark which enlightens all sides, a Brilliant Flame in the zenith of the heavens, will teach thee that which thou dost not know of the facts of the universe and of the divine doctrine.[82]

Finally, 'Abdu'l-Bahá writes in another Tablet:

Judaism, Zoroastrianism, Buddhism, Christianity, Islam, the Bábí Faith and the Bahá'í Faith.

[81] On behalf of Shoghi Effendi, 6 October 1954, quoted in The Compilation of Compilations. Prepared by the Research Department of The Universal House of Justice 1963–1990, vol. 2 (Ingleside, NSW, Australia: Bahá'í Publications Australia, 1991.) 24–5, sec. 1334.

[82] Tablets of Abdul-Baha Abbas, 3 vols. (New York: Bahá'í Publishing Society, 1909–1915.) 706–7, from now on Tablets.

> Nothing can demonstrate to a man that what happens in his heart is a divine inspiration, beside the Effusion of Merciful. It is demonstrated by the following passage: "And thou shalt surely guide into the right way" [Koran 42:52]. The intermediary is the Supreme Intermediary, and the niche of the light of guidance, and any inspiration is a ray emanating from this lodestar, which guides and enlightens [coming] from this Luminary.[83]

Similar words echo in another Tablet: "O thou maid-servant of God! The aim of the theosophists is to attain to Truth, but the Truth is unattainable except through the favor of the Holy Spirit. The light hath a center and if one desire to seek it otherwise but from the center, he can never attain to it."[84]

These words seem to imply that without the assistance of the Intermediary, that is the Manifestation of God, it is very difficult for a human being to be divinely inspired. They are reminiscent of Augustine of Hippo (354–530 AD), considered as one of the greatest Christian thinkers of all times, who in the 4th century AD set forth a very similar concept in his well-known doctrine of enlightenment: God is Light that enables man to know.

In another Tablet 'Abdu'l-Bahá explains how this fifth criterion of truth works:

> A real, spiritual connection between the True One and the servant is a luminous bounty, which causeth an ecstatic (or divine) flame, passion and attraction. When this connection is secured (or realized) such an ecstasy and happiness become manifest in the heart that man doth fly away (with joy) and uttereth melody and song. Just as the soul bringeth the body in motion, so that spiritual bounty and real connection likewise moveth (or cheereth) the human soul.[85]

---

[83] Makátíb 398.
[84] Tablets 592.
[85] Tablets 196.

All these words are reminiscent of words ascribed to Plotinus by Vaughan:

> You ask, how can we know the Infinite? I answer, not by reason. It is the office of reason to distinguish and define. The Infinite, therefore, cannot be ranked among its objects. You can only apprehend the Infinite by a faculty superior to reason, by entering into a state in which you are your finite self no longer — in which the divine essence is communicated to you. This is ecstasy [Cosmic Consciousness]. It is the liberation of your mind from its finite consciousness. Like only can apprehend like; when you thus cease to be finite, you become one with the Infinite. In the reduction of your soul to its simplest self, its divine essence, you realize this union — this identity.[86]

It does not seem that the fifth criterion of knowledge may be developed through a mere intellectual effort. Rather it seems that it is the result of a process of inner transformation, depending on the achievement of that which the Bahá'í texts conceive as spirituality. 'Abdu'l-Bahá said that spirituality is "the awakening of the conscious soul of man to perceive the reality of Divinity," made possible "through the breathes of the Holy Spirit."[87]

Knowledge is always a divine bounty. It becomes "certainty" on the one hand "through the help of the Holy Spirit which comes to man"[88] and bestows upon man the spirit of faith, on the other, through the effort exerted by the seeker who strives to acquire the capacity of recognizing this bounty out of his "love of reality."[89] These concepts are summarized in the following passage of the Seven Valleys:

---

[86] Plotinus. "Letter to Flaccus," quoted in Vaughan, in his book *Hours with the mystics* 80, http://archive.org/stream/hourswithmystics1893vaug#page/n123/mode/2up/search/dialectic, retrieved on 3 July 2018.

[87] *Promulgation* 142. The Persian notes of this talk are recorded in Majmú'ih 378.

[88] *Some Answered Questions* 296, sec. 83; Mufáviḍát 208.

[89] *Promulgation* 49.

And if, confirmed by the Creator, the lover escapes from the claws of the eagle of love, he will enter the Valley of Knowledge and come out of doubt into certainty, and turn from the darkness of illusion to the guiding light of the fear of God. His inner eyes will open and he will privily converse with his Beloved; he will set ajar the gate of truth and piety and shut the doors of vain imaginings.[90]

THE INTUITIVE KNOWLEDGE OF
THE MANIFESTATIONS OF GOD

This fifth criterion of knowledge is reminiscent of the "intuitive" knowledge, or "knowledge of being... [which] is like the cognizance and consciousness that man has of himself," and which "is not the outcome of effort and study. It is an existing thing; it is an absolute gift," mentioned by 'Abdu'l-Bahá,[91] as typical of the Manifestations of God. 'Abdu'l-Bahá describes it as follows:

But the universal divine mind, which is beyond nature, is the bounty of the Preexistent Power. This universal mind is divine; it embraces existing realities, and it receives the light of the mysteries of God. It is a conscious power, not a power of investigation and of research. The intellectual power of the world of nature is a power of investigation, and by its researches it discovers the realities of beings and the properties of existences; but the heavenly intellectual power, which is beyond nature, embraces things and is cognizant of things, knows them, understands them, is aware of mysteries, realities and divine significations, and is the discoverer

---

[90] Baha'u'llah. *The Seven Valleys and the Four Valleys*. Translated by Marzieh Gail in consultation with Ali-Kuli Khan (Wilmette, IL: Bahá'í Publishing Trust, 1991) 11, from now on Seven Valleys.

[91] *Some Answered Questions* 156, sec. 40, paras. 4 and 5.

of the concealed verities of the Kingdom. This divine intellectual power is the special attribute of the Holy Manifestations and the Dawning-places of prophethood; a ray of this light falls upon the mirrors of the hearts of the righteous, and a portion and a share of this power comes to them through the Holy Manifestations.[92]

This passage explains that "the universal divine mind" is "the special attribute of the Holy Manifestations and the Dawning-places of prophethood," but does not exclude that human beings may have a limited share of it: "a ray of this light falls upon the mirrors of the hearts of the righteous, and a portion and a share of this power comes to them through the Holy Manifestations." In the Manifestations of God this power is inborn and perfect. In human beings it is potential and limited and can be progressively and partially quickened through the divine confirmations and the efforts exerted by seeker, while struggling to acquire capacity and preparedness. As to the divine confirmations, 'Abdu'l-Bahá wrote that they are "the rain of the bounties of God... and the heat of the Sun of Reality."[93] He explains that they "change a gnat into an eagle, a drop of water into rivers and seas, and an atom into lights and suns;"[94] make "the weak strong, the lowly mighty, the child grown, the infant mature and the small great;"[95] they "dilate... [human] breasts through the fragrances of joy and happiness;"[96] bestow "the utmost eloquence, fluency, ability and skill in teaching;"[97] give the power to "withstand all who inhabit the earth"[98] and to "quicken the souls."[99] Through those con-

---

[92] *Some Answered Questions* 217, sec. 58, para. 4.
[93] *The Tablets of the Divine Plan: Revealed by 'Abdu'l-Bahá to the North American Bahá'ís* (Wilmette, ILL: Bahá'í Publishing Trust, 1997) 64, sec. 9, para. 8.
[94] Ibid. 73, sec. 10, para. 13.
[95] *Tablets* 274.
[96] Ibid. 367.
[97] Ibid. 243.
[98] Ibid. 460.
[99] Ibid. 674.

firmations "tongues... become fluent... hearts like clear mirrors flooded with the rays of the Sun of Truth... thoughts expanded... comprehension more vivid and... [human beings] progress in the plane of human perfections."[100] As to capacity and preparedness, we are reminded of the following words by 'Abdu'l-Bahá:

> The Sun of Reality is shining upon you, the cloud of mercy is pouring down, and the breezes of providence are wafting through your souls. Although the bestowal is great and the grace is glorious, yet capacity and readiness are requisite. Without capacity and readiness the divine bounty will not become manifest and evident. No matter how much the cloud may rain, the sun may shine and the breezes blow, the soil that is sterile will give no growth... Therefore, we must develop capacity in order that the signs of the mercy of the Lord may be revealed in us. We must endeavor to free the soil of the hearts from useless weeds and sanctify it from the thorns of worthless thoughts in order that the cloud of mercy may bestow its power upon us. The doors of God are open, but we must be ready and fitted to enter... Unless the eyes of perception be opened, the lights of the sun will not be witnessed... Therefore, we must endeavor night and day to purify the hearts from every dross, sanctify the souls from every restriction and become free from the discords of the human world. Then the divine bestowals will become evident in their fullness and glory. If we do not strive and sanctify ourselves from the defects and evil qualities of human nature, we will not partake of the bestowals of God.[101]

---

[100] Promulgation 458.
[101] *Promulgation* 195–6.

FINAL REMARKS

The fifth criterion of knowledge described by 'Abdu'l-Bahá deserves a number of observations. First, it seems that in our days very few persons think that their inmost heart may be important in their search. And yet 'Abdu'l-Bahá explains that "through the faculty of meditation man... receives the breath of the Holy Spirit — the bestowal of the Spirit is given in reflection and meditation."[102] He explains that "You cannot apply the name 'man' to any being void of this faculty of meditation; without it he would be a mere animal, lower than the beasts."[103] These words are reminiscent of the following warning by Bahá'u'lláh: "we must labor to destroy the animal condition, till the meaning of humanity shall come to light."[104] May we deduct from these words that the inmost heart is especially developed in a spiritually progressed human being?

Second, it seems that the development of the inmost heart, as the fifth criterion of knowledge, is a gradual process related to the purification of the heart from the "whispers (*wasáwis*) which are influxes of the ego (*khuṭúrátin nafsiyyatin*),"[105] or, metaphorically, of Satan intended as "the evil ego within us, not an evil personality outside."[106] However, Shoghi Effendi remarks that

> The only people who are truly free of the "dross of self" are the Prophets, for to be free of one's ego is a hall-mark of perfection. We humans are never going to become perfect, for perfection belongs to a realm we are not destined to enter. However, we must constantly mount higher, seek to be more perfect.[107]

---

[102] *Paris Talks* 187, sec. 54, para. 11.

[103] Ibid. para. 10.

[104] *Seven Valleys* 34.

[105] Makátíb 397.

[106] *Promulgation* 286.

[107] On behalf of Shoghi Effendi, 8 January 1949, Lights of Guidance: A Bahá'í Reference File Compiled by Helen Basset Hornby (New Delhi: Bahá'í Publishing Trust, 1996) 114, no. 389. Prophets may be intended as the Manifestations of God.

And thus, human beings are invited to strive towards "perfection," even if they are aware that they will never reach it, in the awareness that this struggle will yield a rich harvest of personal and collective progress. 'Abdu'l-Bahá may have mentioned this concept when he said:

The confirmations of the Spirit are all those powers and gifts which some are born with (and which men sometimes call genius), but for which others have to strive with infinite pains. They come to that man or woman who accepts his life with radiant acquiescence.[108]

> Third, it seems that "unveiling (al-mukáshifat)" and "contemplation (ash-shuhúd)," resulting from the development of one's inmost heart, may be sometimes accompanied by mystical experiences. 'Abdu'l-Bahá mentions "ecstasy and happiness," born of the "spiritual connection between the True One and the servant."[109] Shoghi Effendi clarifies the nature and meaning of these kinds of experiences. He says that these experiences "are very rare,"[110] come "to an individual through the grace of God, and not through the exercise of any of the human faculties,"[111] and that "[i]t is very difficult to distinguish between true visions which are true spiritual experiences of the soul and imaginations which have no reality in spiritual truths."[112] Therefore, as precious as such experiences may be considered by the individ-

---

[108] 'Abdu'l-Bahá in London Addresses and notes of Conversations. Rpt. (London: Bahá'í Publishing Trust, 1982) 120; see also Divine Philosophy 22.

[109] Tablets 196, see above.

[110] On behalf of Shoghi Effendi, 25 October 1942, in Bahá'í News (A monthly news journal published by the National Spiritual Assembly of the Bahá'ís of the United States. Wilmette, IL: National Spiritual Assembly of the Bahá'ís of the United States, 1924–), no. 152 (April 1942) 2.

[111] On behalf of Shoghi Effendi, 6 May 1952, quoted in Bahá'í Institutions 114.

[112] On behalf of Shoghi Effendi, 26 November 1939, Bahá'í News, no. 152 (April 1942) 2.

ual who had them, they "should under no circumstances, be construed as constituting an infallible source of guidance, even for the person experiencing them."[113] He warns his addressees not to "place much importance on" them,[114] and not "to go groping about in the darkness of... [one's] imagination after the true thing,"[115] since "[i]f we are going to have some deeply spiritual experience we can rest assured God will vouchsafe it to us without our having to look for it.".[116] He says: "'[w]hen a person endeavors to develop faculties so that they might enjoy visions, dreams etc., actually what they are doing is weakening certain of their spiritual capacities; and thus under such circumstances, dreams and visions have no reality, and ultimately lead to the destruction of the character of the person'."[117]

Therefore, "through the grace of God, and not through the exercise of any of the human faculties,"[118] a person may have meaningful personal mystical experiences, that is, "ecstasy and happiness," born of the "spiritual connection between the True One and the servant,"[119] and "that mystic feeling which unites Man with God,"[120] which are quite different from the sorts of dreams, visions, and psychic experiences about which Shoghi Effendi said, as it was mentioned above, that they "should under no circumstances, be construed as constituting an infallible source of guid-

---

[113] On behalf of Shoghi Effendi, 1 November 1940, in Bahá'í News, no. 152 (April 1942) 2.

[114] On behalf of Shoghi Effendi, 9 April 1948, quoted in Bahá'í Institutions 113.

[115] On behalf of Shoghi Effendi, 25 October 1942, Bahá'í News, no. 152 (April 1942) 2.

[116] On behalf of Shoghi Effendi, 25 October 1942, Bahá'í News, no. 152 (April 1942) 2.

[117] On behalf of Shoghi Effendi, 6 May 1952, quoted in Bahá'í Institutions 114.

[118] On behalf of Shoghi Effendi, 6 May 1952, quoted in Bahá'í Institutions 114.

[119] 'Abdu'l-Bahá. Tablets 196.

[120] On behalf of Shoghi Effendi, 8 December 1935, Bahá'í News, no. 102 (August 1936) 3.

ance, even for the person experiencing them."[121] And the mystic search after holiness, enjoined upon each human being, is not intended as aiming to achieve these experiences, but to acquire virtues and spiritual powers, which may be used at the service of the cause of the commonweal of humankind. Likewise, unveiling and contemplation, seemingly the result of the development of one's inmost heart, are not a goal we should consciously and willingly pursue. It seems that they will be the spontaneous fruit, which will gradually come to maturation, as the sincere seeker will earnestly struggle on the path of search. This search is not an abstract and intellectual effort, it is an ongoing attitude of service to the common good of humankind.

Fourth, it seems that today most people are interested in attaining a kind of limited knowledge, a kind of knowledge, which is achieved through sense perception, reason, and quite seldom inspiration. 'Abdu'l-Bahá's words sound as a call to pursue the path of inner perfection, trusting that it will assist us to develop the required capacities and preparedness so that our "inmost heart" may gradually become our fifth criterion of knowledge, and we may achieve "unveiling" and "contemplation." In this case the range of our knowledge will be greatly widened; our interest will not be limited to the material world but will be extended to the spiritual worlds. And this expansion is very important, because human beings are not only physical bodies, they also, and especially, are spirits. Therefore, human beings should understand both worlds, if they want their lives on earth to be conducive to personal and collective progress. They should finally find a balance between science and religion. As 'Abdu'l-Bahá said:

> Religion and science are the two wings upon which man's intelligence can soar into the heights, with which the human soul can progress. It is not possible to fly with one wing alone! Should a man try to fly with the wing of religion alone he would quickly fall into the quagmire

---

[121] On behalf of Shoghi Effendi, 1 November 1940, in Bahá'í News, no. 152 (April 1942) 2.

of superstition, whilst on the other hand, with the wing of science alone he would also make no progress but fall into the despairing slough of materialism.[122]

Perhaps a deeper awareness of this fifth criterion of truth and a wider use of it may be one of the features of the "new race of men"[123] that is gradually arising in this day of "the coming of age of the human race"[124] announced by Bahá'u'lláh.[125]

Last but not least, the development of the inmost heart depends on spiritual progress. Spiritual progress or spirituality, intended as "the awakening of the conscious soul of man to perceive the reality of Divinity," made possible "through the breaths of the Holy Spirit,"[126] is characterized by a progressively deeper consciousness of one's divine nature.[127] This deeper consciousness implies for our intellect and insight to become keener, embracing both the material and spiritual worlds. It also implies for our understanding of tradition or Scripture to become deeper, and immune from superstition, fanaticism and exclusivism. We will thus acquire a kind of knowledge that will make the heart fearful and mindful of its Creator, submitted to His will, as it is revealed in His Scripture. That knowledge is the knowledge of God and of one's true self, that is, the recognition of the image of God engraved in one's soul. There is but one Teacher from whom such knowledge is to be learned and who manifests the primal

---

[122] *Paris Talks* 147, sec. 44, para.15. The Persian notes of this talk are recorded in Majmú'ih 161–4.

[123] Shoghi Effendi. *The Advent of the Divine Justice* (Wilmette, IL: Bahá'í Publishing Trust, 1984) 16.

[124] Shoghi Effendi. *The World Order of Bahá'u'lláh: Selected Letters* (Wilmette, IL: Bahá'í Publishing Trust, 1955) 206.

[125] See Julio Savi. "The newly born babe of that Day." Mysticism in the age of the maturity of humankind. Lights of 'Irfán. Papers Presented at the 'Irfán Colloquia and Seminars. Book Seven (Evanston, Illinois, 2006) 201–20.

[126] *Promulgation* 142.

[127] The divine nature of man is his power of expressing in the material plane of existence the divine attributes engraved in his soul. See Julio Savi. *The Eternal Quest for God. An Introduction to the Divine Philosophy of 'Abdu'l-Bahá* (Oxford: George Ronald, 1989) 91–3, 96–9 etc.

reason, the divine, universal mind: the Manifestation of God. His school is the best one, because it teaches "the science of the love of God."[128] And when a human being has learnt that science, he will adopt a correct standard of behaviour. Life will be easier for him, because he will more easily accept the divine decrees and recognize tests as opportunities. Otherwise, intellectual knowledge alone, with the sense of accomplishment and superiority that it sometimes implies, can be a real trap for the heart that is deceived by it, a great test for a person and for those about him. Bahá'u'lláh dwells on the theme of knowledge at length in His writings, explaining how both intellectual and inner knowledge are praiseworthy, but that as far as results are concerned intellectual knowledge is subordinate in importance to spiritual knowledge. For example, He writes:

> That which is of paramount importance for the children, that which must precede all else, is to teach them the oneness of God and the laws of God. For lacking this, the fear of God cannot be inculcated, and lacking the fear of God an infinity of odious and abominable actions will spring up, and sentiments will be uttered that transgress all bounds… parents must exert every effort to rear their offspring to be religious, for should the children not attain this greatest of adornments, they will not obey their parents, which in a certain sense means that they will not obey God. Indeed, such children will show no consideration to anyone, and will do exactly as they please.[129]

As to the children:

> We have directed that in the beginning they should be trained in the observances and laws of religion; and thereafter, in such branches of knowledge as are of benefit, and in commercial pursuits that are distinguished

---

[128] *Seven Valleys* 52.
[129] Bahá'u'lláh, quoted in Compilation of Compilations 1:248, no. 565.

for integrity, and in deeds that will further the victory of God's Cause or will attract some outcome which will draw the believer closer to his Lord. We beg of God to assist the children of His loved ones and adorn them with wisdom, good conduct, integrity and righteousness. He, verily, is the Forgiving, the Clement.[130]

'Abdu'l-Bahá commented on this theme:

Training in morals and good conduct is far more important than book learning... The reason for this is that the child who conducts himself well, even though he be ignorant, is of benefit to others, while an ill-natured, ill-behaved child is corrupted and harmful to others, even though he be learned. If, however, the child be trained to be both learned and good, the result is light upon light.[131]

In the light of such knowledge the satanic whispers will abate; the divine inspiration will be stronger and more easily recognized.

---

[130] Bahá'u'lláh, quoted in Compilation of Compilations 1:250–1, no. 575.
[131] *Selections* 135–6, sec.110.

Ethics Based on Science Alone?

IAN KLUGE
Wilmette Institute

INTRODUCTION

Can ethics be based on science alone? Is it possible to develop a coherent and internally sufficient ethical system without relying on a transcendental power as the ground and/or goal of our existence as moral beings? Despite the confident assurances of such contemporary authors as Paul Kurtz, Greg M. Epstein and Sam Harris, there still are numerous reasons to doubt why this is possible. These authors maintain that it is possible to establish a viable system of personal and social ethics on a strictly empirical basis provided by the sciences, most especially neuro-science, psychology, physiology sociology and anthropology. Each of these sciences can supply the objective, physical, quantitative and universal knowledge needed by individuals and collectives to establish moral codes and make moral decisions. In short, science alone is necessary and sufficient.

Before proceeding, it is important to clarify our two key terms — ethics and science — as precisely as we can. At the foundational level, ethics concerns itself with obligations, i.e. it is prescriptive in telling us what we must do or not do. It concerns value judgments of good and evil; right and wrong; virtuous and blameworthy; and just and unjust. For its part, science is the empirical study of the natural world. For a thing or an event to be an appropriate object of scientific study, it must be

(1) physical/material;
(2) susceptible to empirical direct or indirect observation by the human's senses or instruments;
(3) measurable or quantifiable;
(4) observer independent
(5) disprovable or falsifiable by observation and/or experiment, at least in principle.
(6) universal, i.e. applicable everywhere under the same circumstances

While ethics concerns *prescription*, science concerns *description* about the attributes and behaviors of natural beings. The advocates of basing ethics on science, i.e. on the description of empirical facts, believe that science alone is both necessary and sufficient to prescribe behavior without any appeal to a transcendental ground or goal. As Greg Epstein puts it, "God is beside the point."[1]

In this paper we shall argue that while science is necessary for developing a coherent ethical system, it is not sufficient to achieve this goal. By that we mean that an ethics based on science alone is irremediably deficient in regards to the establishment of values and obligations; in regards to its criteria for moral evaluations; and in regards to internal self-sufficiency. How shall we determine values and obligations? How can we establish standards by which to judge? How can we acquire internal self-sufficiency so that our arguments do not need to go beyond the boundaries of empiricism and science?

Greg Epstein recognizes this problem when he states, "Can you rationally justify your unconditional adherence to timeless values without implicitly invoking the existence of God?"[2] In our view — which we hope to prove below — the answer is neg-

---

[1] Greg M. Epstein. *Good Without God*, New York: Harper, 2009, p. 14.
[2] Ibid, p. 31.

ative. Making up the inherent deficiencies of a strictly empirical science-based ethics, logically requires an implicit or explicit appeal to something transcendent to the phenomenal world, i.e. 'God.' Otherwise, our reasoning remains trapped in the empirical realm, and that is precisely one of the chief logical problems of a strictly science-based ethic. In short, to ground a coherent ethical system, science and religion or religion-based ethics must work together.

To forestall any misunderstanding, we hasten to emphasize that this is not an argument to diminish the role of science in establishing morals and making ethical decisions. For the Bahá'í Writings, science is much too important to be shunted aside. 'Abdu'l-Bahá summarizes the Bahá'í view of the importance of science:

> If we say religion is opposed to science, we lack knowledge of either true science or true religion, for both are founded upon the premises and conclusions of reason, and both must bear its test.[3]

Elsewhere he asserts,

> We may think of science as one wing and religion as the other; a bird needs two wings for flight, one alone would be useless. Any religion that contradicts science or that is opposed to it, is only ignorance — for ignorance is the opposite of knowledge.[4]

Given the inter-dependence of science and religion — and by implication, ethics — the question is not *if* science has a role in ethics but *what kind* of role it has and what are the parameters of that role? To discover the parameters of science's role in ethics, we shall have to examine its limits and go on from there to establish its appropriate function. As this paper will attempt to show,

---

[3] 'Abdu'l-Bahá. The *Promulgation of Universal Peace*, 2nd ed., Wilmette: Bahá'í Publishing Trust, 1982, p. 107.

[4] 'Abdu'l-Bahá. *Paris Talks*. London: Bahá'í Publishing Trust, 1971, p. 130.

both science and religion are required to ground necessary and sufficient ethical principles in a rational and incoherent manner.

SEPARATING ETHICS AND RELIGION

The goal of separating ethics from religion and, thereby, building ethics on a strictly empirical and/or scientific basis is not new in the history of Western ethics. The three best known attempts are Hume's emotivism and communitarianism, Kant's deontology and Bentham and Mill's utilitarianism. Unlike other attempts to establish a fully empirical and scientific ethics such as Social Darwinism and Communism, emotivism and communitarianism, deontology and utilitarianism have survived as viable alternatives in contemporary ethical debates and have numerous intellectual off-spring. Although Hume, Kant or Bentham and Mill do not specifically refer to science as the basis of their ethics, but science-based ethics are a logical extension of their insistence on a strictly empirical basis for morality.

For Hume, sentiment or feelings are the foundation of ethics. Indeed, he states that the "notion of morals implies some sentiment common to all mankind,"[5] to which he adds,

> The hypothesis which we embrace is plain. *It maintains that morality is determined by sentiment.* It defines virtue to be whatever mental action or quality gives to a spectator the pleasing sentiment of approbation; and vice the contrary.[6]

Feeling, and the community's approbation or condemnation determine that

> we must at last acknowledge, that the *crime or immorality is no particular fact or relation, which can be the object of the understanding,* but arises entirely from the

---

[5] David Hume. *An Enquiry Concerning the Principles of Morals.* Part II, p. 64, www.gutenberg.org/files/4320/4320-h/4320-h.htm.
[6] Ibid, p. 73.

> sentiment of disapprobation, which, by the structure of
> human nature, we unavoidably feel on the apprehension
> of barbarity or treachery.[7]

Hume emphasizes that the morality (or lack of it) of an act is found in "entirely" in personal and community sentiment and that there is nothing in the act itself that makes it good or evil. This view reminds us of Hume's famous is/ought distinction (sometimes known as Hume's Guillotine) by which he shows that a description of a fact cannot logically lead to a prescription of how we ought to behave. As we shall see, this distinction is one of the key weaknesses of all empirical and scientific ethics. The importance of sentiment is further emphasized in his statement that

> though reason, when fully assisted and improved, be suf-
> ficient to instruct us in the pernicious or useful tenden-
> cy of qualities and actions; *it is not alone sufficient to
> produce any moral blame or approbation.* Utility is only a
> tendency to a certain end; and were the end totally in-
> different to us, we should feel the same indifference to-
> wards the means. *It is requisite a sentiment should here
> display itself, in order to give a preference to the useful
> above the pernicious tendencies. This sentiment can be no
> other than a feeling for the happiness of mankind, and a
> resentment of their misery;* since these are the different
> ends which virtue and vice have a tendency to promote.
> Here therefore reason instructs us in the several ten-
> dencies of actions, and humanity makes a distinction in
> favour of those which are useful and beneficial.[8]

Three points must be noticed here. First, we need for sentiment or feeling to motivate us. Second, this sentiment is for the happiness of humankind and rejection of its misery, and that this sentiment is in favour of the "useful and beneficial actions." The third point concerns the role of reason which can guide our senti-

---

[7] Ibid, p. 75; emphasis added.
[8] Ibid, p. 72; emphasis added.

ments into proper directions once such sentiments exist but cannot arouse such sentiments by itself. Reason cannot, in Hume's, view to motivate us to choose "the useful above the pernicious tendencies." Consequently, Hume writes that "Reason is, and ought only to be the slave of the passions and can never pretend to any other office than to serve and obey them."[9]

From the foregoing discussion we may conclude that the basis of Hume's ethic is immanent to the phenomenal world. The actual decision as to whether an act is right or wrong belongs to the individual and the community and not to any transcendent entity for whom there is actually no need. In short, the community and its customs have replaced God as the arbiter of virtue and vice and consequently, have provided an empirical foundation for ethical issues. By separating ethics from religion in this manner, Hume helps clear the way for a scientific approach to ethics.

Immanuel Kant's deontological ethics took another major step of separating ethics from religion. Unlike Hume, who saw the power of reason as quite limited, Kant's ethics are based on pure rationality. His goal was to develop an ethical system based only on reason and nothing else. In the "Preface to the First Edition" of *Religion Within the Limits of Reason Alone* (1793), Kant writes,

So far as morality is based upon the conception of man as a free agent who, just because he is free, binds himself through his reason to unconditioned laws, it *stands in need neither of the idea of another Being over him,* for him to apprehend his duty, nor of an incentive other than the law itself, for him to do his duty. At least it is man's own fault if he is subject to such a need; and if he is, this need can be relieved through nothing outside himself.[10]

---

[9] David Hume. *A Treatise of Human Nature.* Part III, Section 3, p. 253, http://www.gutenberg.org/zipcat2.php/4705/4705-h/4705-h.htm#link2H_4_0023.

[10] Immanuel Kant. "Preface to the First Edition" of *Religion Within the Limits of Reason Alone,* trans. by Theodore M. Greene and Hoyt M. Hudson, https://www.marxists.org/reference/subject/ethics/kant/religion/religion-within-reason.htm.

The gist of these statements is clear: "morality" is independent of everything except reason which is the basis of all moral injunctions; ethics cannot rely upon God. If we are to devise a system of ethics it must work strictly within the empirical realm and must have no other basis than reason. In his earlier book, *Religion Within the Limits of Reason Alone*, Kant goes even further in the direction of a scientific ethic than he did in *Critique of Practical Reason* (1788) in which he says that the idea of God is a practical necessity for an ethical system. However, he reminds us that this does not give us "the least encouragement to run riot into the transcendent."[11] As a transcendent being, God has no place in rational ethics.

Utilitarianism and its offshoot consequentialism are another attempt to uncouple ethics and religion. Despite some differences in emphasis both assert "that actions are right or wrong according to their consequences rather than any intrinsic features they may have."[12] For utilitarianism which began with Jeremy Bentham in nineteenth century England, that consequences that mattered were pleasure and pain. Utilitarianism is based on

> the *greatest happiness or greatest felicity* principle… which states the greatest happiness of all those whose interest is in question, as being the right and proper, and only right and proper and universally desirable, end of human action… [This forms the]… *standard of right and wrong*, by which alone the propriety of human conduct, in every situation, can with propriety be tried.[13]

Although Bentham speaks of "happiness" in general, his ideas focus more on pleasure which he believed we could measure em-

---

[11] Immanuel Kant. *Critique of Practical Reason.*, trans by Thomas Kingsmill Abbott, Ch. 1, http://pinkmonkey.com/dl/library1/book1133.pdf.

[12] Tom L Beauchamp. *Philosophical Ethics.* New York: McGraw Hill Inc., 1991, p. 129.

[13] Jeremy Bentham. *An Introduction to the Principles of Morals and Legislation.* p. 11, http://www.econlib.org/library/Bentham/bnthPML.html. This note was added to Chapter 1 by Bentham in July, 1822.

pirically by means of his "hedonistic calculus" (or "felicific calculus") on a quantitative scale including such factors as intensity, duration, predictability (certainty) and purity, i.e. the absence of later pain. Mill, however, centers his deliberations on "happiness," a far more encompassing term than 'pleasure.' He writes,

> The creed which accepts as the *foundation of morals, Utility,* or the Greatest Happiness Principle, holds that actions are right in proportion as they tend to promote happiness, wrong as they tend to produce the reverse of happiness.[14]

Mill associates happiness with "well-being"[15] which is also something we can measure empirically in order to build a moral system. Mill differed from Bentham insofar as Mill thought there were qualitative differences between experiences. Some pleasure or happiness is of a higher quality than others and, therefore, more desirable. "It is better to be a human being dissatisfied than a pig satisfied; better to be Socrates dissatisfied than a fool satisfied."[16] As we shall see, Mill's doubts about the hedonistic calculus also point to some problems with "well-being" in Harris's attempt to establish a strictly scientific ethic.[17]

The goal of this critical analysis of the attempts to establish an ethic based on science alone is to show that the inherent deep-seated problems in these attempts revive the viability of transcendentally based ethics as a worthwhile alternative.

---

[14] John Stuart Mill. *Utilitarianism*. London: Longmans, Green, 1901, p. 9; emphasis added.

[15] Ibid, pp. 33, 88.

[16] Ibid, p. 14.

[17] Sam Harris. *The Moral Landscape: How Science Can Determine Human Values*. New York: Free Press, 2010, p. 2.

THE FIRST PROBLEM: THE SCIENTIFIC METHOD

The most obvious problem in developing an empirical and science-based ethics is the scientific method itself. As noted above, for a thing to be a proper object of scientific study, it must, among other things be physical/material, quantifiable, observer independent and testable. In addition, it must be subject to the process of observing facts, forming a hypothesis, testing the hypothesis and forming a testable explanation of the findings. The insurmountable difficulty with a strictly science-based ethics is that the scientific method makes this impossible. Obligations, values, prescriptions and judgments cannot meet any of the criteria of appropriate objects for scientific study: they are not physical/material, quantifiable or necessarily observer independent. Nor can we conceive of or set up an experiment to show that a certain act is 'immoral.' Such concepts do not fit into the scientific method. Consequently, concepts of morality have to be imported from outside the boundaries of empirical science to arrive at any conclusion about ethics. Those concepts are not empirical — a fact already noted by Hume who writes,

> we must at last acknowledge, that the *crime or immorality is no particular fact or relation, which can be the object of the understanding*, but arises entirely from the sentiment of disapprobation, which, by the structure of human nature, we unavoidably feel on the apprehension of barbarity or treachery.[18]

Because morality is not one of the things for which empirical science can test, any strictly science-based ethical system lacks internal self-sufficiency in its reasoning since it must import its moral categories from beyond empirical science. Therefore, it is inherently incomplete and fails to establish its own intellectual foundations.

---

[18] David Hume. *An Enquiry Concerning the Principles of Morals.* Part II, p. 75; emphasis added. www.gutenberg.org/files/4320/4320-h/4320-h.htm.

A second and equally serious problem for science-based ethics is the is/ought or facts/value distinction, sometimes known as Hume's Guillotine. According to Hume,

> In every system of morality, which I have hitherto met with, I have always remark'd, that the author proceeds for some time in the ordinary way of reasoning, and establishes the being of a God, or makes observations concerning human affairs; when of a sudden I am surpriz'd to find, that *instead of the usual copulations of propositions, is, and is not, I meet with no proposition that is not connected with an ought, or an ought not.* This change is imperceptible; but is, however, of the last consequence. For as this ought, or ought not, expresses some new relation or affirmation, 'tis necessary that it shou'd be observ'd and explain'd; and at the same time that a reason should be given, for *what seems altogether inconceivable, how this new relation can be a deduction from others, which are entirely different from it...* [I] am persuaded, that this small attention wou'd subvert all the vulgar systems of morality, and let us see, that the distinction of vice and virtue is not founded merely on the relations of objects, nor is perceiv'd by reason.[19]

Hume's argument is devastatingly simple: we cannot argue from *description* to *prescription*, from an *is* to an *ought*, from a *statement of fact* to a statement of *obligations*. As Hume notes, the "crime or immorality is no particular fact or relation, which can be the object of the understanding."[20] The moral status of an act is not intrinsic to the act, it is not an empirically observable fact, and, therefore is not an appropriate object for science. That being the case, drawing an ethical conclusion from a factual premise is a

---

[19] David Hume. *A Treatise of Human Nature.* Book III, Part 1, Section 1, http://www.gutenberg.org/zipcat2.php/4705/4705-h/4705-h.htm#link2H_4_0023.

[20] David Hume. *An Enquiry Concerning the Principles of Morals.* Part II, p. 75, www.gutenberg.org/files/4320/4320-h/4320-h.htm.

logical *non sequitur*. This error applies to all science-based ethics. The only way to remedy this error is to begin with facts that already imply intrinsic values — something which theist ethics are able to do.

Let us examine this argument more closely. The problem is that if we wish to establish a strictly empirical and scientific system of morality, it is necessary to close the gap between empirical facts which are established by the scientific method and human values which are the products of human judgments *about* those facts. From a purely empirical perspective, valuation is something that we bring to the facts; the facts themselves do not give us an evaluative judgment, although they do give us the material on which to base such judgments. For example, nothing in the strictly empirical evidence from a body sprawled on the sidewalk allows us to establish that this death is 'sad,' 'wrong' or 'evil' or even a 'crime.' Such moral evaluations are not scientifically testable because moral values are not physical, measurable, physically observable, observer independent, objective or disprovable.' No coroner's report will say that certain physical evidence shows the moral evil of this death. How could the scientific method even begin to investigate the 'evil' nature of such an event — even when the evil is as egregious as the Holocaust, Stalin's Gulags or Mao's Red Guards? How could scientific experimentation establish the moral 'rightness' of picking a flower or saving a child from drowning? The inescapable conclusion is that moral values are not proper scientific objects, i.e. they are not suited to discovery or exploration by the scientific method.

We may, of course, show that a certain act is more advantageous to some people, but advantage and morality are not the same kinds of things. This is well illustrated in 'The Hospital' scenario.[21] There are five people desperately requiring an organ transplant (a different organ in each case) when the chief surgeon realizes he has a healthy young man with a multiply fractured

[21] Julia Driver. *Ethics: The Fundamentals.* Malden, MA: Blackwell Publishing, 2010, p. 131.

leg available to him. By transplanting the organs from the young man, he can save five lives — the greatest good for the greatest number — and bring the advantage of life to the five. Although the advantage to the five is clear, few would consider the advantage to be moral. Advantages may be moral — but do not necessarily have to be.

It is important not to confuse the process of reaching ethical judgments with the sociological and psychological study of the judgments that people actually make. The latter study measures the popularity of opinions, and the intensity with which they are held but does not measure the moral value of the act *per se*. Hume's fact/value distinction is clearly at work. The fact that a certain opinion has a popularity rating of 80% cannot in itself make that opinion morally right; it is a fact *about which* we can make a moral judgment but is not a moral judgment in itself.

The significance of Hume's argument cannot be exaggerated because it undercuts the possibility of establishing moral rules on an empirical or scientific basis. This negates the logical foundations of ethics in utilitarianism, consequentialism, hedonism, egoism, "self-realizationism,"[22] pragmatism, scientific ethics, situation-ethics and deontological ethics. We must especially remember that advantages to one or many, practical, or 'best' results, pleasure, logical consistency and agreement with science are in themselves neither moral nor immoral — they are simply facts *about which* we must make ethical judgments. By themselves such results are morally neutral, and we cannot use them to 'bootstrap' our way to moral imperatives. An act is what it is — and no strictly empirical scientific argument can demonstrate that it is inherently more than that.

---

[22] William S Sahakian. *Ethics: An Introduction to Theories and Problems.* New York: Barnes and Noble, 1974, p. viii.

A REPLY FROM HARRIS AND KURTZ

Although Harris seems unaware of the problem concerning the non-scientific nature of values and obligations, he is fully aware of Hume's is/ought difficulty. In his view, "the divide between facts and values is illusory"[23] and he states that "the division between facts and values is intellectually unsustainable especially from the perspective of neuroscience."[24] He begins his argument by asserting that

> Questions about *values* — about meaning, morality, and life's larger purpose — are really questions about the *well-being* of conscious creatures. Values, therefore, translate into facts that can be scientifically understood... The more we understand ourselves *at the level of the brain*, the more we will see that there are right and wrong answers to questions of human values.[25]

He adds,

> "good" [is] that which supports well-being... it makes no sense at all to ask whether maximizing well-being is "good." It seems clear that what we are really asking whether a certain state of pleasure is "good," is whether it is conducive to or obstructive of, some deeper form of well-being.[26]

According to Harris, brain-states are a reliable way to determine whether or not an action contributes to our well-being. Because neuroscience is able to determine the attributes of the brain-state of well-being, it is possible for us — so says Harris — to measure whether or not well-being, i.e. the moral good, is being

---

[23] Sam Harris. *The Moral Landscape: How Science Can Determine Human Values*. New York: Free Press, 2010, p. 14.

[24] Ibid, p. 24.

[25] Ibid, pp. 1–2; emphasis added.

[26] Ibid, p. 12.

achieved. This will even work across cultures.[27] In other words, brain-states provide physical/material, quantifiable, objectively observable and testable standards by which to measure moral goodness or well-being. For this reason, Harris says,

> science can, in principle, help us understand what we *should* do and *should* want — and, therefore, what *other people* should do and want in order to live the best lives possible.[28]

In other words, brain-states can cross the chasm between is and ought, between description and prescription and between what we do and what we should do.

However, only a little reflection reminds us that Harris' argument is not safe from Hume's Guillotine. The problem is that the brain-scans are facts i.e. descriptions of reality, and facts by themselves cannot logically lead to prescriptions without committing the logical *non sequitur* fallacy. Furthermore, there is also a category mistake in such attempts. Facts belong to one logical category — namely, statements of that which is actually the case — while prescriptions belong to another — statements of what *should, ideally be* the case.

To rebut Harris' claim that an fMRI brain scans can give a scientific proof of well-being, and, thereby, of moral good, we need only point out that even the most positive brain-scan imaginable, is still only a brain scan, i.e. an objective piece of scientific data *about which* one must pass judgment and which is still subject to all the limitations of the scientific method. As Hume has already pointed out, nothing in the data provided by a brain scan itself tells us whether this state of mind or state of brain or the action that accompanies it is morally 'good,' 'virtuous,' 'blameworthy' or conducive to well-being. There is no empirical evidence in the brain-scan to instruct us whether we are obligated or have a duty to avoid or cultivate such acts or their correlated brain-states. The judgment

---

[27] Ibid, p. 60.
[28] Ibid, p. 28; original emphasis.

that certain brain-states are morally good must be imported from outside the scientific framework — illustrating thereby, that such a science-based science is not internally self-sufficient.

This problem is not just a matter of awaiting future refinements in fMRI technology; rather the problem is intrinsic to the scientific method and the fMRI machines themselves. Such equipment is not designed to detect moral evaluations because such evaluations do not meet the criteria of being scientific objects, i.e. they are not physical, measurable, physically observable, observer independent, objective or disprovable. What Harris tries to do is to substitute a physical state — well-being as measured by fMTRI — for a moral condition — being ethically justified. This, too, is a logical category mistake since a physical and a non-physical state cannot be interchanged without destroying his argument since he is, in effect, changing the subject. Moreover, this exchange seems to work until we ask if all positive brain-states are moral? It is not difficult to imagine that a man like Dr. Mengele had positive brain-states while subjecting victims to vivisection 'in the name of science.' His brain-states may have been just as positively correlated with well-being as Mother Teresa's because both believed they were serving humanity and doing the morally 'right thing'. We might also recall the surgeon in "The Hospital Story' mentioned earlier; she, too, might have fully positive brain-scans while sacrificing the healthy young man to the lives of five transplant candidates. The problem is obvious: the evidence provided by even the most positive brain-scans is insufficient to define the moral good.

Of course, science can tell us that people who have a lot of type X brain scans tend to be a lot physically healthier than people who have a lot of type O's. However, science cannot tell us why we are morally obligated to prefer type X scans, why we 'ought' to, or why it is our 'duty' to facilitate type X scans in as many people as possible. Interestingly enough Harris admits as much: "Science cannot tell us why, *scientifically*, we should value health."[29] In effect, he concedes that science has nothing to say about moral val-

---

[29] Ibid, p. 37; original emphasis.

uations or obligations and, thereby, undermines his own thesis. It seems clear that if "scientifically" speaking there is no reason to value something as self-evidently important as health, then there is not much hope of building an ethical system — with all its complex questions — on science alone.

How, for example, could science-based ethics help us in the following situation which often played out in the twentieth century? You believe in always telling the truth, but one night, you are hiding an innocent man from unjust persecution by the state police. The police come and ask if you have anyone in your house. Most people would probably lie (or like to think they would) but the real point of recounting this story is that no conceivable scientific experiment has the slightest bearing on the morality of your act one way or the other. Science is simply not intended or equipped to answer these kinds of questions that do not involve mass, measurability, repeatability, predictability, objectivity and falsifiability.

Interestingly enough, Harris tries to dismiss the question *"why* the well-being of conscious beings *ought* to matter to us."[30] He says he does "not think anyone sincerely believes this kind of moral skepticism makes sense."[31] He misses the point of the question which is not to doubt that well-being is worthwhile but to show that science cannot establish the moral 'goodness' of this goal — which he admits several pages later, saying "Science cannot tell us why, *scientifically*, we should value health."[32]

In the last analysis, Harris is left with the problem so clearly articulated by Daniel Dennett: "If 'ought' cannot be derived from 'is,' just what *can* it be derived from?"[33] That is exactly the problem to which Harris' argument about science-based ethics is unable to provide a logically coherent answer.

In *Forbidden Fruit: The Ethics of Secularism*, secular humanist Paul Kurtz also seeks to develop a science-based ethics, the

---

[30] Ibid, p. 32.
[31] Ibid, p. 32.
[32] Ibid, p. 37.
[33] Daniel Dennett, quoted in Sam Harris, ibid, p. 196; original emphasis.

sciences in this case being physiology, evolutionary science and anthropology. He calls his approach "eupraxsophy,"[34] which he defines as "good practical wisdom."[35] Kurtz, like Harris, believes that "The intrinsic value we seek to achieve is *eudaemonia*: happiness or well-being."[36]

The heart of Kurtz's ethical philosophy is the concept of "the common moral decencies"[37] which are "transcultural in their range."[38] They are universal because they are based on the needs of human nature which, in Kurtz's view is grounded in biology. (One cannot help remembering Maslow's hierarchy of needs at this point.) Therefore, we can expect that humankind, including the specific societies within it, already possess a number of [these] principles... as binding."[39] Among the major "decencies" we find truthfulness; promise-keeping; trustworthiness; justice and fairness; tolerance and benevolence and cooperation to name a few. Without these attributes, human individuals could not survive as members of society and societies could not maintain unity and function successfully, i.e. survive. As Kurtz says, "They no doubt grow out of the long evolutionary struggle for survival."[40]

According to Kurtz, these "common moral decencies" provide a scientific foundation for ethics because they have an empirical

> *socio-biological* basis; they are rooted in the nature of the human animal and the *processes of evolution* by which the species adapts and survives. Human beings are social animals, and our young require an extended

---

[34] Paul Kurtz. *Forbidden Fruit: The Ethics of Secularism.* New York: Prometheus Books, 2008, p. 22.

[35] Ibid, p. 22.

[36] Paul Kurtz. "The Ethics of Humanism Without Religion." *Free Inquiry.* Volume 23, Number 1, Winter, 2002/2003, https://www.secularhumanism.org/index. php/cont_index_23.

[37] Kurtz. *Forbidden Fruit*, p. 93.

[38] Paul Kurtz. *Free Inquiry.* Volume 23, Number 1, Winter, 2002/2003, https://www.secularhumanism.org/index. php/cont_index_23.

[39] Kurtz. *Forbidden Fruit.* p. 105.

[40] Paul Kurtz. *Free Inquiry.* Volume 23, Number 1, Winter, 2002/2003, https://www.secularhumanism.org/index. php/cont_index_23.

> period of nurturing for survival. Given this, a number
> of moral rules that govern behavior have developed...
> Moral codes thus have an adaptive function; one can
> postulate that those groups which had some effective
> regulation for conduct were better able to survive, re-
> produce and compete with other species or human
> groups... The test of the truth of these principles was
> their consequences.[41]

In these words, Kurtz makes clear the empirical science-based nature of his ethical system vis-à-vis its "socio-biological" and evolutionary basis as well as the anthropological study of "moral codes" among various groups. As noted before, the aim is not only survival but also well-being. As a result of the socio-biological and evolutionary processes working in individuals and societies, the "common moral decencies" are rooted in human nature and, therefore, they "need not be divinely ordained to have moral force, for they are tested in the last analysis by their *consequences* in practice."[42] In other words, the ontological basis of ethics lies in human nature which, at bottom, is given to each human being; we have no choice about being born human with a particularly defined nature.

These "socio-biological" needs are the ontological basis on which the "socio-cultural"[43] and the "historical"[44] moral codes are built. In this way, Kurtz answers his own challenge about the necessity for building moral systems on ontological foundations. He says that the

> central issue about moral and ethical principles con-
> cerns their ontological foundation. If they are neither
> derived from God nor anchored in some transcendent
> ground, are they ephemeral?... The moral and ethical

---

[41] Kurtz. *Forbidden Fruit*, pp. 97–98.
[42] Paul Kurtz. *Free Inquiry*. Volume 23, Number 1, Winter, 2002/2003, https://www.secularhumanism.org/index. php/cont_index_23.
[43] Kurtz. *Forbidden Fruit*. p. 97.
[44] Ibid, p. 100.

> principles that we live by and to which we are commit-
> ted are "real": that is, we can make factual descriptive
> statements about their centrality of human behavior.[45]

In Kurtz's view, because the "common moral decencies" are empirically verifiable and can be studied by the scientific method, there is no need to appeal beyond empirical phenomena to any transcendental entity as a basis for morality. Therefore, he argues that we can make "factual descriptive statements" about ethics since they are "part of nature"[46] and therefore protected from subjective relativism. He rejects subjective relativism by stating:

> Ethical principles are not simply subjective emotional
> attitudes or states unamenable to any critical justifica
> tion. There are important objective criteria that we use
> to evaluate ethical principles.[47]

Kurtz aims at establishing reason and critique as integral parts of making ethical judgments and to remove reliance on faith i.e. on unexamined presumptions, on authority and tradition.[48]

There are at least three problems with Kurtz's argument. The first is that it cannot escape Hume's Guillotine. The fact that the "common moral decencies" are found everywhere and seem necessary to individual and/or societal well-being and/or survival does not make them morally obligatory. It makes them advantageous but being advantageous and being moral are not the same things. Advantage is an *aspect* of morality but it does not exhaust the concept of morality, as we have already seen in the hospital dilemma, and in various problems with utilitarianism and consequentialism. Letting the old and sick die might be financially advantageous to a society, i.e. the greatest good for the greatest number, but the morality of that is dubious. The "common moral

---

[45] Ibid, p. 95.
[46] Ibid.
[47] Ibid, p. 104.
[48] Ibid.

decencies" may also be seen as necessary vis-à-vis survival, but how do we distinguish them from the "common moral *indecencies*" such as slavery, the suppression of women and the rule of paterfamilias which many societies regarded as necessary to survival and even moral? In other words, the fact that the "common moral decencies" are/were ubiquitous and could be important to survival is not sufficient to bridge the gap between description and prescription.

There is a second difficulty: by what standard are we to distinguish between the "common moral decencies" and the common moral indecencies? It is not difficult to argue that slavery, the suppression of women and the paterfamilias contributed to survival in the past. To say that their 'time is over' simply appeals to an argument that has no basis in science or empirical evidence since there is no scientific way to prove that we are morally obligated to give up practices that no longer contemporary preferences even though they do not threaten human survival. Indeed, someone might argue that we should keep these practices because they have served us so well for so long. Such a morally perverse argument becomes possible precisely because there is no scientific way to exclude it without some standard by which to do so — and science cannot provide that standard.

A third, similar, difficulty arises vis-à-vis the actual applications of the "common moral decencies" which sound positive if we implicitly assume they are intended for all human beings. Few if any of these decencies were missing in Nazi, Fascist or Soviet society, for example, because they are rooted in human nature and in the humanity's "socio-biological" nature. However, few would defend their application of these decencies as moral. These societies — and others like them in the past — applied these decencies to a limited circle, i.e. family, tribal, racial or national members. However, by what empirical or scientific standard can we judge them as 'immoral'? This problem undermines Kurtz's argument because it clearly shows that within his empirical/scientific framework, there is no answer to the question of what is really good and really bad. At best, we have individual or societal preferences. Ultimately, Kurtz's argument falls into the very relativism it seeks to avoid.[49]

Strangely, both Kurtz and Harris recognize that they cannot produce a compelling scientific obligation to act for well-being or the "common moral decencies." As Harris notes, "Science cannot tell us why, *scientifically*, we should value health."[50] Kurtz asks, why should we be moral, "Why ought I to perform *this* obligation or *that* duty?"[51] These questions point to the heart of the problem: if a science-based ethic cannot give us science-based reasons for being moral — or even determine what constitutes morality and a moral standard — then something is missing in that ethic. It is not internally self-sufficient, which is to say, it must import the ethical concepts of obligation and value from outside empirical science.

At this point it is important to remind ourselves that the lack of self-sufficiency and the problems caused by Hume's is/ought division do not completely invalidate Harris' and Kurtz's arguments. Only their limitations are revealed. The information they provide can, as we shall see, be used in other arguments that complete the foundation for ethics by other means.

'IS' TO 'OUGHT" IN THE BAHÁ'Í WRITINGS

Before beginning this discussion about the is/ought distinction in the Bahá'í Writings — and, by implication — other theistic systems, two introductory remarks must be made regarding the invocation of God. First, the critique that invoking the transcendent God is simply a desperate resort to the so-called 'God-of-the-gaps' to solve otherwise insoluble problems is weak since the argument is easily turned around: the denial of God is simply a tactic to remove an otherwise insoluble problems for strictly empirical views about ethics. For example, it might be argued the

[49] Ibid, pp. 95–96.
[50] Harris. *The Moral Landscape*. p. 37
[51] Kurtz. *Forbidden Fruit*. p. 196.

concept of God is merely an artifice to give absolute grounding to a specific moral position; on the other hand, it can be equally argued that the denial of God is a way of avoiding the consequences of the existence of absolute moral standards. In other words, this criticism of the Bahá'í and theistic position is moot, giving neither side an advantage. Second, the censure that God's existence is an illegitimate assumption, whereas the assumption that He does not exist is somehow allowable also fails. Both are assumptions and proving that one assumption or the other is 'more justified' simply leads us to an infinite regress of assumptions that cannot — even in principle — decide the problem. For these two reasons, and the implications of Hume's is/ought problem, we maintain that the most rational response is evaluate the theist and non-theist positions on the basis of their internal logical coherence and self-sufficiency, and on their ability to answer logical problems such as the is/ought distinction.

In contrast to empiricist ontologies, the 'is-ought' problem does not exist in Bahá'í ethics or in the ethics of other theistic systems. In this paper, we shall focus on the Bahá'í Writings but it will become clear that none of the theistic religions fall victim to Hume's Guillotine. The reason is clear. Empiricism and the scientific method cannot find more in nature than can be revealed by the scientific method — and obligations, values, judgments and goodness or evil cannot be found in that way. However, the Bahá'í Writings — like all theistic religions — do not see nature as exclusively material. As 'Abdu'l-Bahá says, "there is a sign (from God) in every phenomenon."[52] More specifically, Bahá'u'lláh says,

> Whatever is in the heavens and whatever is on the earth is a direct evidence of the revelation within it of the attributes and names of God, inasmuch as within every atom are enshrined the signs that bear eloquent testimony to the revelation of that Most Great Light. Methinks, but for the potency of that revelation, no

---

[52] 'Abdu'l-Bahá. *Paris Talks*. p. 174.

being could ever exist. How resplendent the luminaries of knowledge that shine in an atom, and how vast the oceans of wisdom that surge within a drop… all things, in their inmost reality, testify to the revelation of the names and attributes of God within them. Each according to its capacity, indicateth, and is expressive of, the knowledge of God.[53]

Bahá'u'lláh makes it clear that there is more to reality than what is empirically perceptible and scientifically measureable, i.e. the "signs… of that Most Great Light." Indeed, physical reality reveals the "names and attributes of God" which appear in all things to an appropriate degree. These signs are ontologically real "spiritual realities"[54] even though they are not available for empirical analysis and can only be known if we "awaken [our] spiritual susceptibilities"[55] (As a quick digression, we note that science, too, requires the cultivation of special 'susceptibilities' and understandings for us to become aware of certain scientific truths, as in, for example, quantum physics. Thus, the requirement for "spiritual susceptibilities" is not an extraordinary claim made by religious thought.) Through the signs and knowledge revealed or instantiated in His creations, God makes His will known to a degree consistent with humankind's abilities to understand. Therefore, it is not necessarily a logical error to extract an ethical argument, i.e. an 'ought' or a prescription, from a natural fact, an 'is.' A particular argument may be faulty due to its own inherent flaws but, in principle, the procedure of reasoning from an 'is' to an 'ought' in a universe preternaturally charged with spiritual significances is valid. That is because prescriptions based on natural facts are grounded in an ontology that gives spiritual — in this case, ethical — significance to natural facts. Thus, spiritually speaking, there is an intrinsic connection between the subject matter and the moral to be learned. Natural

---

[53] Bahá'u'lláh. *Gleanings from the Writings of Bahá'u'lláh*. Wilmette: Bahá'í Publishing Trust, 1976, p. 177.

[54] 'Abdu'l-Bahá. *The Promulgation of Universal Peace*. p. 302.

[55] Ibid, p. 7.

facts have "spiritual significance"[56] which is not just a pleasing but fictitious analogy but is, rather, ontologically real, like "the luminaries of knowledge that shine in an atom."[57]

This non-materialist outlook on the phenomenal world provides an ontological foundation for our ethical systems. For example, 'Abdu'l-Bahá states,

> all humanity must be looked upon with love, kindness and respect; for what we *behold in them are none other than the signs and traces of God Himself.* All are evidences of God; therefore, how shall we be justified in debasing and belittling them, uttering anathema and preventing them from drawing near unto His mercy? This is ignorance and injustice, displeasing to God; for in His sight all are His servants.[58]

In other words, we must treat all created beings — and especially humankind — in a morally upright fashion precisely because they contain spiritual value as direct references to God. This is straightforward 'is' to 'ought' reasoning which, in a Bahá'í or theist context, is valid because the conclusion we draw is already implicit in the premise or the 'is.' Of course, theists may disagree about which specific moral imperative may be taken from certain natural facts, but that does not invalidate the effort to go beyond mere material knowledge. Here is another example. 'Abdu'l-Bahá states,

> For Christ declared, "Love your enemies... and pray for them which... persecute you; that you may be the children of your Father which is in heaven: for he maketh his sun to rise on the evil and on the good, and sendeth rain on the just and on the unjust."[59]

---

56 'Abdu'l-Bahá. *Paris Talks*. p. 98.
57 Bahá'u'lláh, *Gleanings*, p. 177.
58 'Abdu'l-Bahá. *The Promulgation of Universal Peace*. p. 231; emphasis added.
59 Ibid, p. 86.

From this natural example, he extracts a moral lesson, an 'ought,' an obligation, a prescription for human behavior. We are to be like the rain and offer good to everyone. From an empiricist perspective, this is an illogical violation of the 'is/ought' distinction. Of course, it might be argued that 'Abdu'l-Bahá simply uses rain as a convenient metaphor just as an empiricist might. However, for an empiricist, this metaphor is at best a clever and pleasing analogy; there is no intrinsic connection between the example and the lesson drawn from it. The connection is purely accidental. Consequently, the metaphor cannot give authority to any argument on which it is based. This is not true of the Bahá'í Writings in particular and theism in general. 'Abdu'l-Bahá's use of this natural illustration is grounded in an ontology that gives spiritual — in this case, ethical — significance to natural facts. Therefore, 'Abdu'l-Bahá's example is not merely a pleasing embellishment but points to a real ethical truth. From this it follows that there is an intrinsic connection between the subject matter and the moral explicated by 'Abdu'l-Bahá.

All this is not to say that God created rain solely for the purpose of teaching humans about doing good to all. Rain, like anything else, has other reasons for being, but it also performs a spiritual function for those who are spiritually awake and are "informed of the mysteries of the world of significances."[60] They will understand that these "significances" are not merely subjective phenomena but are ontologically real aspects of reality since, as, Bahá'u'lláh tells us, everything that exists reveals God's names and attributes. In short, ethics have an ontologically real foundation.

To sum up our foregoing argument: the exemption of the Bahá'í Writings (and other theistic systems) from Hume's is/ought distinction is of tremendous logical significance because it legitimizes the move from 'is' to 'ought.' Therefore, unlike scientific and empirically based ethics, theistic ethics can build on the factual descriptions of nature — be they fMRI brain-scans or "socio-biological" discoveries about human nature or scientific stud-

---

[60] Ibid, p. 303.

ies of well-being — to lead to prescriptive conclusions because values are already in the premise, i.e. in the natural data. Whether or not this possibility is always used well is another matter. What counts is that the principle has been established. On this issue, the Bahá'í Writings and other theistic ethics are internally self-sufficient and coherent, i.e. they do not have to import concepts from beyond the framework they have adopted.

THE PROBLEMS OF LEGITIMACY, AUTHORITY/POWER AND UNIVERSALITY

The belief in God helps us deal with three basic issues that any system of ethics must deal with: legitimacy, authority and universality. Legitimacy deals with the questions, 'Who — if anyone — has the legitimacy or qualifications to lay down moral principles and precepts for the human race? Who or what — if anything — has the knowledge, understanding and intrinsic goodness necessary to legitimize a demand for obedience? Who — or what — is inherently entitled to make obedience a condition for attaining 'rightness,' or true value and appropriate worth as a human being?' Clearly, no human individual or collective has the unlimited knowledge needed to dispense perfect justice, understanding and compassion. Human beings are fallible and fickle, have personal interests, lack absolute independence from all things, are susceptible to outside influence, interference and coercion. Therefore, it is virtually self-evident that no individual and no collective inherently possess such legitimacy by virtue of their human nature. This leaves science-based ethics in a weak position regarding the legitimacy of any ethical system it might adopt because no one has the qualifications that justify making particular demands. Of course, we may give governments or social institutions the power to do so but this is legal not moral legitimacy. On the other hand, in Bahá'í or in any other theist ethical system, God is not only unaffected by the aforementioned deficiencies, but He is also the actual maker of the world and the nature of everything in it. Consequently, it is difficult to imagine who else could be better qualified and possess the moral legitimacy to legislate for humanity.

All ethical systems must also deal with the issue of authority or power which refers to the power to enforce ethical commands in some way or another, i.e. to ensure that some kind of consequence follows moral or immoral behavior, just as consequences follow all behaviors in the natural world. Without power, legitimacy remains purely theoretical, in effect, impotent, thereby undermining and endangering one of the main *raisons d'être* of ethics, i.e. providing unity and the basis for co-operation among people.

In the last analysis, science-based ethics are forced to rely on political power to impose their ethical standards; they rely on government or social institutions to make their moral standards effective in the world. Here, too, they show their lack of internal self-sufficiency because they need to import an essential aspect of their ethical systems from beyond the scientific domain. What experiment could possibly tell us which political decision — regardless of how it is made — is correct? Neither political nor moral correctness can be measured by the scientific method. Bahá'í, and by implication, theistic ethics, do not suffer this deficiency because the question of power is soluble within their conceptual frameworks. They are logically coherent on these foundational matters.

The third challenge for scientific and empirical ethics is 'universality' by which we mean the applicability of ethical standards everywhere, at all times and under all circumstances. Harris deals with this by referring to the human brain which is substantially the same among all ethnicities and which is part of the body that humans have evolved over the last three million years. For his part, Kurtz relies on the "common moral decencies" that he believes underlie all human culture because human "socio-biology" requires them. Because the is/ought divide is an insurmountable problem in establishing brain-scan results or "common moral decencies" as moral obligations, it is impossible to maintain any claims to universality. From the perspective of the Bahá'í Writings, these suggestions are not so much mistaken as incomplete insofar as the Manifestations of God in every time and place "restate the eternal verities"[61] i.e. the basic religious truths which, of course, include the moral truths. These truths may appear in different forms under different circumstances but are always fundamentally the same. However, the problem with the science-based ethics is that they can neither bridge the is/ought divide nor definitively establish their legitimacy, authority and universality on the basis of their own premises. Here, too, they reveal their lack of internal conceptual self-sufficiency which undermines their claims.

CONCLUSION

In this paper we have examined two claims that a science-based ethics is a viable alternative to theist-based ethics such as we find in the Bahá'í Writings. We have found these claims to be untenable for three major reasons. First, they cannot logically bridge the divide between 'is' and 'ought' as explained by David Hume. Second, because of their inability to bridge the is/ought divide, they are not internally self-sufficient, i.e. they have to import ethical concepts from outside their empirical framework. Science simply cannot prove 'goodness' or 'obligation.' Third, because of their failures in the foregoing two endeavors, they cannot adequately assert claims to legitimacy, authority/power and universality. The fact that science-based ethics cannot establish their conceptual framework and work within it, indicates that the serious logical deficiencies undermine their project. As our examples from the Bahá'í Writings have shown, theist ethical systems do not suffer from these difficulties and, therefore, remain a logically viable alternative to science-based ethics.

---

[61] Shoghi Effendi. *The Promised Day Is Come*. Wilmette, Illinois: Bahá'í Publishing Trust, p. 108.

Arguments for the Existence of God in 'Abdu'l-Bahá's Writings

Mikhail Sergeev
University of the Arts

> *"...if the inner perception be open, a hundred thousand clear proofs [of God's existence] become visible..."*
>
> 'Abdu'l-Bahá

INTRODUCTORY REMARKS

The Bahá'í Faith is a monotheistic religion, and the notion of one supreme Deity occupies the central place in Bahá'í thought. On various occasions 'Abdu'l-Bahá stressed the importance of formulating the rational proofs of God's existence. The purpose of human life on earth consists of spiritual progress. However, one cannot strive toward this goal rationally without achieving some certainty about the source of spirituality and life after death. Hence, acquiring the knowledge of God may serve as the first step in the human intellectual journey — an important step that would facilitate our further spiritual advancement. As 'Abdu'l-Bahá admonishes his audience during one of his public addresses:

> Day and night, you must strive that you may attain to the significances of heavenly Kingdom, perceive the signs of Divinity, acquire certainty of knowledge and realize that this world has a Creator, a Vivifier, a Provider,

an Architect — knowing this through proofs and evidences and not through susceptibilities, nay, rather,
through decisive arguments and real vision.[1]

In many of his talks and writings 'Abdu'l-Bahá points out,
however, that the essence and the nature of the Supreme Being
are hidden from human cognition. The "reality of the Godhead,"
he writes in one letter,

> ...is beyond the grasp of the mind... how could it be
> possible for a contingent reality, that is, man, to under-
> stand the nature of that preexistent Essence, the Divine
> Being?.. man graspeth his own illusory conceptions
> but the Reality of Divinity can never be grasped... That
> Divinity which man doth imagine for himself existeth
> only in his mind, not in truth.[2]

Since no one can ever have knowledge of God-in-himself, the
only way for humans to acquire some understanding of divinity is
to turn to the effects of God's work on the human plane or, in other
words, to prove the reality of God-for-others. "The utmost one can
say," 'Abdu'l-Bahá argues, "is that [the Ultimate Reality's] existence
can be proved, but the conditions of Its existence are unknown."[3]
And although "the Divine Essence is unseen of the eye, and the existence of the Deity is intangible," he adds in another tablet,

---

[1] 'Abdu'l-Bahá. The Promulgation of Universal Peace (PUP), in *Writings
and Utterances of 'Abdu'l-Bahá*. New Delhi, India: Bahá'í Publishing
Trust, 2000, p. 1002.

[2] Selections from the *Writings of 'Abdu'l-Bahá* (SW), ibid, pp. 321–22.
'Abdu'l-Bahá repeats his arguments for the impossibility of knowing
the nature of God in many of his writings. In "The Tablet to Dr. Forel"
(TF), for example, he writes: "Now concerning the essence of Divinity:
in truth it is on no account determined by anything apart from its own
nature and can in nowise be comprehended. For whatsoever can be conceived by man is a reality that hath limitations and is not unlimited; it is
circumscribed, not all-embracing. It can be comprehended by man, and
is controlled by him... Moreover, differentiation of stages in the contingent world is an obstacle to understanding. How then can the contingent
conceive the reality of the absolute?" Ibid, p. 646.

[3] 'Abdu'l-Bahá, SW, ibid, p. 326.

> ...yet conclusive spiritual proofs assert the existence of that unseen Reality... For instance, the nature of ether is unknown, but that it existeth is certain by the effects it produceth: heat, light and electricity being the waves thereof. By these waves the existence of ether is thus proven. And as we consider the outpourings of Divine Grace we are assured of the existence of God.[4]

My paper thus aims at the systematic exposition in the historical and philosophical context of the arguments for God's existence that 'Abdu'l-Bahá uses in his various writings and speeches.

HISTORICAL BACKGROUND

Philosophical reflections about divine reality had already originated in antiquity. The Bible preserves for us, perhaps, the earliest examples of that. In the final book of the Torah, *Deuteronomy*, Moses taught his people how to distinguish false from true prophecies. He said: "If a prophet speaks in the name of the LORD but the thing does not take place or prove true, it is a word that the LORD has not spoken."[5] In other words, Moses' argument was that God's existence should be inferred from the results of his actions that can be predicted by the prophets — the messengers of God's will in the human world. And if the outcomes of those actions, as well as the prophecies themselves, do not turn out to be right, then the divine will have nothing to do with it.

Classical Greek philosophers Plato (428–348 BCE) and Aristotle (384–322 BCE) developed the first known logical arguments for the existence of God. Both thinkers,

> ...Plato... in *Laws X,* and Aristotle... in *Metaphysics XII,* argued that the finitude or contingency of objects or

---

[4] 'Abdu'l-Bahá, TF, ibid, p. 647.
[5] New Revised Standard Version. Deuteronomy, 18:15, 20–22. *The Complete Parallel Bible Containing the Old and New Testaments with the Apocryhal*/Deuterocanonical Books, New York — Oxford: Oxford University Press, 1993.

events in the world… could not provide adequate grounds for the world's coming into being. An endless chain of contingent or finite causes, they argue, remains implausible. Similarly, movement or change within the world points to a Being who is changeless, or the ground of change; to a Being who is "necessary" rather than contingent.[6]

In the Middle Ages this approach was revived and expanded upon by a variety of arguments not only within the Muslim and Christian religious traditions but also in the Hindu philosophical speculation.[7] In Modern times, and especially in the nineteenth and twentieth centuries, the debates over the existence of God took a new turn considering the most recent scientific developments in cosmology, biology, and human psychology.

TYPOLOGY OF PROOFS – INNER PERCEPTION

The basic typology of arguments for the existence of God can be traced back to the early Fathers of the Christian Church. A second-century Christian thinker Clement of Alexandria (b.c. 150 CE), for instance, already distinguished between the arguments from the observation of nature and from the contemplation of the soul. The external cosmological proofs and the inner realization of the innate idea of God in one's soul, however, according to Clement, can only lead to the belief in God's existence but not to the discovery of God's nature or to the meaning of divine actions.[8]

---

[6] Anthony C. Thiselton. *God, arguments for the existence of. A Concise Encyclopedia of the Philosophy of Religion.* Grand Rapids, MI: Baker Academics, 2002, p. 117.

[7] See, for example, a selection from Udayana Ācārya's (10th century AD) Kusumāñjali: The Kusumāñjali or Hindu Proof of the Existence of a Supreme Being, in A Source Book in Indian Philosophy, eds. Sarvepalli Radhakrishnan and Charles A. Moore, Princeton, NJ: Princeton University Press, 1973, pp. 379–385.

[8] Mayorov, G. G. *Formirovanie srednevekovoi filosofii. Latinskaia patristika* [Formation of Medieval Philosophy: Latin Patristics], Moscow: "Mysl'," 1979, p. 88.

In modern philosophical terminology these two types of arguments are called *a priori* (internal proofs) and *a posteriori* (external proofs). The *a priori* proofs of the existence of God were also discussed in the early Christian theology. A second-century Christian thinker Athanagoras, for example, was the first in the history of Christian thought to provide a philosophical argument for the existence of one God against the belief of pagan polytheism. Sometimes called "topological," his argument states that by its very definition, God is limitless. If one admits, however, the existence of more than one God, then, those gods will limit each other, thus contradicting the basic premise of the argument. Hence, Athanagoras concludes, there must exist only one God.[9]

The classic formulation of the *a priori* proof, which is known in the history of philosophy as the ontological argument, belongs, however, to the medieval Christian thinker, the Archbishop of Canterbury St Anselm (1033–1109 CE). In his *Proslogion*, St. Anselm wrote that God

...exists so truly that it cannot be thought not to exist. For it is possible to think that something exists that cannot be thought not to exist, and such a being is greater than one that can be thought not to exist. Therefore, if that than which a greater cannot be thought can be thought not to exist, then that than which a greater cannot be thought is not that than which a greater cannot be thought; and this is a contradiction. So that than which a greater cannot be thought exists so truly that it cannot be thought not to exist.[10]

---

[9] Ibid, p. 67. Mayorov points out that the topological argument, as Athanagoras formulated it, presupposes the spatial and, therefore, the bodily existence of God.

[10] St Anselm and Gaunilo, "The Ontological Argument," from Monologion and Proslogion, with the replies of Gaunilo and Anselm, in God, Hackett readings in philosophy, edited, with Introduction, by Timothy A. Robinson, Indianapolis/Cambridge: Hackett Publishing Company, 1996, pp. 2–3.

In Modern times it was René Descartes (1596–1650) who revived St. Anselm's position and in the twentieth century Alvin Plantinga (b. 1932) discussed it in the context of modal logic of probabilities.[11]

The founder of German Idealism, Immanuel Kant (1724–1804), proposed another version of the *a priori* argument — in his case, from the freedom of human will. Kant rejected any proofs that were based on observation of the external world since they rely on the nature of human experience that reflects the workings of the mind rather than the world as it actually is. Instead he appealed to the moral imperative as a necessary pre-condition of God's existence because, without the fear of divine retribution, humanity would lose its most vital incentive for good moral behavior. Kant's reference to morality, however, is not, strictly speaking, a valid proof but rather a postulate of practical reason that in no way — according to Kant himself — can be supported by the conclusions arrived at by theoretical reason. As a result, the Kantian approach turns into a paradox — in order for humanity to pursue moral virtues God must exist although we cannot prove that he does.

The third argument from inner perception addresses human emotions, especially those associated with faith and religiosity. The feelings of reverence and love toward God, the fear of losing connection with divinity, by the virtue of their very existence, seem to prove the existence of the object of those feelings. An Anglo-Catholic thinker, A. E. Taylor (1869–1945), provided a modern restatement of the argument in his essay "The Vindication of Religion." He wrote here about the uniqueness of religious experience:

It is universal voice of the mutable and temporal brought face to face with the absolutely eternal... As nearly as we can express our attitude towards that which awakens this sense of being immediately in the presence of

---

[11] See, for example, Alvin Plantinga. *The Ontological Argument*. New York: Doubleday, 1965.

the "other-worldly" by any one word, we may say that it is the attitude of "worship."[12]

This attitude of worship and the sense of the holy that are universally present in all of human civilizations, in Taylor's view, already represent a sufficient proof of the reality of God.

CLASSICAL *A POSTERIORI* ARGUMENTS

In contrast to the *a priori* proofs, the *a posteriori* arguments for the existence of God rely on the observation of the external world. Thus, the holy book of Islam, the *Qur'ān*, for instance,

> ...teaches that God's revelation has occurred in several forms: in nature, history, and Scripture. [Therefore,] God's existence can be known through creation [that] contains pointers or "signs" of God... [through the] history of the rise and fall of nations [that provide the] lessons of God's sovereignty and intervention in history [and] through a series of messengers.[13]

In Islamic, Christian and Jewish philosophy, however, one finds mostly the arguments from the nature of creation that lead to the conclusion of God's existence. The substance of the arguments goes back to Plato and Aristotle who discuss motion and causality and argue for the necessity of the "Prime Mover" in light of the contingency of the physical universe. This line of thought, which is known in the history of philosophy as the cosmological argument, received further development in the Middle Ages.[14]

---

[12] A. E. Taylor, "The Vindication of Religion," in The Existence of God, edited and with an introduction by John Hick, New York: The Macmillan Company, 1966, p. 159.

[13] Esposito, John L. Islam: The Straight Path. New York – Oxford: Oxford University Press, 1991, p. 19.

[14] For a historical exposition of the cosmological argument see, for example: Craig, W. I. The Cosmological Argument from Plato to Leibniz. London: Macmillan, 1980.

Medieval Muslim thinkers al-Kindī (c. 813–c. 871 CE) and al-Ghazālī (1058–1111 CE), for instance, held that the universe was created and, therefore, finite, which made the infinite regress of "caused causes" in this universe impossible. Other Muslim philosophers, such as Ibn Sīnā (Avicenna, 980–1037 CE) and Ibn Rushd (Averroes, 1126–98 CE), distanced themselves from the Islamic theology of *kalam* by rejecting the doctrine of creation *ex nihilo*. For Ibn Rushd, "the world is eternal but caused; God is eternal and uncaused, since God is God's own ground...and is a 'necessary Being'."[15] Both Ibn Sīnā and Ibn Rushd, furthermore, argued that since our eternal universe contains contingent beings it must have the Necessary Being as its foundation.[16]

Jewish and Christian thinkers — Moses Maimonides (1135–1204 CE) and Thomas Aquinas (1225–74 CE)—took the middle way between the interpretations of Muslim *kalam* and the speculations of Islamic philosophy. They sided with Muslim theologians in affirming the doctrine of creation, which is explicitly stated in the scriptures. At the same time, they supported the rationalism of Muslim philosophers with respect to the laws of nature and in contrast to the providentialism of al-Kindī and al-Ghazālī who argued, "God is the only true causal agent of every event."[17]

Overall, the following table can represent the different positions of Muslim, Christian and Jewish thinkers with respect to the cosmological argument:

---

[15] Thiselton, "Cosmological argument for the existence of God" in *A Concise Encyclopedia of the Philosophy of Religion*, p. 52.

[16] For a modern version of Avicenna's cosmological proof see an article by a Bahá'í philosopher William S. Hatcher "From Metaphysics to Logic: A Modern Formulation of Avicenna's Cosmological Proof of God's Existence" in his book Logic and Logos: Essays on Science, Religion and Philosophy. Oxford: George Ronald, 1990, pp. 60–80.

[17] Thiselton, "Cosmological argument for the existence of God," A Concise Encyclopedia of the Philosophy of Religion, p. 52.

	Universe is finite	Universe is infinite
God created the Universe and is the only true cause agent of every event.	al-Kindī (c. 813 – c. 871) al-Ghazālī (1058–1111)	
God created the Universe but is not the only true cause agent of every event.	Maimonides (1135–1204) St. Thomas Aquinas (1225–74)	Ibn Sīnā or Avicenna, (980–1037) Ibn Rushd or Averroes, (1126–98)

The doctor of the Christian Church, St. Thomas Aquinas, is especially known for his formulations of the *a-posteriori* arguments for God's existence. In his *Summa Theologica*, Aquinas wrote about the "Five Ways" one could prove the existence of the Almighty. The first three of them represent various versions of the cosmological argument that arrives at its conclusion on the basis of the existence of motion or change, causation and contingency in the world. The fourth way proceeds "from the gradation to be found in things" that points to the superlative degree of existence or divine perfection, to "something which is to all beings the cause of their being, goodness, and every other perfection; and this we call God."[18] Finally, the fifth way presents the teleological argument that postulates the purposive character of the universe, which, in its turn, refers back to the existence of its Designer.

The *a posteriori* arguments that appeal to history and divine revelation, to my knowledge, have not been sufficiently explored in the Christian tradition. Their examples, however, can be traced in medieval Hindu speculation, more specifically in the Nyāya school of religious philosophy. Here, for instance, one finds proofs, which are based on the authority of scriptural texts

---

[18] St Thomas Aquinas, "The Five Ways," from *Summa Theologica*, Part I, Question 2, articles 1 & 3, in God, Hackett readings in philosophy, p. 16.

and the very nature of religion and religious rituals that originate in sacred scriptures:

> The right knowledge caused by testimony is one which is produced by a quality in the speaker, viz., his knowledge of the exact meaning of the words used; hence the existence of God is proved, as he must be the subject of such a quality in the case of the [Hindu scripture of the] Veda.[19]

Or: "The knowledge produced by the Veda is produced by a virtue residing in its cause, because it is right knowledge, just as is the case in the right knowledge by perception..."[20]

'ABDU'L-BAHÁ'S ARGUMENTS FROM NATURE

As far as I know, in his writings and public addresses, 'Abdu'l-Bahá never mentions the *a priori* arguments for God's existence. Sometimes he hints at the inner perception as the source of those arguments but even then, he does not explore this line of thought in more details. In *Some Answered Questions* he mentions the depth of inner perception as a sign of strength and adds that the external arguments are needed for those whose spiritual understanding is limited and whose souls are weak. He says, "if the inner perception be open, a hundred thousand clear proofs become visible...but for those who are deprived of the bounty of the spirit, it is necessary to establish external arguments."[21]

All of the proofs of God's existence that 'Abdu'l-Bahá discusses are, therefore, the *a posteriori* arguments, which are based on our observation of the external world. Furthermore, most of them involve the order and composition of the natural universe

---

[19] Udayana Ācārya's (10th century AD) Kusumāñjali: The Kusumāñjali or Hindu Proof of the Existence of a Supreme Being, in A Source Book in Indian Philosophy, p. 381.
[20] Ibid, p. 384.
[21] 'Abdu'l-Bahá. *Some Answered Questions* (SAQ), in Writings and Utterances, p. 133.

and echo the "Five Ways" of St. Thomas Aquinas. Thus, in his various writings and talks, 'Abdu'l-Bahá formulates his own versions of the cosmological argument, which Aquinas divided into three separate parts that address change, causation and contingency of the world. With regard to change, for instance, in *Some Answered Questions* 'Abdu'l-Bahá notes, that "the least change produced in the form of the smallest thing proves the existence of a creator: then can this great universe, which is endless, be self-created and come into existence from the action of matter and the elements?"[22] The logic behind the argument is that change or motion in the world necessarily requires the existence of an entity, which set the world in motion, and that is what people call God.

In "The Tablet to Dr. Forel" 'Abdu'l-Bahá turns to the second part of the cosmological argument, which is related to causation. He writes:

> As we…reflect with broad minds upon this infinite universe, we observe that motion without a motive force, and an effect without a cause are both impossible; that every being hath come to exist under numerous influences and continually undergoeth reaction…Such process of causation goes on, and to maintain that this process goes on indefinitely is manifestly absurd. Thus such a chain of causation must of necessity lead eventually to Him who is the Ever-Living, the All-Powerful, who is Self-Dependent and the Ultimate Cause.[23]

The third part of the argument that involves the existence of contingent beings as proof of the reality of the Necessary Being, takes several forms in 'Abdu'l-Bahá's writings. In *Some Answered Questions*, for example, he argues, "a characteristic of contingent beings is dependency, and this dependency is an essential necessity, therefore, there must be an independent being whose

---

[22] Ibid, p. 133.
[23] 'Abdu'l-Bahá, TF, ibid, p. 647.

independence is essential."[24] In another place, 'Abdu'l-Bahá correlates dependency, which is essential to the entities in the contingent world, with limitations and mutual influences that follow from this notion. He points out: "although all created things grow and develop, yet are they subjected to influences from without." He writes,

> Thus, each one of these entities exerteth its influence and is likewise influenced in its turn. Inescapably then, the process leadeth to One Who influenceth all, and yet is influenced by none, thus severing the chain. And further, all created beings are limited, and this very limitation of all beings proveth the reality of the Limitless; for the existence of a limited being denoteth the existence of a Limitless One."[25]

Yet another version of the same argument in 'Abdu'l-Bahá's writings is related to the creation of man — the highest creature who is still a contingent being that has limited abilities and depends on divine help in his intellectual and spiritual growth. "One of the proofs and demonstrations of the existence of God," he writes, "is the fact that man did not create himself...the creator of man is not like man because a powerless creature cannot create another being. The maker, the creator, has to possess all perfections in order that he may create."[26]

The "Fourth Way" of St. Thomas Aquinas is based on the gradations of things and various degrees of perfection, which

---

[24] 'Abdu'l-Bahá, SAQ, ibid, p. 133.

[25] 'Abdu'l-Bahá, SW, ibid, p. 323.

[26] 'Abdu'l-Bahá, SAQ, ibid, p. 132. 'Abdu'l-Bahá repeats the same argument in PUP: "It is perfectly evident that man did not create himself and that he cannot do so...Therefore, the Creator of man must be more perfect and powerful than man. If the creative cause of man be simply on the same level with man, then man himself should be able to create, whereas we know very well that we cannot create even our own likeness." (Ibid, p. 876.)

presuppose the necessity of the superlative degree or God. 'Abdu'l-Bahá makes a similar argument in *Some Answered Questions* where he says that the "imperfections of the contingent world are in themselves a proof of the perfection of God" and, hence, "the smallest thing proves the existence of a creator."[27] In the "Tablet to Dr. Forel" he uses the idea of limitation in the same context:

> ...limitation itself proveth the existence of the unlimited, for the limited is known through the unlimited; just as weakness itself proveth the existence of wealth... Darkness itself is a proof of the existence of light, for darkness is the absence of light.[28]

The "Fifth Way" of St. Thomas Aquinas is known as the teleological argument, and it states that the natural order and harmony of the universe must have the intelligent Designer as their ultimate source. 'Abdu'l-Bahá often makes use of this argument in his speeches and writings. In "The Tablet to Dr. Forel," for instance, he points out "as we observe the coming together of elements giveth rise to the existence of beings, and knowing that beings are infinite, they being the effect, how can the Cause be finite?" Later in his letter to Dr. Forel, 'Abdu'l-Bahá elaborates on this point in greater details.

He begins with the assumption that "formation is of three kinds and of three kinds only: accidental, necessary and voluntary." As for the first one, he argues, the "coming together of various constituent elements of beings cannot be accidental, for into every effect there must be a cause. It [also] cannot be compulsory," he continues,

---

[27] 'Abdu'l-Bahá, SAQ, ibid, pp. 132–33.

[28] 'Abdu'l-Bahá, TF, ibid, p. 648. 'Abdu'l-Bahá, repeats the same argument in PUP: "Among the proofs of the existence of a divine power is this: that things are often known by their opposites. Were it not for darkness, light could not be sensed. Were it not for death, life could not be known... Therefore, our weakness is an evidence that there is might...In other words, demand and supply is the law, and undoubtedly all virtues have a center and source. The source is God, from Who all these bounties emanate." (Ibid, p. 647.)

...for then the formation must be an inherent property of the constituent parts and the inherent property of a thing can in nowise be dissociated from it...Thus under such circumstances the decomposition of any formation is impossible, for the inherent properties of a thing cannot be separated from it.

Hence, only one possibility remains, namely, that of the voluntary formation, meaning, "an unseen force described as the Ancient Power, causeth these elements to come together, every formation giving rise to a distinct being.[29]

Therefore, as 'Abdu'l-Bahá concludes, "this infinite universe with all its grandeur and perfect order could not have come to exist by itself." And "[a]s one's vision is broadened and the matter observed carefully," he goes on,

...it will be made certain that every reality is but an essential requisite of other reality. Thus to connect and harmonize these diverse and infinite realities an all-unifying Power is necessary, that every part of existent being may in perfect order discharge its own function.[30]

To sum up, the perfect composition of the natural world presupposes its intelligent Designer in the same way as a "piece of bread proves that it has a maker."[31] Similarly, as 'Abdu'l-Bahá points out,

---

[29] 'Abdu'l-Bahá, TF, ibid, pp. 647–48. The argument is restated on page 650: "...every arrangement and formation that is not perfect in its order we designate as accidental, and that which is orderly, regular, perfect in its relations and every part of which is in its proper place and is the essential requisite of the other constituent parts, this we call a composition formed through will and knowledge. There is no doubt that these infinite beings and the association of these diverse elements arranged in countless forms must have proceeded from a Reality that could in no wise be bereft of will or understanding."

[30] Ibid, pp. 648–49.

[31] 'Abdu'l-Bahá, SAQ, ibid, p. 133.

...what has been written presupposes and proves the existence of a writer. These words have not written themselves, and these letters have not come together of their own volition...And now consider this infinite universe. Is it possible that it could have been without a Creator? Or that the Creator and cause of this infinite congeries of words should be without intelligence?[32]

'ABDU'L-BAHÁ'S ARGUMENTS FROM HISTORY

One has to note that 'Abdu'l-Bahá provides significantly less arguments for the existence of God regarding history and historical events than he does with respect to the nature and order of the universe. His detailed explanations of the function of prophecy belong rather to the field of philosophical anthropology while his discussions of the evolution of religion and progressive revelation constitute an integral part of his philosophy of history. Nevertheless, one finds in 'Abdu'l-Bahá's writings one implicit argument from history that is supposed to deliver a definite proof of divine existence. It involves the effects, or, in Biblical terms, the fruits of the lives and teachings of the prophets.

"A Cause which all the governments and peoples of the world, with all their powers and armies, cannot promulgate and spread, one Holy Soul can promote without help or support!" — 'Abdu'l-Bahá exclaims in *Some Answered Questions* and asks his readers: "Can this be done by human power?" He continues: "For example, Christ, alone and solitary, upraised the standard of peace and righteousness, a work which all the victorious governments with all their hosts are unable to accomplish." "What I mean," he says in conclusion, "is that Christ sustained a Cause that all the kings of the earth could not establish!"[33] This achievement alone, according to 'Abdu'l-Bahá, stands as a definite proof of the divine source of Christ's power. It also represents, we may

---

[32] 'Abdu'l-Bahá, PUP, ibid, p. 876.
[33] 'Abdu'l-Bahá, SAQ, ibid, p. 135.

add, the mother of all proofs that relate to history, and can be extended to the teachings of all the prophets and founders of world religions as well as to the influences, which the sacred writings exert on people, and to the survival of religious minorities despite severe persecutions and cruel conquests by countless empires — the list of derivative historical proofs of the existence of God and his involvement in human affairs could be multiplied almost *ad infinitum.*

CONCLUSIONS

The aim of my paper was to systematize and present in the context of world philosophy the arguments for the existence of God that are scattered throughout the numerous writings and utterances of 'Abdu'l-Bahá. From a Bahá'í perspective, 'Abdu'l-Bahá occupies a unique place in religious history and Bahá'ís believe that his knowledge was inspired by the Holy Spirit. From the standpoint of comparative philosophy, one could also make the following conclusions:

(1) Most of the arguments that 'Abdu'l-Bahá explicitly uses are known in the history of philosophy as the so-called *a posteriori* proofs of the existence of God;

(2) Although 'Abdu'l-Bahá never mentions St. Thomas Aquinas, most of the arguments he discusses — with certain individual variations — fall under the rubric of Aquinas' "Five Ways." Since medieval Christian thought was largely influenced by classical Muslim philosophy and theology, it is possible that 'Abdu'l-Bahá was well versed in and may have drawn from the Muslim thought on the subject.

(3) 'Abdu'l-Bahá never wrote a systematic philosophical treatise on the subject of proofs and, therefore, was not obliged to analyze the historical development of the topic. In his writings and public addresses, he usually does not mention the names of individual philosophers but rather goes to the heart of the argument with the intention of strengthening the faith of his readers

or listeners. Still, in my opinion, it is significant that he does not address modern Western thought on the subject of proofs, more specifically, the Kantian rebuttal of *a priori* and *a posteriori* arguments from his *Critique of Pure Reason*[34] and especially Kant's critique of the ontological argument, which (the argument), as far as I know, 'Abdu'l-Bahá never discusses. It seems to me that 'Abdu'l-Bahá may have been less familiar with modern Western thought on the subject than with classical philosophical arguments for the existence of God.

---

[34] See: Kant, Immanuel. *Critique of Pure Reason*, trans. Norman Kemp Smith, New York: St. Martin's Press, 1965, Ch. III, Sections 3–6, pp. 495–524, where Kant unfolds his critique of traditional arguments for the existence of God.

A Look at Harmony and Unity as Common Principles in the Confucian System and the Bahá'í Faith

BENJAMIN B. OLSHIN

The University of the Arts

INTRODUCTION

One may well ask the purpose of a comparison of two systems of philosophy or belief. More particularly, why a comparison of the Confucian system and the Bahá'í Faith, especially given the existence of a book that looks at this very subject, with Confucianism in the broader context of Chinese belief systems?[1] To answer the latter question first: This paper focuses exclusively on Confucianism, in part because Confucianism can be considered the driving philosophy — even if it is not always articulated consciously — at the root of most East Asian cultures.[2] In many ways, it is more fundamental in shaping the ethics and even daily practices of East Asian cultures than Buddhism, Daoism, or the

---

[1] Phyllis Ghim Lian Chew. *The Chinese Religion and the Bahá'í Faith* (Oxford: George Ronald, 1993).

[2] For one look at the development of Confucian thought in China, Korea, and Japan, see John H. Berthrong. *Transformations of The Confucian Way* (Boulder, CO: Westview Press, 1998).

various animist beliefs that continue to exist either independently or in a syncretic form in those cultures.[3]

As for the formalized comparison of the Confucian thought with the Bahá'í Faith presented here, the rationale lies in the continuing need to understand these kinds of systems as attempts to create cohesive, living social structures, rather than simply abstract "sets of beliefs." If one looks at Confucian ethical principles and those of the Bahá'í Faith, it is clear that they are sophisticated attempts to bring rational and — in the case of the Bahá'í Faith — spiritual teachings to bear in organizing human behavior. The ultimate goal of both systems — and many other systems, of course — is for human beings to live in a society characterized by *harmony*, a goal achieved by the *unity* of a shared ethical practice.

The reader should understand that in the Bahá'í Faith, this concept of "unity" also exists beyond the idea of shared ethical practice (although this paper will focus on the latter). In the Bahá'í Faith, the concept of unity relates directly to the single nature of humanity as a whole ("Oneness of Mankind"), and reflects a truly universal vision:

> Let there be no mistake. The principle of the Oneness of Mankind — the pivot round which all the teachings of Bahá'u'lláh revolve — is no mere outburst of ignorant emotionalism or an expression of vague and pious hope. Its appeal is not to be merely identified with a reawakening of the spirit of brotherhood and good-will among men, nor does it aim solely at the fostering of harmonious cooperation among individual peoples and nations... Its message is applicable not only to the individual but concerns itself primarily with the nature of those essential relationships that must bind all the states and nations as members of one human family.[4]

---

[3] I wish to thank Prof. Mikhail Sergeev for giving me the opportunity to explore this subject through the present paper.

[4] Shoghi Effendi. *The World Order of Bahá'u'lláh*, as quoted in Kenneth E. Bowers *God Speaks Again: An Introduction to the Bahá'í Faith*

Note that the declarations here are of a broader vision, but at the same time there is — as in the writings of Confucius — a pragmatic element: this is, Shoghi Effendi states, "no mere outburst of ignorant emotionalism or an expression of vague and pious hope". As one commentator puts it, "The Bahá'í vision is not some utopian fantasy — it is the next inevitable stage in the long process of human social evolution."[5] The overall message, moreover, is that this is not just about the "individual"; Shoghi Effendi goes on to say:

It implies an organic change in the structure of present-day society, a change such as the world has not yet experienced... It calls for no less than the reconstruction and the demilitarization of the whole civilized world — a world organically unified in all the essential aspects of its life, its political machinery, its spiritual aspiration, its trade and finance, its script and language...[6]

Again, the concept is visionary and broad, even as the terms — "political machinery," "spiritual aspiration," "trade and finance," and so on, are quite practical.

Confucius outlines specific virtues, examined in detail in this paper, to build his model of ethical practice, while the Bahá'í Faith in some sense works in reverse, providing broad principles — such as love and tolerance — under which humans can then practice particular ethical behaviors, such as being free from prejudice.

Both Confucianism and the Bahá'í Faith represent complex and multi-faceted systems of philosophy, practice, and belief, and the reader is asked here to accept a somewhat simplified representation of those systems for the sake of a clear and concise study. Moreover, for Confucianism, this paper will draw almost exclusively from the *Analects* (論語 *Lúnyǔ*), again for the sake of presenting what one might call the "core" ethical system of

---

(Wilmette: Bahá'í Publishing Trust, 2004), 227; also see William S. Hatcher and J. Douglas Martin. *The Bahá'í Faith: The Emerging Global Religion* (Wilmette: Bahá'í Publishing Trust, 1998), 76.

5 Bowers, 227.
6 Ibid., 227.

Confucius.[7] We will not explore, for example, the philosophy of Neo-Confucianism and its parallels with the Bahá'í Faith — which could indeed, however, serve as the basis for an interesting subsequent study.[8] In terms of the Bahá'í Faith, we will draw primarily from the writings of Bahá'u'lláh here.

Finally, this paper is not a "survey" comparison of Confucianism and the Bahá'í Faith; that has been done well elsewhere.[9] Rather, we focus here — through a close reading of the texts — on particular aspects of each system that resonate most strongly with each other.

CONFUCIAN THOUGHT AND THE BAHÁ'Í FAITH: ORIGINS AND CONTEXTS

Given the importance of Confucius and his philosophy, it is remarkable how little is known about him. In Chinese, he is typically known as 孔子 (Kǒngzǐ), which simply means "Master Kong." Another appellation is 孔夫子 (Kǒngfūzǐ), the source of the Latinized version of his name, "Confucius."

The actual dates of his life are uncertain, although they are traditionally given as 551–479 B.C.E. It seems that Confucius came from an aristocratic family, but one which was no longer wealthy in his lifetime. Confucius himself never held a high political post, although he indeed was an educated man. In fact, his goal was to realize his philosophy through serving a ruler, and so much of his life was spent moving from place to place, looking for the head of a feudal state who might be interested in his principles. Yet Confucius never gained any fixed role or position, and in the end, he returned to his native state of Lu (魯國 Lǔ guó).

---

[7] All reference to the *Analects* in this paper are from Roger T. Ames and Henry Rosemont, Jr., eds., *The Analects of Confucius: A Philosophical Translation* (New York: Ballantine Books, 1998).

[8] For a good introduction to Neo-Confucianism, see Anne D. Birdwhistell, *Transition to Neo-Confucianism: Shao Yung on Knowledge and Symbols of Reality.*

[9] See Chew's *The Chinese Religion and the Bahá'í Faith*, cited in n. 1.

Confucius lived during a time of marked instability, with various states engaged in

> escalating internecine violence, driven by the knowledge that no state was exempt, and that all comers were competing in a zero-sum game — to fail to win was to perish. The accelerating ferocity of battle was like the increasing frequency and severity of labor pains, anticipating the eventual birth of the imperial Chinese state.[10]

Not surprisingly, the Bahá'í Faith appeared at a similar nexus of historical change. The fertile, even volatile, period of the mid-nineteenth century saw the rise of the Bábí movement, that later led to the founding of the Bahá'í Faith. The founder of the Bábí movement, Siyyid 'Alí Muḥammad Shírází (1819–1850), later known as the *Báb* (literally, "gate"), was similar to Confucius in his awareness of his location in history, and the need for societal change. One study notes:

> His principle book, the Bayán, envisioned a time when Persia's accumulated legacy of misspent energy would be entirely destroyed and the intellectual capacities of its people liberated from superstition. He spoke of a coming age in which entirely new fields of scholarship and science would emerge and in which the knowledge of even young children would far surpass the learning current in his own time.[11]

Confucius, as we shall see, similarly rejected superstition, and as to youth, he similarly wrote:

> The young should be held in high esteem. After all, how do we know that those yet to come will not surpass our contemporaries?[12]

---

[10] Ames and Rosemont, 2.
[11] Hatcher and Martin, 24.
[12] Ames and Rosemont, 131.

As in Confucian thought, the Bábí movement drew from the past while envisioning a very different future:

> The Báb's way... was to create the concept of an entirely new society, one that retained a large measure of cultural and religious elements familiar to hearers, but which, as events were to show, could arouse powerful new motivation. He called upon the Shah and the people of Persia to follow him in the establishment of this society... [and] he elaborated a system of laws for the conduct of public affairs [and] for the maintenance of peace and public order...[13]

The Bábí leader who was to found the Bahá'í Faith was Bahá'u'lláh (meaning "Glory of God"), born Mírzá Ḥusayn-'Alí Núrí (1817–1892).[14] Again, much like Confucius, he had a "reputation for personal integrity"[15] and lived in a period of complex geopolitical and social change — the beginnings of the slow death of the Ottoman Empire, struggles between the European powers for influence in the Middle East and Central Asia, and the broader conflict between the modernity wrought by the nineteenth-century Western ideas and traditional beliefs.

As with many remarkable thinkers, Confucius gained renown posthumously. His idealized role as a teacher developed during the Han Dynasty (206 B.C.E. — 220 A.D.). Eventually, of course, his philosophical principles became deeply influential in education and even political philosophy, not just in China but also other parts of East Asia. Bahá'u'lláh was much more influential in his own lifetime, although he seemed to have been little known to Westerners.[16]

Confucius' ideas are framed on a basic model that includes both the universe and mankind's role in that universe. Confucian

---

[13] Hatcher and Martin, 25.
[14] For a brief overview of Bahá'u'lláh's life, see Hatcher and Martin, 28–49.
[15] Hatcher and Martin, 28–29.
[16] Ibid., 48.

philosophy draws from the fundamental idea that the universe is ordered and has a pattern, and second, that mankind can exist in natural harmony with this pattern. Moreover, Confucius considers humans to be social beings, who have to engage in the world and in relationships with each other. Such relationships will be harmonious, Confucius notes, if they are clearly articulated and bound by "authoritative conduct." The key relationships are five in number: (1) sovereign-subject; (2) husband-wife; (3) parent-child; (4) elder brother-younger brother; and (5) friend-friend. These relationships require each individual to carry out their role to the utmost, in terms of responsible behavior, so that one is an integral part of a community — in short, "role ethics."[17] The connection between relationships and this "authoritative conduct" is nicely defined by the Chinese term for the latter, 仁 (*rén*), which is "the foremost project taken up by Confucius."[18] The character itself is composed of two Chinese characters: for "person" 人 (*rén*) and the character for "two" 二 (*èr*). As one study notes:

> This etymological analysis underscores the Confucian assumption that one cannot become a person by oneself — we are, from our inchoate beginnings, irreducibly social.[19]

Confucius thus believes both that mankind should adhere to proper conduct and that any kind of unified society would arise only through harmonious relationships. In such a society, moreover, a ruler's primary role was to be a model in terms of conduct and have strong relationships to both the divine order of the universe and the subjects of the earthly realm. The ruler was to serve in some sense as an exemplar for the people, and as a conduit between the people and the divine order.

---

[17] On this concept, see Ames *Confucian Role Ethics: A Vocabulary* (Honolulu: University of Hawai'i, 2011)

[18] Ames and Rosemont, 48.

[19] Ibid., 48.

The teachings of Bahá'u'lláh do not have such an explicit emphasis on relationships, although there is the similar idea that our individual spiritual growth happens in a social context. In other words, because, "we are social beings, our greatest progress is made through living in association with others."[20] This idea of association, even communality, is clearly outlined in the three basic principles of the Bahá'í Faith: "(1) the oneness of God; (2) the oneness of mankind; and (3) the fundamental unity of religion."[21] In this paper, we will focus particularly on the Bahá'í idea of "the oneness of mankind," as that is where Bahá'í thought is most akin to Confucian philosophy.

Despite what appears to us to be the profoundly novel way of thinking exhibited by Confucius, he viewed himself not as an originator, but as a transmitter — he claimed that he was simply passing on the wisdom of the ancients. In *Analects* 7.1, Confucius says, "I do not forge new paths; with confidence I cherish the ancients."[22] This claiming of a heritage from a lost "golden age" is not unusual in Chinese thought, nor is it particular to Chinese culture. However, that is not to dismiss its importance in this particular case: Confucius wished to apply a "corrective" to the decadent practices and abuses of power that he saw around him, and by harkening back to the past he could put some weight behind his critiques. For Confucius, the past supplied a sound, irrefutable standard.

In a similar manner, the founders of the Bahá'í Faith — while presenting some quite new ideas — at the same time saw themselves as part of the continuum of the Islamic tradition.[23] In a broader sense than in the Confucian system, the Bahá'í see a very particular place for themselves, moreover, not only in that Islamic history, but also in the religious history of the world." Indeed, the "interventions by God in human history" are seen as "progressive, each revelation from God more complete than those which

---

[20] Hatcher and Martin, 104–105.
[21] Ibid., 74.
[22] Ames and Rosemont, 111.
[23] See the comments in Hatcher and Martin, 2 et ff.

preceded it, and each preparing the way for the next."[24] In this continuum, Islam is the result of the most recent such intervention before the Báb, and historically served as the background for the rise of the Bahá'í Faith.[25] More particularly, just as Confucius wished to correct the decadence of his age, the Bábí movement that preceded the formalized Bahá'í Faith arose in opposition to a world that, as one study describes it, "had changed little from medieval times, except to become more obscurantist, isolated, and fatalistic."[26]

SOME CONTRASTS

The most fundamental contrast between Confucianism and the Bahá'í Faith, perhaps, is their place in history. Simply put, viewed from the present, Confucianism is old, while the Bahá'í Faith in some sense is "new," so that the latter addresses directly several contemporary issues, such as the equality of men and women; the elimination of prejudice; and the use of spiritual approaches to the solving of economic problems. Confucian principles certainly can be applied to these issues, but Confucius himself in the *Analects* does not quite address them directly. In terms of historical *contexts*, however, both Confucianism and the Bahá'í Faith arose in similarly unstable, troubled times, as highlighted earlier.

The other key contrast, of course, is that Confucian ethics are not drawn directly from any complex theological structure, although there is an idea of the transcendent in the *Analects* and in other Confucian and Neo-Confucian works.[27] The Bahá'í Faith and its principles are based on a belief in God. It is interesting to note, however, that in the texts of Bahá'u'lláh, we see some prag-

---

[24] Ibid., 2–3.
[25] Ibid., 3.
[26] Ibid., 25.
[27] See the discussion in Yong Huang, "Confucian Theology: Three Models," *Religion Compass* 1.4 (July 2007): 455–478.

matic approaches to religion, which actually serve as a contrast to Confucian ideas:

> It is not necessary to undertake special journeys to visit the resting-places of the dead.[28]

In Analects 1.9, however, a disciple of Confucius, states:

> Be circumspect in funerary services and continue sacrifices to the distant ancestors, and the virtue of the common people will thrive.[29]

But these are small differences. Given the vast separation in time between the Confucian *Analects* and the rise of the Bahá'í Faith, and their quite different cultural contexts, it is actually remarkable how similar their principles are.

POINTS OF CONVERGENCE

Even a quick reading of the *Analects* with certain Bahá'í texts also at hand shows some rather clear points of convergence. But this is not surprising in that these two systems — like many other such systems — are broad attempts to wrestle with human behavior in an attempt to create a better world. Yet even when we look more closely here, we still see this convergence, and on a rather detailed level.

A fruitful place to look, in fact, is in the writings of Bahá'u'lláh. We begin with the *Tablets of Bahá'u'lláh*, a collection of writings comprising selected tablets that cover such subjects as teachings and laws, personal character, knowledge of God, and the development of mankind.[30]

---

[28] Bahá'u'lláh. *Writings of Bahá'u'lláh: A Compilation.* 3rd ed. (New Delhi: Bahá'í Publishing Trust, 1998), 212.

[29] Ames and Rosemont, 73.

[30] The full title of this work is *Tablets of Bahá'u'lláh Revealed After the Kitáb-i-Aqdas.* See Bahá'u'lláh. *Tablets of Bahá'u'lláh Revealed After the Kitáb-i-Aqdas.* Compiled by the Research Department of the Universal House of Justice..., trans. Habib Taherzadeh (Wilmette: Bahá'í Publishing Trust, 1994).

In Bahá'u'lláh's *Bishárát* ("Glad Tidings"), for example, we find a number of analogues to passages in the *Analects*. In the "fifth Glad-Tidings," we read:

> In every country where any of this people reside, they must behave towards the government of that country with loyalty, honesty and truthfulness.[31]

This passage reflects the idea that individual followers of the Bahá'í Faith are to keep the faith separate from political matters and questions. A follower of this faith, wherever they might reside, should obey a government, as long as that government is duly constituted. Recall that one of the underlying principles of both Confucian thought and the Bahá'í Faith is for human beings to live in a society characterized by *harmony*, and one aspect of achieving such a goal is abiding the law. In *Analects* 1.2, we read the words of one of the Confucian disciples, Master You:

> It is a rare thing for someone who has a sense of filial and fraternal responsibility to have a taste for defying authority. And it is unheard of for those who have no taste for defying authority to be keen on rebellion. Exemplary persons concentrate their efforts on the root, for the root having taken hold, the way [道 *dào*] will grow therefrom. As for filial and fraternal responsibility, it is, I suspect, the root of authoritative conduct.[32]
>
> The key part here is the first line — "It is a rare thing for someone who has a sense of filial and fraternal responsibility to have a taste for defying authority" — and the third line: "Exemplary persons concentrate their efforts on the root, for the root having taken hold, the way [道 *dào*] will grow therefrom." What Confucius is saying here is not to "obey authority," but rather to concentrate on the matter at hand — as in the Bahá'í

---

[31] Bahá'u'lláh. *Writings of Bahá'u'lláh*, 209.
[32] Ames and Rosemont, 71.

Faith, this means one's own direct moral and social responsibilities.

There are several implications in the *Analects* passage. The first is that it is wise to avoid getting involved in outright rebellion. Second implication is that good governance at a larger scale will follow *naturally* from individuals concentrating on their own "filial and fraternal responsibility," i.e., at a smaller, local scale. Finally, individuals engaging in these responsibilities will create a model for others to follow, and thus bring about change "organically" rather than through confrontation and revolt.

One can certainly read the *Bishárát* passage above in the same way. Indeed, in a letter written by Shoghi Effendi (1897–1957), who was the head of the Bahá'í Faith from 1921 until 1957, we find a comment that explicates this passage from the *Bishárát*:

> The cardinal principle which we must follow... is obedience to the Government prevailing in any land in which we reside... We see, therefore, that we must do two things — shun politics like the plague and be obedient to the Government in power in the place where we reside... [T]he Bahá'ís must turn all their forces into the channel of building up the Bahá'í Cause and its Administration. They can neither change nor help the world in any other way at present. If they become involved in the issues the Governments of the world are struggling over, they will be lost. But if they build up the Bahá'í pattern they can offer it as a remedy when all else has failed.[33]

Note here the idea of disengagement from broad-scale politics, as in the *Analects*. Note, too, the idea that one could become "lost" in the sense of one's moral compass if involved in political issues. Most important, however, is the last line. In the *Analects*, "filial and fraternal responsibility" can be the "root" of a world

---

[33] See Shoghi Effendi. *Directives from the Guardian*. comp. Gertrude Garrida (New Delhi: Bahá'í Publishing Trust, 1974), 56–57.

that runs with proper "conduct," and here in Shoghi Effendi's commentary we see the very similar idea that the "Bahá'í pattern" can be a "remedy" to a world that is "struggling." This is also the fundamental idea introduced at the beginning of this paper: the *unity* of a shared ethical practice can serve as the road to a society characterized by *harmony*, or a remedy for a society that suffers from disharmony.

Confucius, of course, was greatly concerned with governance and its relation to achieving a better society. In *Analects* 2.1, we read:

> Governing with excellence can be compared to being the North Star: the North Star dwells in its place, and the multitude of stars pay tribute.[34]

This passage can be read, too, as resonant with Bahá'í thought. As a metaphor for leadership, the North Star is carefully chosen by Confucius — and not just because of its use in navigation. Perhaps drawing from a typically contrarian Daoist perspective, Confucius has chosen a *passive* object as an exemplar of leadership. The North Star does not *try* to be a leader; it governs by simply being what it is: a fixed star in the heavens.

Even as fine a detail as the role of clothing is found both in the Confucian *Analects* and Bahá'u'lláh's *Bishárát*. In *Analects* 10.6, we read:

> Persons of nobility do not use reddish black or dark brown for the embroidered borders of their robes, nor do they use red or purple in casual clothing. In the heat of summer, they would wear an unlined garment made of fine or coarse hemp but would invariably wear it over an undergarment to set it off. With black upper garments they wear lambskin; with undyed silk upper garments, fawn fur; with yellow-brown upper garments, fox fur. Casual fur robes were long overall, but the right

---

[34] Ames and Rosemont, 76.

sleeve was somewhat short. They are certain to have a nightcoat half his body in length. They use the thick fur of the fox and badger for sitting rugs. Outside of the mourning period, they wear whatever girdle ornaments they please. Apart from pleated ceremonial skirts, they would invariably have their skirts tailored. A lambskin coat and a black cap could not be worn on funeral occasions. On New Year's Day, they would invariably go to court in full court attire.[35]

Similarly, in *Analects* 10.7, we read that, "In periods of purification, Confucius would invariably wear a spirit coat made of plain cloth."[36] To the modern reader, the description in the passage above seems obsessive, if not outright absurd. But in the Confucian system, how one dresses is part of adherence to ritual — and that is, in turn, part of propriety (禮 *lĭ*). Propriety is an idea, interestingly, which appears rarely in Western philosophical systems. In its most literal sense, it the "performance of a ritual action."[37] But by extension, then, it is the way an individual should behave so that society — which, to Confucius is the sum of careful, reflective individuals behaving with propriety — can function.

While the *Bishárát* does not include such a prescriptive passage concerning clothing, we do indeed read the following:

The choice of clothing and the cut of the beard and its dressing are left to the discretion of men. But beware, O people, lest ye make yourselves the playthings of the ignorant.[38]

Here, we see an obvious reference to clothing as regulated by religious edicts. But note the message here: One the one hand,

---

[35] Ames and Rosemont, 136.

[36] Ibid., 136–137.

[37] For an extended definition, see Roger T. Ames and David L. Hall. *Focusing the Familiar: A Translation and Philosophical Interpretation of the* Zhongyong (Honolulu: University of Hawai'i Press, 2001), 34.

[38] Bahá'u'lláh. *Writings of Bahá'u'lláh*, 209.

there is the idea of a breaking away from particular strictures. But on the other hand, there is also an admonition. The subtext here may be the same, then, as in the passage from the *Analects*: however, one dresses, and even given freedom of choice, *observe propriety*.

Connected with the idea outlined above is the sense that when a person dresses and goes out, they are on display — and must be self-aware so as to not "lose face" (丢臉 *diū liǎn*). This concept of "face" and the culture of shame often are considered uniquely Chinese, but actually can be found in other cultures as well.[39] As pertains to Bahá'í thought, the "first leaf" of Bahá'u'lláh's *Kalimát-i-Firdawsíyyih* ("Words of Paradise") states that

> there existeth in man a faculty which deterreth him from, and guardeth him against, whatever is unworthy and unseemly, and which is known as his sense of shame. This, however, is confined to but a few; all have not possessed and do not possess it.[40]

Confucius ties together, too, the idea of shame and the concept of good governance in *Analects* 2.4:

> Lead the people with administrative injunctions and put them in their place with penal law, and they will avoid punishments but will be without a sense of shame. Lead them with excellence and keep them orderly through observing ritual propriety and they will develop a sense of shame, and moreover, will order themselves.[41]

---

[39] For a discussion of the role of shame in Chinese culture, see pp.181 et ff. of Heidi Fung, "Affect and Early Moral Socialization: Some Insights and Contributions from Indigenous Psychological Studies in Taiwan," in Uichol Kim, Kuo-Shu Yang, and Kwang-Kuo Hwang, eds., *Indigenous and Cultural Psychology: Understanding People in Context* (New York: Spring, 2006), 175–196. For an example in another culture, see Kofi Agyekum, "The Sociocultural Concept of Face in Akan Communication," *Journal of Pragmatics and Cognition* 12.1 (2004): 71–92.

[40] Bahá'u'lláh. *Writings of Bahá'u'lláh*, 232.

[41] Ames and Rosemont, 76.

Shame, in this view, is another structure to help guide individuals in their ethical development. Such individuals can then "order themselves" — a term that once more suggests the larger goal of creating a better society.

In contrast to this communal model, another early school of Chinese thought, Daoism — especially as articulated in the *Zhuangzi* (莊子 *Zhuāngzǐ*) — seems to advocate at least a certain degree of seclusion and withdrawal from society. In Western philosophy, we find a similar strain, though with some caveats. Epicurus "advocated withdrawal" from mercantile and political affairs[42] However, he also "stressed engagement with neighbors," and "intended to aid humanity as a whole through his philosophy."[43] Confucius seems to be more of the Epicurean strain, and here again we will see a connection to an idea in Bahá'í thought. *Analects* 18.6 addresses the issue directly:

> Old Marsh and Boldly Sunk were out in harness ploughing the field. Confucius, passing their way, sent Zilu to ask them where to ford.
>
> Old Marsh asked him, "Who is that man holding the reins of your carriage?"
>
> "He is Confucius," replied Zilu.
>
> "The Confucius of Lu?"
>
> "Indeed."
>
> "Then he already knows where the ford is."
>
> Zilu turned and asked Boldly Sunk where to ford.
>
> "Who are you?" asked Boldly Sunk.
>
> "I am Zilu."
>
> "You are that follower of Confucius of Lu?"
>
> "The very one."

---

[42] See Yonder M. Gillihan. *Civic Ideology, Organization, and Law in the Rule Scrolls: A Comparative Study of the Covenanters' Sect and Contemporary Voluntary Associations in Political Context* (Leiden: Brill, 2012), 98.

[43] Ibid., 88–89; also see Jeffrey Fish and Kirk R. Sanders, eds. *Epicurus and the Epicurean Tradition* (Cambridge: Cambridge University Press, 2011), 76.

He then said, "We are inundated like floodwaters. And the whole world is the same. Who then is going to change it into a new world? You follow after a teacher who avoids people selectively. Wouldn't you be better off following a teacher who avoids the world altogether?" As he spoke he continued to turn the earth over the seeds.

Zilu left to inform Confucius. Confucius, with some frustration, replied, "We cannot run with the birds and beasts. Am I not one among the people of this world? If not them, with whom should I associate? If the way [道 *dào*] prevailed in the world, I wouldn't need to change it."[44]

A closely related idea is found in the subsequent passage, *Analects* 18.7, where Zilu, a disciple of Confucius, speaks:

To refuse office is to fail to do what is important and appropriate. If the differentiation between young and old cannot be abandoned, how could one think of abandoning what is appropriate between ruler and subject? This is to throw the most important relationships into turmoil in one's efforts to remain personally untarnished. The opportunity of the exemplary person to serve in office is the occasion to effect what is judged to be important and appropriate.[45]

The careful handling of the issue of seclusion appears also in the *Bishárát*:

The pious deeds of the monks and priests among the followers of the Spirit... are remembered in His presence. In this Day, however, let them give up the life of seclusion and direct their steps towards the open world

---

[44] Ames and Rosemont, 214.
[45] Ibid., 216.

and busy themselves with that which will profit themselves and others.[46]

Again, in both sources, we see the idea of engagement with the world, rather than withdrawal. Another text by Bahá'u'lláh, the *Kalimát-i-Firdawsíyyih* ("Words of Paradise") reiterates this concept. In the "tenth leaf" we read:

> O people of the earth! Living in seclusion or practising ascetism is not acceptable in the presence of God. It behoveth them that are endued with insight and understanding to observe that which will cause joy and radiance... In former times and more recently some people have been taking up their abodes in the caves of the mountains while others have repaired to graveyards at night... Abandon the things current amongst you and adopt that which the faithful Counsellor biddeth you. Deprive not yourselves of the bounties which have been created for your sake.[47]

We clearly see the idea here that those who possess what Bahá'u'lláh calls "insight and understanding" should — as the Confucian disciple Zilu puts it — "serve... to effect what is judged to be important and appropriate."

While engagement is emphasized in both the Confucian system and Bahá'í thought, there are also admonitions against distractions from worldly goods. Near the beginning of the *Kalimát-i-Firdawsíyyih*, we read:

> Man's distinction lieth not in ornaments or wealth, but rather in virtuous behaviour and true understanding. Most of the people in Persia are steeped in deception and idle fancy. How great the difference between the condition of these people and the station of such valiant souls as have passed beyond the sea of names and

---

[46] Bahá'u'lláh. *Writings of Bahá'u'lláh*, 210.
[47] Ibid., 236–237.

pitched their tents upon the shores of the ocean of detachment.[48]

Note the use of the term "detachment"; so, while engagement in the world is a key part of these systems, there still must be a separation, one brought about through adherence to virtue and the seeking of understanding. Confucius, not surprisingly, also speaks of kind of detachment from the material:

> To eat coarse food, drink plain water, and pillow oneself on a bent arm — there is pleasure to be found in these things. But wealth and position gained through in appropriate means — these are to me like floating clouds.[49]

In the same passage of the *Kalimát-i-Firdawsíyyih*" cited above, we also read:

> People for the most part delight in superstitions. They regard a single drop of the sea of delusion as preferable to an ocean of certitude. By holding fast unto names they deprive themselves of the inner reality and by clinging to vain imaginings they are kept back from the Dayspring of heavenly signs. God grant you may be graciously aided under all conditions to shatter the idols of superstition and to tear away the veils of the imaginations of men.[50]

So, not only may "ornaments or wealth" distract mankind, but also spurious beliefs. We find a very tersely expressed but quite similar idea in *Analects.* 7.21:

> The Master had nothing to say about strange happenings, the use of force, disorder, or the spirits.[51]

---

[48] Ibid., 228.

[49] *Analects* 7.16, in Ames and Rosemont, 114.

[50] Bahá'u'lláh. *Writings of Bahá'u'lláh*, 228.

[51] Ames and Rosemont, 115; see the brief comments concerning Confucius and superstition in Karl Ludvig Reichelt. *Meditation and Piety in the Far East* (Cambridge: James Clark, 2004), 127–128.

The emphasis here is on engagement, even though not explicitly stated. Confucius's mind was on cultivation of the virtuous individual and engaging the world through sound relationships, not a false harmony achieved through the appeasement of some ephemeral realm.

Connected with the concept of engagement in the word is the shared idea in both Bahá'u'lláh's writing and the *Analects* that idleness is pernicious and loathsome. The "twelfth Glad-Tidings" of Bahá'u'lláh's *Bishárát* states:

> It is enjoined upon every one of you to engage in some form of occupation, such as crafts, trades and the like. We have graciously exalted your engagement in such work to the rank of worship unto God, the True One. Ponder ye in your hearts the grace and the blessings of God and render thanks unto Him at eventide and at dawn. Waste not your time in idleness and sloth. Occupy yourselves with that which profiteth yourselves and others. Thus, hath it been decreed in this Tablet from whose horizon the day-star of wisdom and utterance shineth resplendent.
>
> The most despised of men in the sight of God are those who sit idly and beg. Hold ye fast unto the cord of material means, placing your whole trust in God, the Provider of all means. When anyone occupieth himself in a craft or trade, such occupation itself is regarded in the estimation of God as an act of worship; and this is naught but a token of His infinite and all-pervasive bounty.

The *Analects* (9.23) is more succinct in its admonition, and does not frame the issue of work in such a directly theological context:

> The young should be held in high esteem. After all, how do we know that those yet to come will not surpass our contemporaries? It is only when one reaches forty or

fifty years of age and yet has done nothing of note that
we should withhold our esteem.[52]

That such a philosophy exists in both sources is not that surprising, but what is interesting here is the implication. It is not so much
the Puritanical idea that "idle hands are the Devil's playground"
recounted here, but rather something more subtle. Work and "engagement in such work," as Bahá'u'lláh puts it, are necessary for
both living in accordance with God and for the kind of cohesive,
universal society that the Bahá'í Faith envisages.

Both Confucianism and the Bahá'í Faith are concerned with
character, and in some sense for the same reason: good character
means sound relationships, and sound relationships mean a cohesive society. This is a "bottom to top" model of building a society,
where the fundamental units in their active process of cohesion
yield a solid "whole." If each person engages in virtuous conduct,
then there is unity in practice. If there is unity in practice, then
sound relationships can form; and if there are sound relationships,
a harmonious society will arise.

But both Confucian *Analects* and the writings of Bahá'u'lláh
also present an overall framework, and in a way address the issue
of governance directly, "top to bottom." In the Confucian system — and, one could argue, in much of Chinese thought — there
is a clear model of a heavenly or cosmic *order*. This is expressed
with the term 天 (*tiān*), often translated as "heaven" or "heavens,"
but really having little to do with the Western connotations that
that word bears.[53] Rather, the term signifies the "cosmic order,"
or even more precisely as "the order [of the world] itself, and
what orders it."[54]

More particularly, there is the concept of 天命 (*tiān mìng*),
usually rendered as the "mandate of heaven," but again meaning

---

[52] Ames and Rosemont, 131.
[53] See pp. 46–48 of Ames and Rosemont for a complete analysis of how this
term, 天 (tian), should be understood.
[54] Ibid., 47.

more specifically the "order" or even "propensities"[55] (命 *mìng*) of the "cosmos" (天 *tiān*). What is key, then, is the concept that any ruler of the state must be aligned with this "mandate of heaven." A ruler who does not follow this "cosmic order" or defies it (違命 *wéi mìng*, to "defy the mandate of heaven") is no longer legitimate and can have no authority over the people.

In *Analects* 16.8, Confucius lays it out clearly:

> Exemplary persons hold three things in awe: the propensities of *tian* [天命 (*tiān mìng*)], persons in high station, and the worlds of the sages. Petty persons, knowing nothing of the propensities of *tian*, do not hold it in awe; they are unduly familiar with persons in high station, and ridicule the words of the sages.[56]

Understanding the "propensities of *tian*" is no easy task, of course, and in a famous passage (*Analects* 2.4), we find the following:

> From fifteen, my heart-and-mind was set upon learning; from thirty I took my stance; from forty I was no longer doubtful; from fifty I realized the propensities of *tian*; from sixty, my ear was attuned; from seventy I could give my heard-and-mind free rein without overstepping the boundaries.[57]

For the individual, then, it takes some time to become aware of — and then aligned to — the "propensities of *tian*" or the "mandate of heaven." For a ruler, the process is even more fundamentally important: as an individual, the ruler must be aligned to the "propensities of *tian*" *and* incorporate such propensities into their every act of governance.

How this finds an analogue in Bahá'í thought is not immediately obvious. But implications certainly appear in the writings of

---

[55] As in *Analects* 16.8, discussed below.
[56] Ames and Rosemont, 198.
[57] Ames and Rosemont, 76–77.

Bahá'u'lláh. In the "fifteenth Glad-Tidings" of the *Bishárát*, one finds what is to the modern reader a rather curious passage:

> Although a republican form of government profiteth all the peoples of the world, yet the majesty of kingship is one of the signs of God. We do not wish that the countries of the world should remain deprived thereof.[58]

How does this connect with the Confucian expression of 天命 (*tiān mìng*), the "mandate of heaven"? Note the emphasis on kingship: the idea here is that an *individual*'s majesty is most reflective of God, and the implication is that an individual ruler is best suited to be like God in terms of fairness and ethical rule. At the end of the "fifteenth Glad-Tidings," we see a reinforcement of this reading:

> We earnestly beseech God — exalted be His glory — to aid the rulers and sovereigns, who are the exponents of power and the daysprings of glory, to enforce His laws and ordinances.[59]

Just as in the Confucian model, the ruler's role is to "channel" the "laws and ordinances" from above — from 天 (*tiān*) or from God. This structure and the patterning of the earthly realm on the heavenly realm is clearly articulated in the "sixth leaf" of Bahá'u'lláh's *Kalimát-i-Firdawsíyyih*:

> Verily I say, whatever is sent down from the heaven of the Will of God is the means for the establishment of order in the world and the instrument for promoting unity and fellowship among its peoples.[60]

Bahá'u'lláh's writings emphasize this point in other places, as well. In the "first Ishráq" of the *Ishráqát* ("Splendors"), we have the following

---

[58] Bahá'u'lláh. *Writings of Bahá'u'lláh*, 212.
[59] Ibid., 213.
[60] Bahá'u'lláh. *Writings of Bahá'u'lláh*, 234.

> They that are... invested with authority and power
> must show the profoundest regard for religion. In truth,
> religion is a radiant light and impregnable stronghold
> for the protection and welfare of the peoples of the
> world...[61]

Here, the suggestion is both that human authority must be
based on divine principles and that people can be protected from
the vagaries of secular rule by the power of religious — i.e., divine — principles.

> The "second Ishráq" explicitly states that the "sovereigns of the world" are the manifestations of the power
> of God and the dayspring of his authority. We beseech
> the Almighty that he may graciously assist them in
> that which is conducive to the well-being of their subjects.[62]

Very much as in the *Analects*, we have here rulers as transmitters of the divine or cosmic order.

In addition to this linear model of governance, there is also the
suggestion of the use of merit, and other ways of creating social
order, in both Confucianism and the Bahá'í thought. *Analects* 2.19
has the following:

> Duke Ai of Lu inquired of Confucius, asking: "What
> does one do to gain the allegiance (fu) of the people?"
> Confucius replied: "Raise up the true and place them
> over the crooked, and the allegiance of the people will
> be yours; raise up the crooked and place them over the
> true, and the people will not be yours.[63]

In a close parallel, the "fifth Ishráq" states:

---

[61] Ibid., 270.
[62] Ibid., 270.
[63] Ames and Rosemont, 80.

Governments should fully acquaint themselves with the conditions of those they govern and confer upon them positions according to desert and merit.[64]

A second way of bringing about harmony is by addressing the very question of what is being governed. Is it a collection of individuals? Sovereign states? The "sixth Ishráq" of Bahá'u'lláh's *Ishráqát* includes a very interesting passage on this topic. It looks to a time in the future when

the earth will be regarded as one country and one home... Let not man glory that he loveth his country, let him rather glory in this that he loveth his kind.[65]

The key term here is "one country and one home." In a very similar manner, Confucius saw the larger political entity of the state as no more than a collection of households, and thus itself a household or home. As one commentator notes:

In the writings of Chinese intellectuals and officials, the word *jia* (family or home) is regularly featured as a metaphor for the nation... This is not surprising, since the state (*guo*) is explicitly figured as family in the modern Chinese term for nation or country (*guojia*).[66]

Indeed, still today the term 國家 (*guó jiā*, literally "state + home") is used to refer one's country. For Confucius, the family or household model of society can be realized when the ruler acts in a parental role — not through strictures, however, but through exemplary behavior. In *Analects* 2.20, there is the following:

Ji Kangzi asked: "How do you get the people to be respectful, to do their utmost for you, and to be eager?" The Master replied: "Oversee them with dignity and the people will be respectful; be filial to your elders and

---

[64] Bahá'u'lláh. *Writings of Bahá'u'lláh*, 271.

[65] Ibid., 271.

[66] Gloria Davies. *Worrying about China: The Language of Chinese Critical Inquiry* (Cambridge, MA: Harvard University Press, 2007), 58.

kind to your juniors, and the people will do their utmost for you; raise up those who are adept and instruct those who are not and the people will be eager."[67]

Again, we have a linear structure, where the person in authority rules, but does so as a father who models behavior for his child. Moreover, recall the idea in the "sixth Ishráq" that man should "loveth his kind"; this is not a simple injunction, but rather a way of creating a unified society without use of coercion from above. Similarly, *Analects* 13.6 states:

If people are proper in personal conduct, others will follow suit without need of command. But if they are not proper, even they command, others will not obey.[68]

Exemplary behavior by a ruler leads to effortless rule, and exemplary behavior by other individuals will lead to their fellows doing the same.

Earlier, we noted that both Confucianism and the Bahá'í Faith are concerned with an individual's good character. People of good character make a good society. But what particulars concerning character development do the Confucian system and the Bahá'í Faith prescribe? Again, we can find similar concepts in the *Analects* and the words of Bahá'u'lláh. In Bahá'u'lláh's *Tarázát*, the "first Taráz" has the following:

[M]an should know his own self and recognize that which leadeth unto loftiness or lowliness, glory or abasement, wealth or poverty. Having attained the stage of fulfilment and reached his maturity, man standeth in need of wealth, and such wealth as he acquireth though crafts or professions is commendable and praiseworthy in the estimation of men of wisdom.[69]

---

[67] Ames and Rosemont, 80.
[68] Ibid., 163.
[69] Bahá'u'lláh. *Writings of Bahá'u'lláh*, 215.

At first glance, this seems a rather simplistic philosophy, but the underlying themes here are the very important ones of responsibility, stability, and self-knowledge — part of the over-arching theme of building a harmonious and unified society.

For Confucius, the same holds true, although he approaches the matter in a slightly different way. At the root, there is an emphasis of paying attention to one's role or one's "craft"; in *Analects* 19.7, we have:

> The various craftsmen stay in their shops so that they may master their trades; exemplary persons study so that they might promote their way.[70]

The "sixth Taráz" of Bahá'u'lláh's *Tarázát*" adds:

> Knowledge is one of the wondrous gifts of God. It is incumbent upon everyone to acquire it. Such arts and material means as are now manifest have been achieved by virtue of His knowledge and wisdom which have been revealed in Epistles and Tablets through His Most Exalted Pen — a Pen out of whose treasury pearls of wisdom and utterance and the arts and crafts of the world are brought to light.[71]

The *Kalimát-i-Firdawsíyyih*" adds a definition:

> By the wise it is meant those whose knowledge is not confined to mere words and whose lives have been fruitful and have produced enduring results.[72]

Note the meaning here: knowledge must include the pragmatic, and it must engage the world, a theme examined earlier.

But where does one gain the knowledge to know one's role? Returning to the "first Taráz" in Bahá'u'lláh's *Tarázát,*" we read that "men of wisdom"

---

[70] Ames and Rosemont, 219–220.
[71] Bahá'u'lláh. *Writings of Bahá'u'lláh*, 218.
[72] Ibid., 231.

are, in truth, cup-bearers of the life-giving water of knowledge and guides unto the ideal way. They direct the peoples of the world to the straight path and acquaint them with that which is conducive to human upliftment and exaltation. The straight path is the one which guideth man to the dayspring of perception and to the dawning-place of true understanding and leadeth him to that which will redound to glory, honour and greatness.[73]

Note two subtle points here: first of all, those who have wisdom and knowledge are called "cup-bearers." What they know is not something that they invented themselves; rather these wise figures are preservers and transmitters. The emphasis is not on innovation. Second, we note the idea of the "straight path." This is not exactly like the "path" (道 dào) that we find in Confucius, but in some manner the idea is the same: our journey through life is defined by how well we fulfill our role, and if we each succeed in that, we are on our way to "human upliftment and exaltation."

These two points are also found in Confucius; in Analects 7.28, Confucius states:

There are probably those who can initiate new paths while not understanding them, but I am not one of them. I learn much, select out of it what works well, and then follow it. I observe much and remember it.[74]

The emphasis again is on learning and preserving, not innovation. In Analects 7.20, Confucius again talks about knowledge in terms of the past: "...loving antiquity, I am earnest in seeking it out." Bahá'u'lláh speaks of the "straight path" as "the one which guideth man to the dayspring of perception and to the dawning-place of true understanding..." Analects 1.14 presents a similar idea, in its frequent use of the term dao (道 dào), noted above:

---

[73] Bahá'u'lláh. Writings of Bahá'u'lláh, 215.
[74] Ames and Rosemont, 117

In eating, exemplary persons do not look for a full stomach, nor in their lodgings for comfort and contentment. They are persons of action yet is cautious in what they say. They repair to those who know the way [道 *dào*] and find improvement in their company. Such persons can indeed be said to have a love of learning.[75]

In another passage, Confucius says, "Set you sights on the way know the way [道 *dào*]..."[76] and later, "People who have chosen different ways [道 *dào*] cannot make plans together."[77]

Moreover, both in the writings of Confucius and Bahá'u'lláh, the capacity to follow or forge the right path or way comes from self-knowledge. Note, of course, that in the case of Bahá'í Faith, this self-knowledge has a strong theistic foundation: self-knowledge comes from fully recognizing the Manifestation of God, and obeisance to what He has ordained.

Returning to the "first Taráz" of Bahá'u'lláh's *Tarázát*, we read that through the "loving-kindness of the All-Wise, the All-knowing," "people may discover the purpose for which they have been called into being."[78] As the Bahá'í Faith has a well-articulated concept of God, naturally self-knowledge would come from there. In Confucius, the concept of a deity is not expressed in this way; nonetheless, self-knowledge is paramount. In the famous passage in *Analects* 2.15, we read:

Learning without due reflection leads to perplexity; reflection without learning leads to perilous circumstances.[79]

Similarly, in *Analects* 1.4, we read the words of Confucius' disciple, Master Zeng:

---

[75] Ibid., 74–75.
[76] *Analects* 7.6, in Ames and Rosemont, 112.
[77] *Analects* 15.40, in Ames and Rosemont, 192.
[78] Bahá'u'lláh. *Writings of Bahá'u'lláh*, 215.
[79] Ames and Rosemont, 79.

> Daily I examine my person on three counts. In my undertakings on behalf of other people, have I failed to do my utmost? In my interactions with colleagues and friends, have I failed to make good on my word? In what has been passed on to me, have I failed to carry it into practice?

These three questions embody the Confucian process of gaining self-knowledge. That self-knowledge leads to the practice of becoming a person of integrity who can engage in sound relationships.

The "third Taráz" of Bahá'u'lláh's *Tarázát* reinforces the connection between God, a person's character, and the path of proper conduct:

> A good character is, verily, the best mantle for men from God. With it He adorneth the temples of His loved ones. By My life! The light of a good character surpasseth the light of the sun and the radiance thereof. Whoso attaineth unto it is accounted as a jewel among men. The glory and the upliftment of the world must needs depend upon it. A goodly character is a means whereby men are guided to the Straight Path...[80]

Again, in both the Confucian system and the Bahá'í Faith, self-reflection leads to self-knowledge, and an easing of one's way onto the path. Individuals with sound self-knowledge are sharing a unity of practice. Moreover, they naturally will be drawn to one another, leading to harmonious relationships — something clearly emphasized in the passage above. In Confucianism, it is clear that self-reflection, in turn, ultimately will lead to a harmonious society. The Bahá'í Faith also employs self-reflection, but in terms of building a society characterized by harmony, recognition of God's Manifestation takes a primary role.

---

[80] Bahá'u'lláh. *Writings of Bahá'u'lláh*, 216.

CONCLUSIONS: FUTURE DIRECTIONS IN CONFUCIANISM AND THE BAHÁ'Í FAITH

Both Confucianism and the Bahá'í Faith deal directly with the role of the individual in society, and the future of these systems lies in this core of their philosophical approaches. Without taking a particularly cynical stance, one could argue that we live in an increasingly narcissistic age, and in a society that has for some time now become increasingly "atomized" due to the sparsity of meaningful social interactions. In such an environment, systems such as Confucianism and the Bahá'í Faith at the same time may find both greater challenges in promoting their philosophies and a greater need for those same philosophies.

Confucianism is not global in view, but the *Analects* reveal a system that has such an expansive potential. Individuals of good character, Confucius notes, should associate with each other, and from a modern perspective there is no reason that this cannot mean across the globe. Indeed, one might have to journey far to find a Confucian associate, as we see in *Analects* 7.26:

> The Master said, "I will never get to meet a sage — I would be content to meet an exemplary person."
>
> The Master said, "I will never get to meet a truly efficacious person — I would be content to meet someone who is constant. It is difficult indeed for persons to be constant in a world where nothing is taken to be something, emptiness is taken to be fullness, and poverty is taken to be comfort."[81]

Despite such challenges, Confucius was aware that like minds would benefit from finding each other:

> In taking up one's residence, it is the presence of authoritative persons that is the greatest attraction. How

---

[81] Ames and Rosemont, 116–117.

can anyone be called wise who, in having the choice, does not seek to dwell among authoritative people?[82]

In the "second Taráz" of Bahá'u'lláh's *Tarázát*, a similar idea can be found, although in more poetic language:

They that are endued with sincerity and faithfulness should associate with the peoples and kindreds of the earth with and radiance, inasmuch as consorting with people hath promoted and will continue to promote unity and concord, which in turn are conducive to the maintenance of order in the world...[83]

And what of harmony and unity? At the beginning of this piece, we pointed out that both the Confucian system and the Bahá'í Faith seek a future where human beings live in a society characterized by *harmony*, achieved by the *unity* of a common ethical practice. As noted earlier, Confucius looks to the past in seeking a better state for the future:

Achieving harmony is the most valuable function of observing ritual propriety [禮 *lǐ*]. In the ways of the Former Kings, this achievement of harmony made them elegant, and was a guiding standard in all things large and small. But when things are not going well, to realize harmony just for its own sake without regulating the situation through observing ritual propriety will not work.[84]

So, harmony may be achieved through propriety (禮 *lǐ*) — in this case, a term very particularly defined as understanding one's role. Such understanding and engaging in one's role properly by all individuals is the unity of practice noted above. In *Analects* 16.1, Confucius is engaged in a conversation about a potential attack by clan against a vassal state. But Confucius turns the con-

---

[82] *Analects* 4.1, in Ames and Rosemont, 89.
[83] Bahá'u'lláh. *Writings of Bahá'u'lláh*, 216.
[84] *Analects* 1.12, in Ames and Rosemont, 74.

versation to the issue of avoiding conflict, and a potential ideal situation for society:

> For if the wealth is equitably distributed, there is no poverty; if the people are harmonious, they are not few in number; if the people are secure, they are not unstable. Under these circumstances, if distant populations are still not won over, they persuade them to join them through the cultivation of their refinement and excellence, and once they have joined them, they make them feel secure.[85]

This connection between harmony and unity is also nicely summed up in the "seventh leaf" of Bahá'u'lláh's *Kalimát-i-Firdawsíyyih*:

> O ye men of wisdom among nations! Shut your eyes to estrangement, then fix your gaze upon unity. Cleave tenaciously unto that which will lead to the well-being and tranquillity of all mankind. This span of earth is but one homeland and one habitation. It behoveth you to abandon vainglory which causeth alienation and to set your hearts on whatever will ensure harmony. In the estimation of the people of Bahá man's glory lieth in his knowledge, his upright conduct, his praiseworthy character, his wisdom, and not in his nationality or rank.[86]

The message of the Bahá'í Faith echoes that in the Confucian *Analects*, despite the marked difference in style and tone. First, the *Kalimát-i-Firdawsíyyih* has, as in Confucius, the injunction to cling that which "will lead to the well-being and tranquillity of all mankind." In other words, harmony is the goal, and all pursuits should be those that lead to that end. Further, there is the Chinese idea of the "one homeland and one habitation" — the country as a collection of households but also a *single* household,

---

[85] Ames and Rosemont, 196.
[86] Bahá'u'lláh. *Writings of Bahá'u'lláh*, 234–235.

i.e., 國家 (*guójiā*). Then there is the direct statement to avoid "vainglory," and, again, pursue actions that will "ensure harmony." Finally, the last line mirrors Confucian thought very closely indeed:

> In the estimation of the people of Bahá man's glory lieth in his knowledge, his upright conduct, his praiseworthy character, [and] his wisdom.[87]

All of these values — knowledge, good conduct, and solid character — are ones that Confucius would say precisely comprise the mature individual.

Confucius perceived a world in distress, riven with violence, and run by leaders out of touch with both the "heavenly mandate" above and their subjects below. The Bahá'í Faith arose in a nineteenth-century culture trapped between archaic tradition and encroaching modernity, one that had set the stage for — but was also not quite ready for — new principles, especially the principle of the oneness or unity of mankind. Both the Confucian system and Bahá'í thought urge individuals to transcend existing circumstances and develop beyond human frailties and ignorance. While the Confucian system works primarily on the ethical development of the individual in terms of interpersonal relationships and the Bahá'í Faith looks for broader change based on religious precepts, the goals are the same: a more just and cooperative world.

What is this "broader change" sought by the Bahá'í Faith? Certainly, it is change towards a society structured according to the principles of harmony and unity. But note that in the Bahá'í faith the relation between harmony and unity is shaped by a particular factor — namely, the Bahá'í belief that harmony that is imposed without a clear expression of the need for justice and equity would not lead to genuine unity in society. While Confucius does not always argue about justice in the way it is understood in a contemporary perspective, the Bahá'í teachings do: justice

---

[87] Ibid., 235.

serves as a key component for the dream of unity. As one commentator has noted about justice, "Time and again Bahá'u'lláh addresses this theme."[88] In the "sixth leaf" of Bahá'u'lláh's *Kalimát-i-
Firdawsíyyih*, for example, Bahá'u'lláh states:

> The light of men is Justice. Quench it not with the con-
> trary winds of oppression and tyranny. The purpose of
> justice is the appearance of unity among men.[89]

Bahá'u'lláh also puts it in this way:

> No radiance can compare with that of justice. The or-
> ganization of the world and the tranquility of mankind
> depend upon it.[90]

Bahá'u'lláh here makes an explicit connection between the
concept of justice and the idea of "organization" — that is, the
pragmatic building of a new society.

---

[88] Bowers, 118.
[89] Bahá'u'lláh. *Tablets of Bahá'u'lláh*, 67, as quoted in Bowers, 118.
[90] Ibid., 118.

Alain Locke's Philosophy of Democracy

CHRISTOPHER BUCK

Independent Scholar

There is no formal "Bahá'í philosophy." Yet there are professional philosophers who are Bahá'ís, who therefore may be broadly
characterized as "Bahá'í philosophers."[1] Foremost among Bahá'í
philosophers is Alain Leroy Locke (1918–1954).[2] Columbus
Salley, in *The Black 100*, ranks Locke as the 36th most influential African American ever, past or present.[3] More significantly,
Locke has been acknowledged as "the most influential African
American intellectual born between W. E. B. Du Bois and Martin
Luther King, Jr."[4]

This paper presents Alain Locke's philosophy of democracy,
in nine dimensions, as a contribution to the study of Bahá'í philosophy, in its broader context as philosophical thinking by professional philosophers who were religiously engaged as members
of the Bahá'í Faith. Bahá'í values synergized Locke's philosophy
of democracy or, at the very least, serve as a useful heuristic for

---

1   Christopher Buck, "Alain Locke: Bahá'í Philosopher." *Bahá'í Studies
    Review* 10 (2001/2002): 7–49.
2   Christopher Buck. *Alain Locke: Faith and Philosophy* (Los Angeles:
    Kalimat Press, 2005).
3   Columbus Smalley. *The Black 100: A Ranking of the Most Influential
    African-Americans, Past and Present*. Revised and Updated (Secaucus,
    NJ: Citadel Press, 1999 [1993]), 137.
4   Leonard Harris & Charles Molesworth. *Alain L. Locke: Biography of a
    Philosopher* (Chicago and London: University of Chicago Press, 2008), 1.

understanding and appreciating certain aspects of Locke's philosophy of democracy. Locke's grand (though not systematic) theory of democracy sequenced local, moral, political, economic, and cultural stages of democracy as they arced through history, with racial, social, spiritual, and world democracy completing the trajectory. Adjunct notions of natural, practical, progressive, creative, intellectual, equalitarian democracy crystallized the paradigm.

Locke made history in when he became the first African American Rhodes Scholar in 1907. As one contemporary, writing that same year, has said: "*In what he has achieved, a race has been uplifted.*"[5] Historically, Locke is most closely associated with the Harlem Renaissance (c. 1919–1935), aptly characterized as a movement that sought to achieve "Civil Rights by Copyright."[6] In 1925, Locke edited *The New Negro: An Interpretation*, the historical significance of which Eric King Watts notes: "Only a few claims regarding the Harlem Renaissance are uncontested: that *The New Negro* stands as the 'keystone,' the 'revolutionary' advertisement, and the 'first national book' of African America is one of them."[7]

There is also synergy between the social objectives of the Harlem Renaissance and Alain Locke's philosophy of democracy. As to the purpose behind the Harlem Renaissance, Locke is crystal clear: "The Negro mind reaches out as yet to nothing but American wants, American ideas. But this forced attempt to build his Americanism on race values is a unique social experiment, and its ultimate success is impossible except through the fullest sharing of American culture and institutions." The Harlem

---

[5] William C. Bolivar, "Alain LeRoy Locke." African Methodist Episcopal Church Review 24.1 (July 1907): 19.

[6] David Levering Lewis, When Harlem Was in Vogue (New York: Penguin, 1998), xxviii.

[7] Eric King Watts, "African American Ethos and Hermeneutical Rhetoric: An Exploration of Alain Locke's The New Negro." Quarterly Journal of Speech 88.1 (Feb. 2002): 19–32, citing Houston Baker, Jr., Modernism and the Harlem Renaissance (Chicago: University of Chicago Press, 1987), 85.

Renaissance achieved a major objective of the New Negro movement, which, was to instill a race pride in Blacks and a corresponding respect for Blacks by mainstream America. This race
pride created the group consciousness that was a necessary pre-
condition for the mass mobilization of African Americans led by
Dr. King during the Civil Rights movement. As the acknowledged
"Dean" of the Harlem Renaissance, Locke sought to ennoble the
perception (and self-perception) of African Americans through
"ameliorative use of stereotypes" and "advocacy aesthetics"[8]
whereby art served as a cultural ambassador in promoting ideal
race relations.

As historically important as his pivotal role in Harlem
Renaissance surely was, Locke's legacy as as philosopher may
just as profound, as Leonard Harris points out: "Alain Locke,
I believe, is the sentinel historical figure in the history of African
American professional philosophers because he conjoins an interest in the historically important issues of social well-being crucial to the African American intellectual agenda with central issues in the modern history of philosophy."[9] Locke has been called
"the father of multiculturalism."[10]

Alain Locke was a pragmatist philosopher. Of the pragmatists, John Dewey most influenced democratic theory from the
pragmatist perspective. But the pragmatist whom Locke ad-
mired most was likely Franz Boas, whom Locke called a "ma-

---

[8] Leonard Harris, "Alain L. Locke," in *A Companion to Pragmatism*, edited by John R. Shook and Joseph Margolis (Oxford: Blackwell, 2006),
Chapter 7, pp. 87–93 (91).

[9] Leonard Harris, "The Horror of Tradition or How to Burn Babylon and
Build Benin While Reading A Preface to a Twenty Volume Suicide Note."
Philosophical Forum 24.1–3 (Fall–Spring 1992–93): 94–119. Reprinted
in *African-American Perspectives and Philosophical Traditions*. Edited by
John P. Pittman and Marx W. Wartofsky (New York: Routledge, 1996),
pp. 94–119 [112].

[10] Charles Molesworth, "Alain Locke and Walt Whitman: Manifestos and
National Identity," *in The Critical Pragmatism of Alain Locke: A Reader
on Value Theory, Aesthetics, Community, Culture, Race, and Education*, ed.
Leonard Harris (Lanham, MD: Rowman & Littlefield, 1999), 176.

jor prophet of democracy."[11] Locke is credited with having first coined the term, "critical pragmatism." "The actual phrase, 'critical pragmatism'," writes Alison Kadlec, "appears at least as early as 1935 in Alain Locke's pragmatic theory of valuation. In the context of Locke's work, the idea of a critical pragmatism was supposed to undergird the development of cultural pluralism."[12] Leonard Harris, arguably the foremost scholar on Alain Locke, notes:

> Critical pragmatism was created by Locke and has its religious sensibilities in a place other than Cornel West's prophetic pragmatism and Dewey and James' American forms of Christianity. Locke was affiliated with the B'hai faith (sic; Bahá'í Faith) and thereby a radical cultural pluralist and influenced by the B'hai [Bahá'í] demand, as a tenet of religious faith, that racism is a sin.[13]

Cornel West's "prophetic pragmatism" is said to have been inspired by "his trinity of Christ, Marx, and Dewey."[14] As the Cornel West of the Jim Crow era, Locke's own "critical pragmatism" drew its inspiration from the trinity of Baha'u'llah, Royce, and

---

[11] Alain Locke, "Major Prophet of Democracy" (Review of *Race and Democratic Society* by Franz Boas), *Journal of Negro Education* 15.2 (Spring 1946): 191–92. See also Mark Helbling, "Feeling Universality and Thinking Particularistically: Alain Locke, Franz Boas, Melville Herkskovits, and the Harlem Renaissance," Prospects 19 (1994): 289–314.

[12] Alison Kadlec, "Reconstructing Dewey: The Philosophy of Critical Pragmatism," Polity 38.4 (Oct. 2006): 519–542 (520, n. 3).

[13] Leonard Harris, Review of Pragmatism and the Problem of Race, Bill E. Lawson and Donald F. Koch, editors (Bloomington, IN: Indiana University Press, 2004), Transactions of the Charles S. Peirce Society 41.2 (Spring, 2005): 440–443 [442].

[14] Charles W. Mills, "Prophetic Pragmatism as a Political Philosophy," in Cornel West: A Critical Reader. Edited by George Yancy (Malden, MA and Oxford: Blackwell, 2001), 196, quoting Lewis R. Gordon, "Black Intellectuals and Academic Activism: Cornel West's 'Dilemmas of the Black Intellectual'," in idem, Her Majesty's Other Children: Sketches of Racism from a Neocolonial Age (Lanham, MD: Rowman and Littlefield, 1997), 195.

Boas. One can say that Locke has synergized faith (Baha'u'llah) and philosophy (Royce), reinforced by scientific anthropology (Boas). While all but Josiah Royce among the first white pragmatists had turned a blind eye to race, Locke would agree with Cornel West in characterizing American pragmatism as "unique as a philosophical tradition in the modern world in its preoccupation or near obsession with the meaning and value of democracy."[15] (Here, pragmatism is Cornel West's synecdoche for philosopher John Dewey.) Although West, in *The American Evasion of Philosophy: A Genealogy of Pragmatism* (1989), had excluded him, Locke has finally entered the canon of American philosophy and taken his rightful place in the philosophical pantheon with the appearance of John Stuhr's *Pragmatism and Classical American Philosophy* (2000).[16]

Locke anchored philosophy in human values and formulated his own theory of relativity by way of a naturalized epistemology of human values. One of Locke's lectures captures the essence of his philosophy by its very title: "Cultural Pluralism: A New Americanism."[17] Locke's integrationism was not assimilationism. Locke held to the Bahá'í principle of unity in diversity, which he reformulated as "unity through diversity."

Seeing America as "a unique social experiment," Locke's larger goal was to "Americanize Americans,"[18] with the simple yet profound message that equality benefits everyone, and that democracy itself is at stake. Locke's cosmopolitan paradigm of unity is a "theoretical and praxical transformation of classical American

---

[15] Qtd. in Mills, "Prophetic Pragmatism," 197.

[16] John J. Stuhr (ed.), Pragmatism and Classical American Philosophy: Essential Readings and Interpretive Essays, 2nd edn. (New York: Oxford University Press, 2002).

[17] Alain Locke Papers, Moorland-Spingarn Research Center (hereafter, "MSRC"), Howard University, Box 164–167, Folder 4: 1950–1953 (Programs on which Locke's Name Appears). Sponsored by the Department of Philosophy, Locke's lecture, presented on November 8, 1950, was held in the faculty lounge, Douglass Hall, Howard University.

[18] Alain Locke Papers, MSRC, Box 164–124, Folder 15 ("The Preservation of the Democratic Ideal"), 5.

pragmatism."[19] According to Judith Green, Locke had preco-
ciously conceptualized "deep democracy" as "cosmopolitan unity amidst valued diversity."[20]In raising democracy to a new level
of consciousness, Locke internationalized the race issue, making
the crucial connection between American race relations and international relations. Racial justice, he predicted, would serve as
a social catalyst of world peace.

Locke was trained as a philosopher at Harvard University. The
primary branch of philosophy that Locke studied was the theory
of values. Locke's dissertation was *The Problem of Classification
in Theory of Value: or an Outline of a Genetic System of Values.*[21]
Harvard University conferred Locke's Ph.D. on 25 February
1918, after he had successfully defended his dissertation.[22] That
same year, he adopted the Bahá'í Faith, as documented and discussed in *Alain Locke: Faith and Philosophy.*[23] Locke, moreover,
established the study of philosophy at Howard University — an
institution of higher learning aptly characterized as the equivalent to Harvard University among traditionally black universities.

Leonard Harris credits Alain Locke for having contributed a
"unique version of pragmatism," which "promotes a deep-seated commitment to transforming a world" through "intellectual
engagement" and "aesthetic pluralism whereby beauty-making

---

[19] Segun Gbadegesin, "Values, Imperatives, and the Imperative of
Democratic Values," in Leonard Harris (ed.), The Critical Pragmatism
of Alain Locke: A Reader on Value Theory, Aesthetics, Community,
Culture, Race, and Education (Lanham, MD: Rowman & Littlefield,
1999), 288.

[20] Judith Green, "Cosmopolitan Unity Amidst Valued Diversity: Alain
Locke's Vision of Deeply Democratic Transformation," in Deep
Democracy: Community, Diversity, and Transformation (Lanham, MD:
Rowman & Littlefield, 1999), 96.

[21] Alain Leroy Locke, The Problem of Classification in the Theory of Value:
or an Outline of a Genetic System of Values (Ph.D. dissertation: Harvard,
1918).

[22] Alain Locke Papers, MSRC, Box 164–228, P Oversize (Diploma awarded
by Harvard University 25 Feb. 1918).

[23] Christopher Buck, Alain Locke: Faith and Philosophy (Los Angeles:
Kalimat Press, 2005), "Chapter Four: Conversion," pp. 58–67.

properties are considered subject to transvaluation."[24] And further:

> Locke's theory of valuation, his advocacy aesthetics, his insistence on moral imperatives as a necessary condition for the possibility of a moral community, his pedagogy of discipline and cultural integration, and his views of community as an evolving democratic experiment, all form a unique chapter of American pragmatism.[25]

Beyond his philosophy of values, Locke also developed a comprehensive theory of democracy. By devoting "Chapter Ten" to "Theorizing Democracy" in their definitive biography of Locke, Leonard Harris and Charles Molesworth identify Locke's philosophy of democracy as his greatest contribution as a philosopher, which has yet to be fully understood and appreciated: "Locke's views on democracy deserve fuller study than they have received."[26] In the fall of 1947, Locke taught a course on the "Philosophy of Democracy"[27] at Howard University, where he was a distinguished professor for over forty years. While the notes that have survived are fragmentary at best, it is now possible to reconstruct Locke's philosophy of democracy in its broad conceptual outlines. In an unpublished typescript, Locke sets forth his definition of democracy as follows:

> In a democracy built out of many peoples by this great historical process of immigration, the only safe principle of democracy is that embodied in this conception of

---

[24] Leonard Harris, "Alain L. Locke," in A Companion to Pragmatism, 88. See also idem, "Alain L. Locke, 1885–1954," in The Blackwell Guide to American Philosophy, edited by Armen T. Marsoobian and John Ryder (Blackwell, 2004), Chapter 17, pp. 263–270.

[25] Harris, "Alain L. Locke," in A Companion to Pragmatism, 91–92.

[26] Harris & Molesworth, "Chapter Ten: Theorizing Democracy," Alain L. Locke: Biography of a Philosopher, 328–357 (329).

[27] Alain Locke Papers, MSRC, Box 164–112, Folder 6: "Concept of Democracy." Outline of lecture for Philosophy of Democracy course. 10 Dec. 1947.

democracy: —A democracy is a system of government and corporate living in which there is no distinction between minority and majority rights; and under which life is safe and equally abundant for all minorities. In historical perspective[,] this is really the distinctive foundation[al] principle of American life. Our task today is to make America truly and consistently American.[28]

Locke forged a vital linkage between American democracy and world democracy. In his previously unpublished Bahá'í essay, "The Gospel for the Twentieth Century" (2005), Locke wrote that "[t]he gospel for the Twentieth Century" and its message of "social salvation" must first address "[t]he fundamental problems of current America," which are "materiality and prejudice."[29] The sad irony is that America—"the land that is nearest to material democracy"—happens to be the land that "is furthest away from spiritual democracy."[30] In the same essay, Locke quotes a prophecy from Baha'u'llah (1817–1892), prophet-founder of the Bahá'í Faith: "That all nations shall become one in faith, and all men as brothers; that the bonds of affection and unity between the sons of men should be strengthened; that diversity of religion should cease, and differences of race be annulled. ... These strifes and this bloodshed and discord must cease, and all men be as one kindred and family."[31] As one scholar observes: "In other words,

---

[28] Alain Locke Papers, MSRC, Box 164–141, Folder 14 ([Notes] Democracy — political, economic, cultural).

[29] Alain Locke, "The Gospel for the Twentieth Century," in idem, "Alain Locke in His Own Words: Three Essays." World Order 36.3 (2005): 39–42 [39–40]. (Previously unpublished essays, introduced by Christopher Buck and co-edited with Betty Fisher.)

[30] Alain Locke, "The Gospel for the Twentieth Century," 42.

[31] Baha'u'llah, quoted in Locke, "Gospel for the Twentieth Century." See also Edward Granville Browne, Sir Thomas Adams Professor of Arabic, Cambridge University, interview with Baha'u'llah, Acre, Palestine, April 15, 1890, in 'Ab du'-Baha, A Traveller's Narrative Written to Illustrate the Episode of the Bab, ed. and trans. Edward Granville Browne, vol. 2 (Cambridge: Cambridge UP, 1891) xxxix–xl, reprinted in J. E. Esslemont, Baha'u'llah and the New Era: An Introduction to the Bahá'í Faith, 5th rev. ed. (Wilmette, IL: Bahá'í Publishing Trust, 1980, 1998 printing) 39–40.

Locke was pro-human rather than pro-negro."[32] Of course, he was both.

Democracy is a process of progressive equalizing. It is a matter of degree. For Locke, democracy was a much broader concept than its narrow political definition. Locke proposed a multidimensional model of democracy, against which he measured America's fidelity to its democratic ideal. His model ranged from concepts of "local democracy" all the way up to "world democracy." In the notes on his lecture, "Concept of Democracy," delivered on 10 Dec. 1947, Locke spoke of how the "[i]dea of democracy has evolved." Locke's dimensional model of democracy is not only typological, but evolutionary as well. In a survey of his writings, one may begin to typologize or systematize Locke's thinking on democracy. These are some of the various dimensions of democracy that Locke spoke and wrote about:

(1) Local Democracy;
(2) Moral Democracy;
(3) Political Democracy;
(4) Economic Democracy;
(5) Cultural Democracy;
(6) Racial Democracy;
(7) Social Democracy;
(8) Spiritual Democracy;
(9) World Democracy.

Locke's philosophy of democracy was both historical and phenomenological. It may aptly be characterized as a "grand theory" of democracy — anchored in history, grounded in philosophy, and validated by personal experience. Locke's philosophy of democracy harks back to Athens, arcs through history, and telescopes into the future. His point of departure was, of course, the historical development or evolution of democracy. The first five dimensions may be roughly characterized as "Historical Democracy," as

---

[32] Yvonne Ochillo, "The Race-Consciousness of Alain Locke." Phylon 47.3 (1986): 173–181 (176).

they are sequenced in Locke's paradigm of social evolution. In his farewell address at Talladega College (1941), Locke spoke of local, moral, political, economic, and cultural stages of democracy. The present writer published the speech in 2005.[33] Locke begins his speech by saying:

> And now, I should like to talk about something that we all take for granted — these are things we know least about. The words most frequently used are words understood least[.]—Democracy is one of those words. Thinking Negroes, of course, know much about what democracy is not, and have a more workable conception of what democracy truly means than those who have just enough to be content with or those to whom it is just a commonplace concept and way of life. Democracy, of course, is one of the basic human ideals, but as an ideal of human association it is something quite superior to any outward institution or any particular society; therefore, not only is government too narrow to express democracy, but government from time to time must grow to realize democracy.[34]

Not only is government too narrow a concept of democracy, but democracy started out historically as a narrow concept as well.

Local Democracy: The historical origins of democracy hark back to Athens, as one would expect. And while it is a breakthrough concept of the profoundest historical moment, Locke emphasizes its limitations:

> It may be a little daring in the time we have at our disposal but let us put on seven-league boots and trace

---

[33] Alain Locke, "Five Phases of Democracy: Farewell Address at Talladega College," in idem, "Alain Locke in His Own Words: Three Essays." World Order 36.3 (2005): 45–48.

[34] Alain Locke Papers, MSRC, Box 164–113, Folder 4 ([re: democracy] Departure speech to students at Talladega College, 1941), 1.

democracy — one of the great social concepts. Both in concept and in practice democracy began in Greece — in the Greek city[–]state. In its day it was a great achievement, but in that day democracy was a concept of local citizenship. Our nearest approach to it is the kind of fellowship we find in college fraternities and sororities in which the bonds are of "like-mindedness" excluding others. The rim of the Greek concept of democracy was the barbarian: it was then merely the principle of fraternity within a narrow, limited circle. There was a dignity accorded to each member on the basis of membership in the group. It excluded foreigners, slaves and women. This concept carried over into the Roman empire.[35]

In staging the evolution of democracy, the next developmental phase in the evolution of democracy, accordingly, was Christianity.

Moral Democracy: Christianity, in Locke's estimate of it, provided the ideal basis for a moral democracy. Ideally universal, and socially so in its pristine beginnings, over time Christianity became circumscribed, as Locke, true to his critical temper, points out:

Christianity was responsible for the introduction of the next great revision in the concept of democracy. We owe to Christianity one of the great basic ideals of democracy — the ideal of the moral equality of human beings. The Christian ideal of democracy was in its initial stages more democratic than it subsequently became. It always held on to the essential ideal of moral equality of man within the limits of organized Christianity — anybody else was a potential member only as he became converted. Christianity was thus a crusading ideal in bringing humanity into wider association. But the Christian church was a political institution and in making com-

---

[35] Alain Locke Papers, MSRC, Box 164–113, Folder 4 ([re: democracy] Departure speech to students at Talladega College, 1941), 1–2.

promises often failed in bringing about real human equality.[36]

Notwithstanding its contribution to the evolution of democracy by promoting "the ideal of the moral equality of human beings," Christianity later failed to live up to its own ideals.

Political Democracy: Locke explains the profound influence of the French Revolution on the establishment of American democracy by the Founding Fathers. In one speech, Locke states:

> Then later came that political and secular strand of colonial experience, which out of the fight against tyranny and taxation grew into the issue of political freedom and the liberty of self-government. But even then, when these developments had been fought for and won, and were being institutionalized, it took another strain of radical thinking imported from Revolutionary France to consolidate this into a formally democratic doctrine, the fundamental historical creed of American democracy that we know so well and rightly treasure so highly.[37]

It was the political philosophy of the French that most impressed Thomas Jefferson, and profoundly influenced the development of democracy in America:

> The third great step in democracy came from [P]rotestant lands and people who evolved the ideal of political equality: (1) equality before the law; (2) political citizenship. This **political democracy** pivoted on individualism, and the freedom of the individual in terms of what we know as the fundamental rights of man. It found its best expression in the historic formula of "Liberty, equality and fraternity."[38]

[36] Alain Locke Papers, MSRC, Box 164–113, Folder 4 ([re: democracy] Departure speech to students at Talladega College, 1941), 2.
[37] Alain Locke Papers, MSRC, Box 164–112, Folder 18 ("Creative Democracy"), 2.
[38] Alain Locke Papers, MSRC, Box 164–113, Folder 4 ([re: democracy]

Locke appreciated the Bill of Rights and subsequent
Amendments as milestones in the evolution of American democracy. But the political system — not to mention the social manifestations of democracy — were still far from perfect:

> In terms of this ideology our country's government
> was founded. But for generations after many of the
> fundamentals of our democracy were pious objectives,
> not fully expressed in practice. In the perspective of
> democracy's long evolution, we must regard our coun-
> try's history as a progressive process of democratiza-
> tion, not yet fully achieved, but certainly progressing
> importantly in terms of the [T]hirteenth, [F]ourteenth
> and [F]ifteenth [A]mendments, and the amendment
> extending the right of franchise to women. It is still
> imperfect.[39]

The perfection of democracy requires a "democratic spirit,"
without which democracy, by legislation standing alone, cannot succeed: "[I]f we are going to have effective democracy in
America we must have the democratic spirit as well as the democratic tradition, we must have more **social democracy** and more
economic democracy in order to have or keep political democracy."[40] This statement reveals the cornerstone of Locke's philosophy of democracy: that democratic ideals must be complemented
by democratic attitudes. In other words, the democratic spirit is
what really animates a democracy, not simply its institutions and
legal safeguards. Consistent with this analysis is Locke's stage-
wise progression from political to economic democracy, in which
human values (on which political democracy is ostensibly based)
can and must be linked to economic values.

Departure speech to students at Talladega College, 1941), 2.

[39] Alain Locke Papers, MSRC, Box 164–113, Folder 4 ([re: democracy]
Departure speech to students at Talladega College, 1941), 2–3.

[40] Alain Locke Papers, MSRC, Box 164–124, Folder 15 ("The Preservation
of the Democratic Ideal"), 5.

Economic Democracy: Although Locke was no economist, he clearly understood that reality. It was totally obvious in the ghettoes. Economic reform was a necessary development of democracy:

> The fourth crucial stage in the enlargement of democracy began, I think, with the income tax amendment. Woodrow Wilson tried to put into operation an extension of democracy which may well have been seriously hindered by World War number one. The income tax [A]mendment was an initial step in **social** [economic] **democracy** as distinguished from the purely political, — a step toward economic equality through the partial appropriation of surplus wealth for the benefit of the commonwealth.
>
> In this country for many generations we thought we had economic equality. What we really had was a frontier expansion which developed such surpluses and offered such practical equality of opportunity as to give us the illusion of economic equality. We later learned that we did not have **economic democracy**, and that in order to have this, we must have guaranteed to all citizens certain minimal standards of living and the right to earn a living. Faced with the crisis of unemployment, the New Deal has been confronted with the problem of inaugurating some of these beginnings of economic democracy and of constitutionally implementing a larger measure of social justice. The whole program of what is now called [S]ocial [S]ecurity is directed toward such objectives.[41]

Locke spoke of "the two basic economic roots of war — unequal access to markets and sources of raw materials and wide-

---

[41] Alain Locke Papers, MSRC, Box 164–113, Folder 4 ([re: democracy] Departure speech to students at Talladega College, 1941), 3–4.

spread differentials of living standards and economic security."[42] Locke taught that political freedom ought to lead to economic equality. What Locke means by economic democracy is an "equitable distribution of wealth."[43]Redistribution of surplus wealth is part and parcel of that process. But what about the connection between economic democracy and race? In the conclusion of an unpublished essay, "Peace Between Black and White in the United States," Locke wrote:

> We used to say that Christianity and democracy were both at stake in the equitable solution of the race question. They were; but they were abstract ideals that did not bleed when injured. Now we think with more realistic logic, perhaps, that economic justice cannot stand on one foot; and economic reconstruction is the dominant demand of the present-day American scene.[44]

Cultural Democracy: Locke's next form of democracy is clear enough, although his name for it ("cultural democracy") is not so much "cultural" as it is "communal." Locke sums up the problem he is addressing as follows: "Less acute than race prejudice, but by no means unrelated to it, is the social bias and discrimination underlying the problem of cultural minorities. [...] Cultural bias, like that directed against the Mexican, Orientals, the Jew, the American Indian, often intensifies into racial prejudice."[45] As an antidote to this social ill, Locke advocates cultural pluralism, and rejects "Americanization," whether forced or coerced by social

---

[42] Alain Locke, "Democracy Faces a World Order," Harvard Educational Review 12.2 (March 1942): 124.

[43] Alain Locke Papers, MSRC, Box 164–112, Folder 6 ("Concept of Democracy"). Outline of lecture for Philosophy of Democracy course. 10 Dec. 1947, 1.

[44] Alain Locke Papers, MSRC, Box 164–123: Folder 19 ("Peace Between Black and White in the United States").

[45] Alain Locke, World View on Race and Democracy: A Study Guide in Human Group Relations (Chicago: American Library Association, 1943), 5.

pressures. Think of "culture" in this context as analogous to the idea of a "corporate culture." As Locke explains:

A fifth phase of democracy, even if the preceding four are realized, still remains to be achieved in order to have a fully balanced society. The present crisis forces us to realize that without this also democracy may go into total eclipse. This fifth phase is the struggle for **cultural democracy**, and rests on the concept of the right of difference, — that is, the guarantee of the rights of minorities. Again, in the colonial days, we achieved the basic ideals of this crucial aspect of democracy, but scarcely realized them in fact. Today we have the same problems of the freedom of speech, worship and conscience, but in a complex modern situation these things are even more difficult to work out.

One of our greatest problems then today is a real democratic reciprocity for minorities of all sorts, both as over against the so-called majority and among themselves. These contemporary problems of democracy can be vividly sensed if we realize that the race question is at the very heart of this struggle for cultural democracy. Its solution lies beyond even the realization of political and economic democracy, although of course that solution can only be reached when we no longer have extreme political inequality and extreme economic inequality.[46]

This is where the Harlem Renaissance fits in. During its heyday, and throughout the post-Renaissance period, Locke expressed the hope that "our writers and artists" would achieve a "victory" through "a psychological conquest of racism, prejudice and cultural intolerance."[47] His race loyalty was the gold vein in a rock of solidarity with the rest of humanity. Alain Locke was

---

[46] Alain Locke Papers, MSRC, Box 164–113, Folder 4 ([re: democracy] Departure speech to students at Talladega College, 1941), 4–5.

[47] Alain Locke, "Reason and Race," in Stewart, The Critical Temper of Alain Locke, 320.

both a "race man" and an integrationist. The role of culture in a "cultural democracy" is that of enrichment in full representation:

> Instead of saying, as was said for so long, that we should recognize the Negro because he has been neglected and needs recognition, recent American literature, — and for that matter, American art generally— has come forward, at least in its more creative talents, with a very new and democratic formula: We will recognize Negro materials because they are intrinsically interesting and because the national culture needs them in the picture to be truly representative.[48]

Racial Democracy: Alain Locke was a precursor to Dr. Martin Luther King, Jr. "[T]he race question," wrote Locke in 1949, "has become the number one problem of the world."[49]The next statement follows from the first: "Race," Locke states, "really is a dominant issue of our thinking about democracy[.]"[50] In his small book, *World View on Race and Democracy: A Study Guide in Human Group Relations*, Locke states this another way: "Of all the barriers limiting democracy, color is the greatest, whether viewed from a standpoint of **national** or **world democracy**."[51] Locke sees this as part of "total democracy."[52]

Prophetically, Locke forged a linkage between racism as an American problem and racism as a world problem, as he explicitly states: "race as a symbol of misunderstanding has become fully

---

[48] Alain Locke, "The Negro Minority in American Literature," in The Works of Alain Locke, edited by Charles Molesworth (New York and Oxford: Oxford University Press, 2012), pp. 83–88 [87].

[49] Alain Locke, "Dawn Patrol: A Review of the Literature of the Negro for 1948," Phylon 10:1–2 (1949): 5–14; 167–72. Reprinted in Jeffrey C. Stewart, The Critical Temper of Alain Locke: A Selection of His Essays on Art and Culture (New York and London: Garland, 1983), 337–49 [337].

[50] Alain Locke, "Reason and Race," in Stewart, The Critical Temper of Alain Locke, 325.

[51] Alain Locke, World View on Race and Democracy, 1.

[52] Alain Locke, World View on Race and Democracy, 2, citing Howard H. Brinton (no reference given).

the great tragedy of our time, both nationally and internation-ally."[53] Race is the crux, the litmus test, the hinge on which the entire project of democracy hangs. In a previously unpublished report on racism, Locke writes:

> The American race problem may eventually become just a phase and segment of the world relationship of races, and in slight degree it is already in process of becoming so. Historically, and in the general American thought of it, whether among the Negro minority or the white majority, it is thought of as peculiarly and exclusively a national problem. In some respects, its situations are relatively unique. [...] So, as between the white and the black peoples, the American situation is the acid test of the whole problem; and will be crucial in its outcome for the rest of the world. This makes America, in the judg-ment of many, the world's laboratory for the progressive solution of this great problem of social adjustment.[54]

Locke takes Christianity to task for what today is called self-segregation: "It is a sad irony," Alain Locke wrote, "that the social institution most committed and potentially most capable of implementing **social democracy** should actually be the weak-est and most inconsistent, organized religion."[55] Particularly egregious, in Locke's view, is what today is termed "self-segrega-tion": "Of all the segregated bodies, the racially separate church is the saddest and most obviously self-contradicting. The separate Negro church, organized in self-defensive protest, is nonetheless

---

[53] Alain Locke, "A Critical Retrospect of the Literature of the Negro for 1947," Phylon 9:1 (1948): 3–12. Reprinted in Jeffrey C. Stewart, The Critical Temper of Alain Locke: A Selection of His Essays on Art and Culture (New York and London: Garland, 1983), 329–36 [329].

[54] Alain Locke, "[Through Mrs. Ruth Cranston] Report on The Race Problem in the American Area." Alain Locke Papers, MSRC. Box 164–43, Folder 3 (Writings by Locke — Notes[:] Christianity, spirituality, reli-gion.), 1.

[55] Alain Locke Papers, MSRC, Box 164–105, Folder 34 ("American Education's Latest Task: Teaching Democracy." [incomplete]), 8.

just as anaomolous [sic], though perhaps, more pardonably so."[56] Locke's remark presaged those of the Rev. Billy Graham and the Rev. Martin Luther King, Jr., both of whom later observed that Sunday morning is the most segregated time in America.

Social Democracy: In "Reason and Race" (1947), Locke underscores "the fact that the contemporary world situation clearly indicates that **social democracy** is the only safe choice for the survival of Western and Christian civilization."[57] In the Seventeenth Annual Convention and Bahá'í Congress (5 July 1925), Locke was reported to have said:

> Dr. Alain LeRoy Locke of Washington, D.C., delivered a polished address, portraying the great part which America can play in the establishment of world peace, if alive to its opportunity. The working out of **social democracy** can be accomplished here. To this end we should not think in little arcs of experience, but in the big, comprehensive way. Let our country reform its own heart and life. Needed reforms cannot be worked out by the action of any one group, but a fine sense of cooperation must secure universal fellowship. He praised Green Acre, which he declared to be an oasis in the desert of materiality. He urged all who were favored by this glorious experience to carry forth its glorious message and thus awaken humanity. In final analysis, peace cannot exist anywhere without existing everywhere.[58]

---

[56] Alain Locke Papers, MSRC, Box 164–105, Folder 34 ("American Education's Latest Task: Teaching Democracy." [incomplete]), 8.

[57] Alain Locke, "Reason and Race," in Stewart, The Critical Temper of Alain Locke, 327.

[58] "The Seventeenth Annual Convention and Bahá'í Congress," Bahá'í News Letter, No. 6 (1925): 3. Here, Locke's reference to "Green Acre" is the Green Acre Bahá'í School, Retreat, and Conference Center in Eliot, Maine, where, in 1925, Bahá'í delegates assembled primarily to elect the "National Spiritual Assembly of the Bahá'ís of the United States and Canada" — a council of nine Bahá'í representatives charged with overseeing the affairs of the American and Canadian Bahá'í community at that time. (The National Spiritual Assembly of the Bahá'ís of Canada was

The very integrity of democracy itself is put to test by the state of its race relations.

Spiritual Democracy: Democracy is more than a political system. It is a state of mind, a province of the heart, a radiation of attitudes, from which all actions flow. Spiritual democracy is the democracy of the heart. It's a place, a state of mind that legislation cannot reach. It is the interiority of democracy that Locke emphasized:

> Constitutional guarantees, legal and civil rights, political machinery of democratic action and control are, of course, the skeleton foundation of democracy, but you and I know that attitudes are the flesh and blood of democracy, and that without their vital reinforcement [sic] democracy is really moribund or dead. That is my reason for thinking that in any democracy, ours included, the crucial issue, the test touchstone of democracy is minority status, minority protection, minority rights.[59]

During World War II, Locke wrote of the potential role that religion could play in promoting democracy on a world scale:

> The world crisis has led to the reexamination of the traditional doctrines of human equality and brotherhood among the leading thinkers of the Christian churches. As a result, a fresh crusade for aligning organized religion with the constructive forces of world democracy has come to the vanguard of liberal religious thought and action. Both intercultural, intersectarian and interfaith movements have grown out of these considerations.[60]

---

separately elected beginning in 1948 and was legally incorporated by an Act of Parliament in 1949, while The National Spiritual Assembly of the Bahá'ís of the United States would be elected annually thereafter.)

[59] Alain Locke Papers, MSRC, Box 164–124, Folder 15 ("The Preservation of the Democratic Ideal"), 1–2.

[60] Alain Locke, World View on Race and Democracy, 18.

In attempting to remold the American temperament, Alain Locke led a civil rights movement of the American spirit. Of particular importance are Locke's views on "spiritual democracy"—an aspect of Locke's thought that, so far, has received scant attention. In an evidently unpublished Bahá'í essay, Locke expresses his conviction that "Spiritual Democracy" is the "largest" dimension of democracy as a whole "and most inner meaning." In his unpublished, "The Gospel for the Twentieth Century," Locke states:

> The gospel for the Twentieth Century rises out of the heart of its greatest problems [...] Much has been accomplished in the name of Democracy, but Spiritual Democracy, its largest and most inner meaning, is so below our common horizons. [...] [T]he land that is nearest to material democracy is furthest away from spiritual democracy [...] The word of God is still insistent, [...] and we have [...] Baha'u'llah's "one great trumpet-call to humanity": "That all nations shall become one in faith, and all men as brothers; that the bonds of affection and unity between the sons of men should be strengthened; that diversity of religion should cease, and differences of race be annulled [...] These strifes and this bloodshed and discord must cease, and all men be as one kindred and family.["]

The spirit of democracy is best realized in a spirit of confraternity of the races, as a basis for the social solidarity of society as a whole. In *The Negro in America* (1933), Locke promoted ideal race relations by emphasizing the mutual benefits that true reciprocity would foster:

> If they will but see it, because of their complementary qualities, the two racial groups have great spiritual need, one of the other. It would truly be significant in the history of human culture, if two races so diverse should so happily collaborate, and the one return for

the gift of a great civilization the reciprocal gift of the spiritual cross-fertilization of a great and distinctive national culture.[61]

World democracy: Democracy, ideally, is collective self-destiny. On a world scale, democracy is global self-governance. Locke's universalism is most evident in his discussion of world democracy, for which "internationalism" appears to be a synonym. World democracy is really the logical and pragmatic expansion of the democratic principle, from a national to truly international level. "[W]orld democracy," writes Locke, "presupposes the recognition of the essential equality of all peoples and the potential parity of all cultures."[62] On a radio program, "Woman's Page of the Air," with Adelaide Hawley, broadcast 6 August 1944 while World War II was at its height, Locke said: "Just as the foundation of democracy as a national principle made necessary the declaration of the basic equality of persons, so the founding of *international* democracy must guarantee the basic equality of human *groups*."[63]

Accordingly, Locke noted, "we must find common human denominators of liberty, equality, and fraternity for humanity at large."[64] In the quest to universalize democracy, "color becomes the acid test of our fundamental honesty in putting into practice the democracy we preach."[65]

Exploring the relationship between America and world democracy, Locke postulated that "World leadership [...] must be moral leadership in democratic concert with humanity at large."[66] In so doing, America must perforce "abandon racial and cultural

---

[61] Alain Locke, The Negro in America (Chicago: American Library Association, 1933), 50.

[62] Alain Locke, World View on Race and Democracy, 14.

[63] Alain Locke Papers, MSRC, Box 164–105, Folder 33: [re: America's position in world affairs in relation to race.] Speech over station KMYR, Denver. 6 August 1944, p. 6.

[64] Locke, "The Unfinished Business of Democracy," 455.

[65] Locke, "The Unfinished Business of Democracy," 456.

[66] Locke, "The Unfinished Business of Democracy," 459.

prejudice."[67] "A **world democracy**," wrote Locke, "cannot possibly tolerate what a national democracy has countenanced too long."[68] This is an unmistakable allusion to America and racism.

Conclusions: Alain Locke's philosophy of democracy is unfinished, for the simple reason that he did not systematize it, much less apply it. Superficially, if one accepts the multidimensional nature of Locke's theory of democracy, it appears, at best, to be descriptive. Yet there is a prescriptive element as well. This aspect of Locke's thinking has yet to be fully developed. If one reads his writings closely, the prescriptive elements fall into focus. To sharpen the focus, let us take the following statement from "Cultural Relativism and Ideological Peace," as a point of departure for the prescriptive application of Locke's theory of democracy:

> [T]hree working principles seem to be derivable for a more objective and scientific understanding of human cultures and for the more reasonable control of their interrelationships. They are:
>
> 1. The principle of *cultural equivalence,* under which we would more wisely press the search for functional similarities in our analyses and comparisons of human cultures... . Such functional equivalences, which we might term *"culture-cognates"* or *"culture-correlates,"* discovered underneath deceptive but superficial institutional divergence, would provide objective but soundly neutral common denominators for intercultural understanding and cooperation;
>
> 2. The principle of *cultural reciprocity,* which, by a general recognition of the reciprocal character of all contacts between cultures and of the fact that all modern cultures are highly composite ones, would... [provide] scientific, point-by-point comparisons with their

---

[67] Locke, "The Unfinished Business of Democracy," 459.
[68] Locke, "Democracy Faces a World Order," 128.

correspondingly limited, specific, and objectively verifiable superiorities or inferiorities;

3. The principle of *limited cultural convertibility*, that, since culture elements, though widely interchangeable, are so separable, the institutional forms from their values and the values from their institutional forms, the organic selectivity and assimilative capacity of a borrowing culture becomes a limiting criterion for cultural exchange.[69]

In simpler terms, Locke's prescriptive paradigm proposes a three-step process: (1) Correlate (identify "functional equivalences" as possible "common denominators"); (2) Validate (verify reciprocal character of such "culture-correlates" by objectively making "point-by-point comparisons"); and (3) Reciprocate (justified mutual acceptance of comparable values to pursue intercultural exchange and cooperation). The result would be as follows:

Through functional [1] comparison a much more constructive phase of cultural relativism seems to be developing, promising the discovery of some less arbitrary and more objective norms. Upon them, perhaps we can build sounder intercultural [2] understanding and promote a more equitable [3] collaboration between cultures.[70]

What Locke calls for is "an objective comparative analysis on a world scale of our major culture values."[71] This can be done dimension-by-dimension — in local, moral, political, economic, cultural, interracial, social, spiritual, global, intellectual, natu-

---

[69] Alain Locke, "Cultural Relativism and Ideological Peace," in The Works of Alain Locke, edited by Charles Molesworth (New York and Oxford: Oxford University Press, 2012), pp. 548–554 (550–551).

[70] Locke, "Cultural Relativism and Ideological Peace," in The Works of Alain Locke, p. 552 (bracketed numbers and emphasis added).

[71] Locke, "Cultural Relativism and Ideological Peace," in The Works of Alain Locke, p. 553.

ral, practical, and creative contexts. Locke's proposed method has never been rigorously tested. This quest for intercultural exchange, recognition and cooperation is part and parcel of what Locke called "reciprocity." In and of itself, reciprocity is not a method of conflict resolution *per se* but is a means of cultural diplomacy that promotes peaceful interchange.

Alain Locke's philosophy of democracy does not end with his dimensional paradigm and comparative method for identifying equivalent cross-cultural values and their concomitant moral imperatives. Locke famously wrote:

> All philosophies, it seems to me, are in ultimate derivation philosophies of life and not of abstract, disembodied "objective" reality; products of time, place and situation, and thus systems of timed history rather than timeless eternity... . In de-throning our absolutes, we must take care not to exile our imperatives, for after all, we live by them."[72]

Locke's Bahá'í-inspired vision incorporates the three "basic corporate ideas" of nation, race and religion, of which Locke speaks in his paper, "Moral Imperatives for World Order" (1944).[73] Alain Locke's prophetic words remain true today: "The moral imperatives of a new world order are an internationally limited idea of national sovereignty, a non-monopolistic and culturally tolerant concept of race and religious loyalties freed of sectarian bigotry." In "Pluralism and Intellectual Democracy" (1942), Locke wrote that: "The intellectual core of the problems of the peace... will be the discovery of the necessary common denominators and the basic equivalences involved in a democratic world

---

[72] Alain Locke, "Values and Imperatives," in The Works of Alain Locke, pp. 451–464 (451, 452).

[73] Alain Locke, "The Moral Imperatives for World Order," Summary of Proceedings, Institute of International Relations, Mills College, Oakland, CA, June 18–28, 1944, 19–20. Reprinted in Leonard Harris, ed., The Philosophy of Alain Locke (Philadelphia: Temple University Press, 1989), 143, 151–152.

order or democracy on a world scale."[74] A world democracy is a world order established on both legal and social foundations that command universal assent.

Locke inwardly felt that what America really needed was to embrace Bahá'í principles (and not necessarily the Bahá'í Faith itself). "Dr. Alain Locke of Washington, D.C., speaking on the subject, 'America's Part in World Peace',", according to a news report, "pointed out the priceless value and the great necessity of a good example if America is to perform a real service to the world." Locke proclaimed:

America's democracy must begin at home with a spiritual fusion of all her constituent peoples in brotherhood, and in an actual mutuality of life. Until democracy is worked out in the vital small scale of practical human relations, it can never, except as an empty formula, prevail on the national or international basis. Until it establishes itself in human hearts, it can never institutionally flourish. Moreover, America's reputation and moral influence in the world depends on the successful achievement of this vital spiritual democracy within the lifetime of the present generation. (Material civilization alone does not safeguard the progress of a nation.) Bahá'í Principles and the leavening of our national life with their power, is to be regarded as the salvation of democracy. In this way only can the fine professions of American ideals be realized.[75]

Here, Locke says that Bahá'í principles can contribute to the full realization of the American ideals of democracy.

---

[74] Alain Locke. "Pluralism and Intellectual Democracy." Conference on Science, Philosophy and Religion, Second Symposium (New York: Conference on Science, Philosophy and Religion, 1942). Pp. 196–212. Reprinted in The Philosophy of Alain Locke, 51–66 (62).

[75] Harlan Ober, "The Bahá'í Congress at Green Acre," Star of the West 16.1 (April 1925): 525, on the occasion of the "The Seventeenth Annual Convention and Bahá'í Congress," where Alain Locke delivered an invited presentation.

Locke's philosophy of democracy, in essence, was to "Americanize Americans"—to realize America's ideals in all its dimensions — locally, morally, politically, economically, culturally, interracially, socially, spiritually, globally, intellectually, naturally, practically, and creatively — in order to further democratize democracy. "[B]ut now, it seems to me," Locke told an audience of social workers in 1938, "the soundest, wisest and most appropriate slogan, — if we must have a slogan,[—] is to [A]mericanize Americans in their social attitudes and behavior, to establish democracy in the heart of our social relations."[76] Once that happens, America could have the requisite moral authority to adopt its "world role."[77]

Locke's philosophy of democracy was his signal contribution to the "salvation of democracy," from race relations to international relations, in connecting economic values with human values, and in predicating all other dimensions of democracy on the health and vitality of "spiritual democracy," which Bahá'í teachings enrich with its wealth of principles of unity,[78]from family relations to international relations, and from local democracy to world democracy.

---

[76] Alain Locke Papers, MSRC, Box 164–124, Folder 15 ("The Preservation of the Democratic Ideal"), 5.

[77] Alain Locke, "Democracy Faces a World Order," 126.

[78] See Christopher Buck, "Fifty Bahá'í Principles of Unity: A Paradigm of Social Salvation." Bahá'í Studies Review 18 (2012): pp. 3–44 (published June 2015). https://www.academia.edu/35016378/_Fifty_Bahai_Principles_of_Unity_A_Paradigm_of_Social_Salvation_2017_update_. Accessed July 3, 2018.

An Intoductory Bio-Bibliographical Note

Stephen N. Lambden

Sayyid Kazim ibn Sayyid Qasim al-Husayni al-Rashti
(b. Rasht c. 1213/1798 or 1799 – d. Karbala, 1259/1843)

Sayyid Kazim Rashti, the son of the silk-merchant and scholar Sayyid Qasim al-Husayni, was born in Rasht, northern Persia (now Iran), towards the beginning of the Persian Qajar era, around the mid. 1780s (c. 1199/1784 or 5) or perhaps in the early 1200s AH., corresponding to the 1790s CE. He is best known to-day as the devout, prolific and learned lifetime disciple and first successor (from 1826 CE), to the Arab-born Shaykh Ahmad ibn Zayn al-Din al-Ahsa'i (d. 1241/1826). This latter figure came to be viewed in parts of the Middle-East, India and elsewhere as the innovative, primary generator of the deeply mystical, sometimes heterodox, branch of Imamocentric Shi'i Islam which came to be known (after this Shaykh) as al-Shaykhiyya (loosely, Shaykhism) and al-Kashfiyya ('Exponents of Spiritual Disclosure').

In a vision of Fatima, daughter of the Prophet Muhammad (d. 632 CE), or as a youth living in Ardabil via a vision of a long-deceased Safavid progenitor, Sayyid Kazim is said to have been instructed to visit Shaykh Ahmad in Yazd (Persia, 270 km southeast of Isfahan). This he did and from there he is said to have drunk deep of mystical gnosis. The life of Sayyid Kazim was de-voted to the defence and propagation of the emergent Shaykhi movement or school. Among the last of his major Arabic writ-ings was the 1258/1842 Dalil al-mutahayyirin ('Evidence for the Perplexed'). Within it Shaykh Ahmad is pictured as a mystical and polymathic genius capable of inspired communications from the occulted, heavenly Imams, the alleged successors of the Prophet Muhammad up till the 9th cent. CE. This in numerous, often esoteric, areas of Islamic knowledge; including metrics, music, grammar, hermeneutics, theology and religious jurisprudence, the history of Shi'i savants and worthies, geometry, astronomy, mathematics, philosophy, alchemy, medicine, divination, numerological prognosis, and the sciences of magic squares. Such numerous areas of expertise were, to some degree, communicated over several decades to Sayyid Kazim. They also included the mastery of religious commentary and exposition, encompassing Tafsir (Qur'an commentary) and the explication of hadith / akhbar (religious traditions); these subjects permeate the writings of Shayklh Ahmad and Sayyid Kazim, both of whom were extremely prolific. The Sayyid of Rasht is reckoned to have composed in excess of 172 books and treatises in both Arabic and Persian. Mostly remaining in manuscript, only a small proportion of these writings have been adequately edited, studied, and printed.

As a youth and teenager, Sayyid Kazim was recognized as a deeply spiritual and insightful thinker within the twelver Shi'i-Shaykhi Islamic community of his day. When aged about twenty he composed a lengthy, 7000 or so verse commentary upon the centrally important Qur'anic 'Throne Verse' (Qur'an 2:255), his Tafsir ayat al-kursi ('Commentary upon the verse of the Throne'). A taste of the depth of this complex and little studied Arabic work, is evidenced in its opening lines where we read:

> Praised be unto God Who shed the splendor of His radiance upon the inmost hearts of the mystic knowers so as to actualize the disclosure of the orient-lights of His theophany. He set ablaze the hearts of the mystic wayfarers through the radiant splendors of His Light and explicated the inner retreats of all the worlds for the purpose of dazzlingly illuminating the radiances of His cyclic schemata. And blessings be upon our Master [the Prophet] Muhammad through whom He [God] set-

tled down upon His Throne ('arsh) and His Seat (kursi) for he is the Name through the shadow of which eyes were solaced. Wherefore, there did not emerge from before me, aught save what is of Him for he [Muhammad] is the Hidden, Mightiest Name (al-ism al-a'zam) and the Light of Lights treasured up, the very one through whom the Lights found illumination. Through him were mysteries disclosed and Light irradiated from the Dawn of Eternity. And through him did all existence find realization" (trans. Lambden).

Other similarly complex and lengthy works of Sayyid Kazim include his incomplete though 24,700 verse Arabic commentary on the abstruse 'Sermon of the Gulf' (Khutba al-Tutunjiyya) ascribed to Imam Ali (d. 40/661), the first successor to the Arabian Prophet Muhammad (d. 632 CE). A Tabriz (NW Iran) lithograph printing of this work first appeared in 1270/1853–4, a decade or so after his death. Its deep meanings also with those of his similarly weighty and lithographed around the same time, 'Commentary on the Ode Rhyming in the Letter "L" (Sharh al-Qasida al-Lami-yya), remain to be adequately summed up and translated into European languages.

Sayyid Kazim sometimes lived close to his master in Iran (e.g. Yazd, Kermanshah, Mashhad, Isfahan, Qazvin, etc.) and Iraq (e.g. Najaf and Karbala) where he imbibed Islamic learning in general and esoterica and Shi'i gnosis in particular. He made a pilgrimage to Mecca and often travelled to the great Shi'i centers, the "thresholds" in Ottoman Iraq,

Today the intellectual and spiritual genius of Sayyid Kazim remains little known and greatly under-appreciated. Aside from the many thousands of contemporary Shaykhis who have, in recent decades, begun (re-)publishing a few of his key writings, members of the approximately 5–6 million Bahá'í International community greatly revere Sayyid Kazim Rashti along with his master al-Ahsa'i. In an early work of the Bab (executed Tabriz 1850), Rashti was referred to as "my instructor" (mu'allimi) and

Baha'ullah (d. Acre, 1892) in his Persian Kitab-i iqan (Book of Certitude, c. 1862), referred to al-Ahsa'i and Rashti as "twin shining lights". They who seen therein as saintly harbingers of the Babi and Bahá'í religions. Indeed, in one of his scriptural Tablets, the founder of the Bahá'í religion stated that he took refuge in al-Ahsa'i and al-Rashti and heard from these two what previously had been known to no one save God (Paraphrase of passage from a Tablet of Baha'u'llah to a certain Ahmad cited in Ishraq Khavari (ed.), Ma'ida-i-Asmani, IV:134–5).

Excerpts from *Essay on Shaykhism* by Alphonse Louis Marie Nicolas

TRANSLATED BY PETER TERRY[1]

Part II, Chapter I
The battle between the Balaseri and the Shaykhis —
Siyyid Kazim Rashti

The death of Shaykh Ahmad[2] interposed, for a few days, a break in the battle, and passions seem to have subsided. Furthermore, it was at this time that Islam received a terrible blow and that its power was bruised. The Russian Emperor defeated the Muslim nations and most of the provinces inhabited by the people of this religion fell into the hands of the Moskovite army.[1]

On the other hand, with Shaykh Ahmad dead, his doctrine would disappear with him without returning, and peace endured for almost two years.

But the Muslims returned quickly to their first sentiments as soon as they saw that the light of the doctrine of the deceased still shined forth in the world, due to Siyyid Kazim Rashti,[3],[2] the best, the most faithful student of Shaykh Ahmad and his successor.

---

[1] *Essay on Shaykhism* by Alphonse Louis Marie Nicolas, French Consul at Tabriz (Tauris), was first published in Paris: Librairie Paul Geuthner, 1914. It was translated by Peter Terry in 2015.

[2] *Nicolas:* 28 June 1826.

[3] *Nicolas:* The date of the birth of Siyyid Kazim Rashti bin Qasim al-Husayni is profoundly unknown to the leading Shaykhis, as also his age when he died. Shaykh 'Ali Javan thinks that he died at 45 years of age; Saqatu'l-Islam at 50 years.

It is the same for the famous meeting at Karbala; Saqatu'l-Islam to establish it, wrote me: "In 1241, my grandfather was at Karbala, and he returned to Tabriz in 1253. But, you ask me if the meeting took place Friday 1 Rajab 1243–18 January 1828 or the 1 Rajab 1251–23 October 1835? As my grandfather left a written record of this meeting and he was in Tabriz in 1253–1837, seeing that there is allusion to the meeting taking place a short time after the death of the Shaykh, it seems to me that the date of 1243 is

The Shi'ites criticized him violently for renting the genius of the Shaykh and taking his books as the texts of his lessons.

The response that Rashti gave to them did not lack a certain grandeur:

"The route upon which I have set my foot," he says, "is the knowledge of God and of His names, those of absolute Prophethood and Vilayat, that of the Unity and of its degrees, the denigration of doubts and suspicions that can assail man in his peregrinations in the Unity. If, in these questions, speech become a cause of estrangement between men, then one must then leave Islam far off and say goodbye to it, for, in such conditions, what is the creation for? Why are there Prophets? 'Ali said it: 'The beginning of religion is knowledge, the perfect knowledge is Unity; Unity is the negation of attributes, for the attributes testifies that it is other than the qualitative that qualifies it."

It was pointed out to him that this knowledge that he invoked was philosophy and, in the eyes of faith, philosophy is not only mislead, but also misleads.

To which he replied:

"Is it the word of the philosopher that you reject? If it is truly of this word that you hear spoken, God has said: 'God has not raised up the Prophets except to instruct men in philosophy.' And He also says: 'It is He who brought into existence in the midst of illiterate men an apostle from among them, so that he could tell them of the miracles of the Lord, so as to make them more pure, by teaching them the book and philosophy.'[4, [3]]

"God says, on the subject of David: 'We gave him philosophy and the capacity to make definitive judgments.'[5]

"On the subject of Luqman: 'We gave Luqman wisdom.'[6]

---

the most precise. As for the date of the death of Siyyid Kazim Rashti, it is towards the end of the year that you indicated that it took place."

[4] *Nicolas:* Qur'an 62:2 [al-kitab wa'l-hikmat (the book and wisdom)]
[5] *Nicolas:* Qur'an 38:20 [hikmata wa'l-fasla'l-khitábi]
[6] *Nicolas:* Qur'an 31:12 [al-hikmat]

"And also: 'He gives philosophy to whomsoever He wishes; and whoever has received it, has received an immense good.'[7]

"If it is the meaning of the word philosophy that is difficult for you, philosophy means: 'Knowledge of God and knowledge of His unity.' Philosophy embraces all that concerns this knowledge, for example, the Names of God, the Attributes of God, the Acts of God, the Traces of the Acts of God, which are the very existences of the Creatures and their essenses; the knowledge of the soul for, this is the place of the radiation of the good qualities, of purity of soul and the purification of its bad qualities; the knowledge of the precepts of God relative to prayers, business, contracts, etc. The very word of God proves that the purpose of philosophy is no other than this for He says: 'Here is what God has revealed in fact of philosophy. And, further, do not put any God beside God.'[8]

"All these verses, all these explanations in the science of good manners, are nothing but philosophy: the precepts of religious law are also derived from philosophy. Thus, after the explanation of knowledge of God, of His attributes, of His names, of His acts, of His traces, of those of the Prophet, of the Vali, of the purification of the soul, God says: 'See what God has revealed to you of philosophy.'[9]"

That is, in reality, the foundation of the Iranian religious philosophy and Siyyid Kazim Rashti asks his adversaries why their observations [are so condemnatory] on the subject of so exalted and pure a science, while they do not make any at all, for example, regarding those who are versed in jurisprudence and wherein there are people without faith who introduce innovations into the religious law. If they say that it is because in jurisprudence, discussion generates light, that is to say the distinction between the true and the false, that is even more true of philosophy in which one must profoundly penetrate to arrive at a result.

---

[7] *Nicolas:* Qur'an 2:272 [al-hikmat]

[8] *Nicolas:* 17:39 [al-hikmat]

[9] *Nicolas:* Ibid.

His adversaries retorted that to immerse oneself in philosophy is a considerable work and in which the least error conducts directly to hell: while error in the other sciences is not a cause for perdition.

"It is when one does not profoundly penetrate into philosophy that one cannot differentiate between the true and the false," responded Siyyid Kazim Rashti. "'Ali said: 'A certain category of men chase after every noise like flies, and the lightest breath agitates them.' And God said: 'When you see them, their exterior pleases you; when they speak, you listen to them voluntarily; they are like trusses leaned against the wall; when they hear a cry, they believe it is against them. These are your enemies, avoid them. May God make war against them! They are false!'[10]"

It is certain that if the heart is not perspicacious, there are proofs certain to dispel the doubts that assail them: it does no longer enjoys security, it is always in turmoil, and finishes by no longer believing in the truth.

One day a Shaykh was asked the truth between two prayers: the one promises the eternal heaven, the other extinction: "O Thou Who art before all things! O Thou Who subsists after all things!"

Religion requires that hell and paradise exist eternally and that they never be extinguished. Thus, if we do not believe in the extinction of the fire and of paradise how can we say that God subsists after the extinction of all things?

The Shaykh replied that there were no rules without exceptions and that God is after all things, with the exception of being after Paradise and Hell.

"It is certain," said Siyyid Kazim Rashti, "that if this Shaykh had learned philosophy, he would not have replied in such a stupid fashion; if he had reflected in the knowledge of God, he would certainly have known, he would certainly have understood that there is no change in God, and that there is no being in front of Him. At the very moment in which He is after, He is before;

---

[10] *Nicolas:* Qur'an 63:4

when He is far, He is near. Before and after do not exist for Him. Thus this Shaykh would not have replied with such lying things, if he had known the words of the Imam Sadiq[4] reported in the Saqatu'l-Islam: 'God is empty of His creature, and His creature is empty of him." Or those of the Imam al-Rida[5] to the Caliph Ma'mun:[6] 'What is in the creature cannot be attributed to God.'

Affirmations of this kind are numerous and derive from those who have not profoundly penetrated the knowledge of God. And we see those who are called Learned Ones puzzled by the least question and then prone to cry: "The simple knowledge suffices us! Penetration into the details, discussion of such matters, is forbidden!"

"Yes, certainly! If the abbreviated knowledge is true. If one comes from it to enter into the details without trembling from fear. Yes certainly! If the owner of this knowledge is Muslim, a believer! But jurisprudence requires that the learned one know the details of science, of philosophy, of theology, of the knowledge of the truth of things, in such fashion to be able at least to dispel the doubts that present themselves: and the doctors, and the learned ones and the chiefs of Islam are in agreement on this point with jurisprudence."

"It is only with knowledge that one can truly close all the paths of the Demon, who searches for the least crack to enter into the hearts.

"The science of philosophy is thus a special obligation like that of jurisprudence. The Shi'ite clergy is truly full of strange contradictions! They say: 'Even as brief knowledge suffices in the principles of religion, in the same way the imitation in the consequences suffices in its turn.' So be it! But then why do they believe it necessary that the Creature penetrate profoundly in the knowledge of these consequences? When they forbid the study of Divine knowledge and of principles? Is this because research and examination would be necessary in the "Consequences" and would not be in the Principles? But then, the consequences are superior to the principles? Does it seem that before painting the ceiling, one must build it? For truly, a principle not verified in any way can serve what consequences?

"We examine the intellectual proof first off. In second place the one provided by the verses, and this second proof, we consider it superior to the intellectual proof; then we examine the traditional proof. If all of these proofs are in agreement, the matter in question is demonstrated. Then, in fourth place, we examine religious beliefs: we place these opposite the three first orders of proof: if they are in contradiction with these beliefs, we abandon them, for we believe that religious convictions are the strongest, the surest, and the most tested. Finally, in fifth place, after all of these tests, we examine the signs in the horizons and in the beings, following the saying of God: 'We will cause to appear our signs in the different borders of the earth and in their own selves until it is demonstrated to them that it is the truth.'[11]

"It is only after this work that we decide about the truth of a thing and its decisive quality.

"But then, when a thing victorious passes all of these five tests, should we consider it as not being a truth? Should we believe that the God of the world leads us astray and deceives us? From the moment that in what concerns beliefs and knowledge we speak according to this argument, from what sidetrack, of what shadows can we be fearful? Why do we abandon evident truth? Has not God said: 'What is there outside of truth, if it is not error? How is it that you turn away therefrom?'[12]"

This was the argument of Siyyid Kazim Rashti, before which his adversaries certainly inclined, but telling him that what they could not come to terms with was to watch him follow the path opened by the Shaykh and to promulgate what he called his sciences.

Siyyid Kazim replied to them: "The path that the Shaykh followed, his manner of pursuing it, what misfortune, what error does it present? Do the learned men of Islam reject his science? His greatness? His talents? Are not all the Shi'ite 'ulama in agree-

---

[11] *Nicolas:* Qur'an 41:53
[12] *Nicolas:* Qur'an 10:32

ment to praise him? Hence, if I follow the way of the Shaykh and it I accept the testimony of these illustrious learned men, what kind of strawman can one agitate in front of me? I have, in the study of a guide, myself examined his state and in him I saw nothing but the search for the contentment of God, and of the straight path. The nights, the days, traveling, relaxing, I was with him, I accompanied him. I never saw him preoccupied in any fashion with things of this lower world, and I witnessed from him only prodigious acts, rare traditions. His truth became evident and clear to me. Therefore, what reasons did I have to distance myself from him? In one word either I am Muqallid[13],[7] or I am Muhaqqaq.[14]

"If we consider the first case, I imitate all the 'ulama of Islam in their greatness, the sublimity of their science, their perfect mastery, their incontestable royalty: I do not imitate anyone who is not learned in the sciences. Hence, what observations can the one who does not know the technical terms of the Shaykh present to me? For in the end he does not have[15] in any fashion possession of these sciences, even though he may be well versed in jurisprudence. Besides his father was more spiritual than he, and yet he affirmed that he couldn't understand anything of the words of the Shaykh.

"If we examine the second case, I am charged with requirements from my own comprehension. I must share with humanity from what I have understood. I must tell you that the love of the Shaykh was full of my human nature and that I considered it obligatory to obey him. I ask God that on the day of judgment he will resurrect me with him and that he give me my part of the intercession of the Prophet. So, if you have proofs, arguments that prove that one must distance oneself from the Shaykh, tell them, if you are sincere."

---

[13] *Nicolas:* Muqallid — Imitator, like the majority of men whose religious acts are nothing but the imitation of those of their leaders.

[14] *Nicolas:* Muhaqqaq — learned person acting according to his own judgment and who should be imitated.
Translator: Meaning authenticated, confirmed, verified, certified.

[15] *Nicolas:* Siyyid Kazim alludes here to one of his adversaries, probably the son of A Siyyid Mahdi.

It was then said to him that the 'ulama of that time had not understood what the 'ulama of the earlier era, and that hence today it was impossible to accept their judgment.

"This affirmation," replied the Siyyid, "seems to be the word of your predecessors. Abu Buraida al-Aslami[16] said to them: 'The prophet of God chose 'Ali as caliph. How is it that you rejected his word and named Abi Quhafa[17] the caliph?' They replied: 'We, we were present, and one who is present sees things that are missed by the one who is absent.' Did not the Prophet of God say: "A group of my people will always be in the truth, until the very instant of the hour" which means: the men of my confession cannot unite themselves in error."

Hence, the universal agreement of those learned men is a proof of the truth of the Shaykh.

Siyyid Kazim asked them: "Which of his beliefs do you believe to be perverse? Which of his words do you consider to be lies?"

And adversaries replied to him:

"Four of his affirmations on the subject of four questions. For example:

"1st. What he says on the subject of the Mi'raj. He wishes to show that the Prophet, during this voyage, abandoned in its respective sphere each of the elements of which he was composed: fire, for example, in the sphere of fire, water in that of water, etc. But our religion wants that our Prophet ascended to the sky with the material body with which he was endowed.

---

[16] *Translator:* Not identified.
http://en.wikipedia.org/wiki/Abu_Buraidah_al-Aslami
Citation: Abu Buraidah al-Aslami was a Sahaba of Muhammad and a narrator of hadith. He was one of the Muhajirun [1] and was not among those who supported Abu Bakr during the meeting at the Saqifah.[2]
[17] *Translator:* http://en.wikipedia.org/wiki/Abu_Bakr
Citation: 'Abu Bakr as-Ṣiddīq (Abdullah ibn Abi Quhafa) (Arabic: عبد الله, أبي قحافة, Transliteration: ʾAbd Allāh ibn Abī Quḥāfah, c. 573 CE — 23 August 634 CE) also known as Abū Bakr (Arabic: أبو بكر, meaning Father of the Virgin) was a senior companion (Sahabi) and the father-in-law of the Islamic prophet Muhammad.

"2nd. What he affirms on the subject of the resurrection and which he wants to show that all of the elements of the bodies return to their centers and cannot return, while Islam declares that we must believe in the return of this same material body.

"3rd. What he affirms on the subject of the science of God for he says that God has two sciences, one eternal, the other newly created. Which is to say that this latter one did not exist and was acquired. God becomes thus the place where new things have been manifested.

"4th. His declaration that the Imam is the efficient cause of things. Thus the Imam must have absolute power in his action and that God has delegated to him the caretaking of the creation. Islam affirms that these two hypotheses are lying.

"Hence, the Shaykh, in these four questions separated himself from what Islam considers obligatory. Hence, it is bad to obey him, it is bad to turn oneself towards him. This is why we forbid you to follow his path, we forbid you to promulgate his doctrines."

Siyyid Kazim replied with the retractions we have already had the regret of encountering in Shaykh Ahmad. He added that Islam as a whole was in agreement on this point and that one cannot base an accusation on a book when the writer affirms that this book does not express what he believes.

This battle which had been fairly courteous until then could not suffice to the enemies of Shaykh Ahmad, who wanted more facts and less words. Thus making a final effort to have legality on this side, they organized a great public reunion to which they invited Siyyid Kazim. This one bravely accepted. This gathering was held the Friday 1st of the month of Rajad 1243–1828. We leave it to Siyyid Kazim to describe.

Not one of the persons present were of my friends. Their heads had seated them in groups and I, was in the middle. Someone approached me and said in my ear: "They want to kill you, leave this place, I counsel you."

But, unfortunately, it was impossible to leave, for all of those who were around me were armed, as if they wanted to make holy war against me in the presence of the Imam.

As soon as they were quiet and seated, I asked them: "What reason has thus pushed you to gather in this way? What is the cause of these quarrels? Have you understood coming from me something contrary to the sacred religious law? Have you found in me a heterodox belief? Have I produced something contrary to our Ithna 'Ashari sect? Have you assembled in order to burden me with the weight of your justice?"

"No!" they replied.

"Then," I asked, "what is the cause of this trouble, of this gathering?"

"We wanted to interrogate you," they replied, "about some of the terms employed by the Shaykh, and to prove to you that they are impious."

"Why," I replied, "the first day when I told you: Ask for whatever explanations you desire from me, did you not do so?

"But now that on the subject of the illustrious Shaykh the insanities that you know have been promulgated, now that the ears of men have been filled with lies, now that he himself has left this world, and is no longer here to explain to you what he has in his heart, it is now that you have arrived at this?

"The error of another, what influence can it have on your hearts? How can it bring you damage? Because you have found your guide."

They said: "You must absolute examine these terms. You must respond to us."

[Me:] "The people of lies, among those who preceded you, were numerous. Ave you acted in reference to their beliefs in the same fashion you are acting towards mine? Did you insist?"

[They:] "Those who believe in the Shaykh are numerous, and we fear that they will fall into the shadows of error, and that they will propagate it."

[Me:] "So be it! But remark that among the people of the past, of whom I speak, there were people who believed in these people of lies and imitators thereof: their lying beliefs were thus propagates. If you do not know their names, I will teach them to you. And so, these predecessors, have you cited them in comparison? Have you proven their infidelity? It is thus, but only thus that you have the right to take issue with the words of the Shaykh."[8]

[They:] "All that is nice and good, but we want precise answers."
[Me:] "We come from God and we return to Him! Bring then what you have."[18]

So the charges that I have already mentioned were brought to me. I had earlier explained all of the terms, and no doubt in their sense they conform to the appearance of Islam. The treatise in which I gave the meaning carries the title Kashfu'l-Haqq. This book is well known, but it did not suffice them. They asked for this explanation:

They cried: "The Shaykh said: 'Certainly this material body does not revive'; so! Is that an impiety, yes or no?"

I replied: "Basing myself on what I understand of these terms it is not an impiety! So, tell me, in basing yourself on your sense of the words based on the dictionary, that is after Qamus, Seha, the Majma'ul-Bahrain, what is the meaning of the word Jasad? Outside of the meaning that it has in the technical terms of the philosophers?"

They cried: "We do not know!"

I replied: "Glory be to God! You do not know the meaning of the word Jasad, you do not know the applications that the lexicographers give to it, and you have just claimed that if we say 'This jasad does not return' we are impious!"

*They said: "We understand by **body** what the common folk*[19] *understand."*

And I cried: "Where are the lexicographers, where the intellect of the common folk?"

They insisted and said: "We understand by this word all that is understood by the people present here."

There was no one to make it known that the common folk had nothing to do with such a discussion. Surely, if popular comprehension can count for something then all the books of all the 'ulama are nothing but lies. There is furthermore no doubt that a grocer or a

---

[18] *Nicolas:* The formula that is pronounced when one is in danger of death.

[19] *Translator:* The original French is "vulgare" which has the connotation of those who have a common, an unsophisticated, an uneducated, and therefore, in many cases an erroneous understanding of complicated matters. I have translated it as "common folk" as this is closer to the French than "ignorant".

lumber salesman can not understand the meaning of the commentary of Lum'a,[20] *that they nothing about the question of free arbitration or of predestination that they can not grasp that if an order intervenes, making obligatory the accomplishment of an act, a defense exists that is opposed to the accomplishment of its opposite? Finally, seeing their fear of loyalty, and their excessive violence, I said to them:*

"What do you have against me?"

[They replied:] "We want you to write that all these words are impieties."

I wrote: "These words when they are not explained, when they are neither preceded nor followed with anything, when nothing is derived from them, are, following the comprehension of the common folk, impieties of the same kind as, for example, in this verse: 'The hand of God is chained',[21] *for this is also an impiety in the eyes of the common folk."*

Siyyid Kazim triumphs with the skill that he has deployed and declares that his enemies, disappointed to have arrived at the end of his resistance, require him to prove his quality as mujtahid. For us, we consider that he was wrong to be so content with the a subterfuge, which, fundamentally, is purely and simply a true retraction.

Be that as it may, the president of the assembly remarked that the debate was being sidetracked:

"You spoke, until now, of the impiety of the impiety of these beliefs and upon the divergences with the obligations of Islam. Now that he has proven to us the purity of his doctrine, you want him to prove his quality as mujtahid. Truly if a gathering this numerous is necessary

---

[20] *Nicolas:* Of the first martyr, Shahid Awal.

Translator: http://en.wikipedia.org/wiki/Muhammad_Jamaluddin_al-Makki_al-Amili

Citation: Muhammad Jamaluddin al-Makki al-Amili (1334–1385) also known as Shahid Awwal (Arabic: ash-Shahid al-Awwal الشهيد الأول) was the first Islamic martyr and the author of Al-Lum'ah ad-Dimashqiya(اللمعة Arabic: الدمشقية "The Damascene Glitter"). He was one of the greatest Shi'a scholars.

[21] *Nicolas:* Qur'an 5:69

to prove that one is a Doctor, show us in what gatherings those others, whom you claim to be mujtahids, have proven this quality."

The adhan[22] was recited and the gathering ended. But the troubles continued and some envious Mullas brought the people together at the tomb of His Highness 'Abbas.[9] They raised flags and set to marching, but this demonstration did not attain to its object.

Once again A. Siyyid Mahdi[23] ascended the minbar and declared that Siyyid Kazim Rashti must be banished from the town, inviting the populace to proceed with the execution of this order.

_____

[22] *Translator:* The Muslim call to prayer, which differs in one verse between the Sunnis and the Ithna 'Ashari Shi'is: http://en.wikipedia.org/wiki/Adhan

[23] *Nicolas:* This A. Siyyid Mahdi was known for his piety and his fear of God. He was the son of A. Siyyid 'Ali the author of the book entitled Riaz, better known under the name Sharh al-Kabir. This one had always refused to pronounce on the case of the Shaykh. But men came to him, and based on the excommunication pronounced by the Shahid Salis [Haji Mulla Muhammad Taqi Qazvini — see below], they asked him what their duty was towards the disciples of the Shaykh. Haji Siyyid Mahdi convened an assembly to which he invited Sharif al-'ulama, Haji Mulla Muhammad Ja'afar Astarabadi and Haji Siyyid Kazim Rashti. A discussion took place in the course of which the enemies of the Shaykhis pointed to the obvious impiety of several passages from the books of the Shaykh.

Siyyid Mahdi, who had refused until that point to excommunicate the Shaykh, was forced to do so because of the testimony of these two righteous men: Sharif al-'ulama and Haji Mulla Muhammad Ja'afar Astarabadi. He thus pronounced the brief disparagement of the Shaykh and his disciples.

The following day he went to the mosque, giving a long sermon that he ended with these words: "Today, there are wolves dressed in ewes' clothing: these ones corrupt religion! And these wolves are Shaykh Ahmad Ahsa'i, and all those who follow him. Know that they are impious."

Thus, the first 'ulama who issued the interdiction against the new sect were 1st Haji Mulla Muhammad Taqi Qazvini Shahid Salis; 2nd A. Siyyid Mahdi; 3rd Haji Mulla Muhammad Ja'afar Astarabadi; 4th Akhund Mulla Aqa Darbandi Sharif al-'ulama; 5th A. Siyyid Ibrahim; 6th Shaykh Muhammad Husayn Sahib Fusul; 7th Shaykh Muhammad Najafi the author of Jawahir.

Translator: http://www.imamreza.net/eng/imamreza.php?id=6934

Citation: Shaykh Muhammad Najafi is briefly described, and he is also called Sahib al-Jawahir, and author of Miftah al-Karamah.

The crowd gathered, but it dispersed without any obvious reason before having arrived at its objective.

Such scenes happened constantly, but it is useless to report the details, which would be fastidious. It suffices us to know that the agitation spread everywhere. In Tabriz, for example, a riot broke out because a Shaykhi wanted to go to the baths. The bath manager, knowing his religion, refused him entrance, insulting the Shaykh. It came to blows, those present took one side or the other, and if the Governor had not intervened with his troops, God only knows what would have happened.

The people of Najaf up until then had not taken part in all these quarrels. They reproached A. Siyyid Mahdi and his students for having excommunicated the Shaykh without sufficient reasons. They repeated that nowhere in the religious law of Muhammad was it said that it was permitted for such a disorder to be made because one had read non-orthodox sentences in a book. It was obligated, they remarked, to accept the meaning given to the words by the one who spoke them, and that it was particularly necessary in the case of the successor of Shaykh Ahmad, whose ideas could not be understood, without them being explained. They were not far from believing that A. Siyyid Mahdi was crazy.

But, little by little, they were caught up in the contagion and they turned against Siyyid Kazim. Two incidents served to ignite the gunpowder.

It happened that a Shaykh died at Karbala; he made A. Siyyid Kazim Rashti the executor of his will, leaving him a house and his little children.

Shaykh 'Ali, the son of Shaykh Ja'afar, asked the Siyyid to sell him this house. The Siyyid sold it to him. At the moment of payment, Shaykh 'Ali asked that he not require this money of him: "When one brings the money coming from the alms for the poor," he said, "take the price of this house and bring it there on his account."

The Siyyid told him that that was impossible because the house belonged to orphans. This refusal provoked the anger of Shaykh 'Ali, who attacked Siyyid Kazim on religious grounds.

This one[24] had just published a treatise on the science of manners.[25] Shaykh 'Ali took as a pretext that this book contained phrases such as this: "Turn away from the books of men, and particularly from those of the ignorant ones, for these ones are blind." He went everywhere crying that the Siyyid renounced the mujtahids, the Qur'an and hadith, and that he had brought a new religion.

He cried loud and seemed to be convinced; also, he was listened to, and the troubles started again. And yet, not a month had passed since Shaykh 'Ali had admirably received Siyyid Kazim in Karbala.

It was at Najaf, at the time of the pilgrimage,[26] that disorder broke out.

Siyyid Kazim however wrote him a letter in saying: "Previously you disapproved of A Siyyid Mahdi who attacked me: why, today, do you speak in this way?" But his adversary did not reply to him. Therefore he wrote a treatise in which he explained the very words that were the cause of the whole scandal, but his enemy did not even examine it and sent it back without opening it.

The tumult thus arrived at its climax, passions were unchained, fanaticism was acerbated and men were precipitated against each other, cursing and excommunicating one another.

---

[24] *Translator:* Siyyid Kazim Rashti, Risalat al-suluk fi al-akhlaq wa-al-a'mal, Bayrut: al-Ma'had al-Almani lil-Abhath al-Sharqiyah fi Bayrut, 2004.

[25] *Nicolas:* Akhlaq.
Translator: http://en.wikipedia.org/wiki/Akhlaq
Citation: Akhlaq (Arabic: قلاخا) is an Arabic term referring to the practice of virtue, morality and manners in Islamic theology and falsafah (philosophy). It is most commonly translated in English dictionaries as; disposition, nature, temper, ethics, morals or manners (of a person).[1]

[26] *Translator:* Apparently a reference to the appointment of 'Ali by Muhammad, celebrated among Shi'i Muslims on 18 Dhu al-Hijjah and called Eid al-Ghadeer. Alternatively, this could denote the commemoration of the martyrdom of Imam 'Ali bin Abu Talib, traditionally occurring on Laylat al-Qadr, during Ramadhan. Both are occasions for making pilgrimage to Najaf, and reciting the ziyarat of 'Ali, found here and elsewhere online: https://www.al-islam.org/supplications-month-ramadhan/ziyarat-ameenullah and https://www.majzooban.org/en/index.php/articles/2882-laylat-al-qadr-and-the-martyrdom-of-imam-ali-as

The country was vigorously brought to oppose the Shaykhis. Shaykh 'Ali took the lead, inundating Turkey, India and Iran with letters of denunciation against the Shaykhi leader: "Siyyid Kazim Rashti," he wrote, "has left religion, he is a renegade. All the believers turn away from him and it is obligatory for us to let you know this. It is not permitted to imitate him, to listen to him, and whoever imitates him, God will not pardon him and his ultimate repentance will not be admitted.

One of these letters addressed to Basra, fell into the hands of Siyyid Kazim, and showed him to what lengths his enemies would take their audacity; the persecutions had already begun and already blood was flowing.

Atrocious calumnies were uttered. Abominable letters were written and all that was talked about was this quarrel. Many thought that it was because of fear that the mujtahids did not dare to summon the Shaykhi leader before them.

For two years, all that was heard were the echoes of these disputes. The Muslim land was inundated with calumnious letters some of which were sent to the Siyyid with this sentiment: "It is better to die than to read such infamies against you!"

Finally, the time of the festival of Qadir[27] having arrived, Siyyid Kazim obeyed the order that the Imam Rida[28] gave at another time to Ahmad ibn Basir Bazanti, in saying: "O Ibn Abi Basir, wherever you will be, the day of Qadir, come to the tomb of the Amir of the believers." He thus went towards Karbala.

---

[27] *Translator:* http://www.islamicinvitationturkey.com/2011/11/09/cleric-calls-for-refraining-from-extremism-on-qadir-event/
Citation: Eid al-Ghadeer is a festive day observed by Muslims on the 18th of Dhu al-Hijjah in the Islamic calendar to commemorate the appointment of first Ahl al-Bayt leader Imam Ali ibn Abi Talib by prophet Muhammad as his immediate successor.

[28] *Translator:* https://en.wikipedia.org/wiki/Ali_Al-Ridha
Citation: 'Alī ibn Mūsā al-Riḍhā (Arabic: علي بن موسى الرضا) (commonly known as, 'Alī al-Riḍā, Ali Reza, or Ali Riza) (ca. December 29, 765 — August 23, 818)[1] was the seventh descendant of the Islamic prophet Muhammad and the eighth of the Twelve Imams, according to Shia sect of Islam as well as an Imam of knowledge according to the Zaydi Shia school and Sufis. His given name was 'Alī ibn Mūsā ibn Ja'far.

As soon as he had arrived, someone came to find him on behalf of his enemies saying that an assembly was being convened to examine him, so as to cause the disorder that reigned for much too long to be disappeared.

Siyyid Kazim remarked that discussion could not arrive at conviction for either of the two parties. It must thus be agreed that this gathering would have a president who would be at the same time arbitrator and who would side with one party, be it with the other.

He furthermore expressed his reservations about the choice of this president. In no fashion did he wish to admit any of the 'ulama of 'Iraq. *"However, I do not wish to be difficult so that you will say that I seek escape routes. This year, many are the 'ulama who have come from Bahrain, from Jayzahir, from Lahsa: among them there is Shaykh Muhammad Ahle 'Abdu'l-Jabbar, a knowledgeable and wise mujtahid; A. Siyyid Husayn, son of A. Siyyid 'Abdu'l-Qahhar Bahraini; Shaykh Ahmad ibn Shaykh Khalaf Ahle Usfur, and others. Choose one of them or choose all of them."*

But the enemy did not accept this proposition and told all of the pilgrims of the impiety of the Siyyid. They went as far as to tell them that 19 people had been sent to him to ask him to participate in a gathering to refute claims against him, and that he had refused.

Hearing that, he caused a minbar to be set up in the colonnade outside the tomb of the Amir, and while the crowd was praying, he ascended the steps and cried out:

"O men, today is a respectable day for two reasons. One is that it is the feast of Qadir, the other is that it is Friday. There is a third reason for respect, it is that we are in the presence of 'Ali. Such circumstances rarely happen: that is a good reunion: Thanks be to God!

"Know that no action can be accepted by God unless it is accompanied by one who possesses the truly beliefs on the subject of 'Ali. Know that 'Ali and his brother Muhammad and his pure children and his wife are the ones faithful to God! Bathed in His mercy. They are the keys of Paradise! The places of the Will, the tongue of the desire of God. O men! God has fixed them, do not go beyond them! Do

not exaggerate the sublimity of the Imams: do not think that God has made them responsible for the care of His orders. They are respected slaves of God, they do not seek to pass before God! They always carry out the order of God, and God knows what is among men! The Imams cannot intervene except in favor of the One whom God wishes, and if one of them had said: 'I am God!' his place would be hell.

"O men! They are the Verb of God! The Prophet of God is the slave of God and His chosen one; and God made him great, because he was worthy of that. This Highness with his body, his clothes, his slippers ascended to the heavens. On the day of judgment, the creatures, with their material and sensible body must be resuscitated. The God of this world knows all things before the creation of all things, as after and at the very moment of creation. He is too high for His state to have a change. Obliteration cannot reach Him. He is the Powerful! The Living! The Risen!

"O men! These beliefs are the truth! Whoever is ornamented with them is on the straight path! And on a day like this one, if he makes the pilgrimage, he has the right to recompense from God.

"Whoever does not believe, be it in part, be it in total, all his works are lying, and on the day of judgment, he has right to no recompense.

"O men! See what are my beliefs! See what is my religion! These are my beliefs with which was filled the flour from which I am composed. My books are full thereof and my aim, in all my books, is nothing else, even though it may be written with different terminology.

"I see the 'ulama of this town wish to quarrel with me: if their hatred comes from my beliefs, I persist in them and have no need of those who do not share them. If they claim that I believe something other than what I have just said to you, they lie!

"The 'ulama of this town have asked me to come to a public reunion. I asked them to choose an arbiter, who will decide between us, without insisting too much on the choice of the arbiter, that I insisted only be a stranger and a pilgrim.

"Therefore, I hold myself at their disposition until tomorrow morning. Hence, they should not accuse me of lying, and they should not say that they have proposed a public reunion to me and that I have not accepted."

Siyyid Kazim descended from the minbar after this about face, and remained in the "San" until the next morning.

One asks oneself truly what was Siyyid Kazim's aim in accumulating these lies — for these are indeed lies. He could not believe that he was thus tricking his enemies and that he would turn them away from the path upon which they had set forth. What he could say, or not, for them, was the same thing. That he would succeed, by these adamant harangues, to deceive some naïve ones, that is certain! But can this success compensate what is painful about seeing him renounce himself?

After the sunset, three persons came to find him from his enemies, and Siyyid Kazim sent one of his faithful ones, Mulla Ahsa'in, known by the name Gohar, to bring his propositions: 1st Public reunion with the designation of an arbiter having the qualifications he agreed to. If they did not think that any person existed who could serve as arbiter, then there were two means left. First, either they were, or were not, mistaken with regard to the Siyyid: if they were mistaken, he offered to immediately explain his beliefs; if they were not mistaken, what right entitled them to penetrate the privacy of his thought?

In the Sahar[29] prayer of 'Ali ibn Husayn[10] is it not written: "O my God! In truth men give their faith only by their tongue, in order to preserve their life: and thus they arrive at the object of their desires."

Or 2nd the other option was to make Mubahala,[30] be it at the tomb of 'Ali, be it at that of 'Abbas, be it at that of Husayn.

Finally, in final analysis, 3rd, his adversaries could write a book in which they would report the words of the Siyyid with an explanation: the Siyyid would do the same from his side; if the two commentaries were in agreement, it was good, if they were in contradiction, this would prove that the enemies of the Shaykh were mistaken.

---

[29] *Nicolas:* Sahar means morning.
[30] *Nicolas:* See Seyyed Ali Mohammed dit le Bab, p. 212, note 160.

Mulla Hasan was going to bring his propositions to the adversary camp, and it seems that it was the last that would have rallied the approbations.

But, in the midst of the tumult, nothing was done to follow up this offer, and the calumnies continued their ravages. "They agitated in such manner that the sky was ready to melt, the earth to split open, the mountains to fall into dust."

The struggle continued and a fanatical Shi'ite attacked the Siyyid with dagger raised when he was in the house of Hashim Khan Nizam al-Dowla. Happily he was stopped in time.

Another time, at Karbala, he was shot, but the bullet was badly aimed, and it wounded the hand of one of his companions.

One day, close to the tomb of Husayn, a Friday, while the Siyyid was prostrated for the second time, at the second raka'at[11] of the prayer, someone approached him and violently tore off his turban.

The struggle continued thus, more violent and more savage than ever, and Shaykh Musa ibn Shaykh Ja'afar counseled the Siyyid to seek out allies and recommended that he write a rapid resume of his beliefs, so as to have it signed by Shaykh 'Ali, which was done.

Shaykh Musa sent copies of this document to the enemies, but this served no purpose and Siyyid Kazim again mounted the minbar and once again gave the discourse that we know.

The first to separate from the group of 'ulama was A Siyyid Mahdi, [then] Shaykh Musa and his brothers, Shaykh Husayn and the other 'ulama of Najaf, Shaykh Hasan Sultan, Shaykh Khalaf bin Askir, and the theological students of Karbala; Siyyid 'Abdullah Shubayr and his father Siyyid Muhammad Rida Shubayr, and his sons Siyyid Husayn, Siyyid Hasan, and his nephew 'Ali Shubayr; Siyyid Muhammad, son of recently deceased Shaykh Assadullah, his brother Shaykh Isma'il, did not follow A Siyyid Mahdi in his protests. In Iran, the 'ulama of Kirmanshah for which we have given the names, the two Hujjatu'l-Islam of Isfahan, Siyyid Muhammad Baqir and Haji Muhammad Ibrahim Qilbassy, the children of Sultanu'l-'ulama remained more or less faithful to Shaykh Ahmad, or at least they remained neutral.

In any case, the discussions were, at least in Arab 'Iraq, violently interrupted by the taking of Karbala.

It was in the year 1258 (1842) that this event took place, the day of the feast of Qadir.[31] The armies of Baghdad, under the direction of Najib Pasha overran Karbala, massacring the inhabitants, and pilfering the rich mosques. Almost 9 thousand people were killed, and most were Iranians.[32] Muhammad Shah was seriously enough ill when these events occurred,[33] also the high functionaries concealed them from him.

When the Shah, later on, found out about them, he threw into a great rage and swore to exact a thunderous revenge. But the Russian and British representatives intervened in order to calm things. In the final analysis, Mirza Ja'afar Khan Mushir al-Dowla, returning from this embassy to Constantinople, was sent to Erzurum[34] to meet with the British, Russian and Ottoman delegates.

---

[31] *Translator:* A brief history of Iraq, by Hala Mundhir Fattah, p. 150, writes that the battle in which the Ottoman troops invaded Karbala, resulted in 5000 casualties for the Karbala'i fighters and 400 losses for the Ottomans.

On January 18, 1842 Najib Pasha entered the city, went to the shrine of the Imam Husayn and said prayers. A Sunni governor, Sunni imam and Sunni qadis were imposed upon the population. There is no mention in this brief history of the Ottoman troops killing the population or stripping the Shi'ite shrines of their riches.

[32] *Nicolas:* Haqa'iq al-Akhbar Nasiri.
Translator: Haqa'iq-i-Akhbar-i-Nasiri, by Muhammad Ja'afar Khurmuji, cited in bibliographies including Amanat, Resurrection and Renewal.

[33] *Nicolas:* Tarikh Qajariyyih.

[34] *Translator:* http://en.wikipedia.org/wiki/Erzurum
Citation: Erzurum is a city in eastern Turkey. It is the largest city in and the eponymous capital of Erzurum Province. The city is situated 1757 meters (5766 feet) above sea level. Erzurum had a population of 361,235 in the 2000 census, increasing to 367,250 by 2010...The city was captured by the Russian Empire in 1829, but was returned to the Ottoman Empire under the Treaty of Adrianople (Edirne), in September of the same year. During the Crimean war Russian forces approached Erzurum, but did not attack it because of insufficient forces and th continuing Russian siege of Kars. The city was unsuccessfully attacked (Battle of Erzurum (1877)) by a Russian army in the Russo-Turkish War of 1877–78. However, in February 1878, the Russians took Erzurum withou resistance, but it was again returned to the Ottoman Empire, this time under the Treaty of San Stefano.

Having arrived at Tabriz, the Iranian plenipotentiary fell ill. Haji Mirza Aqasi therefore named in his place Mirza Taqi Khan Farahani, the Vazir Nizam: this one when to Erzurum with 200 officers.

The Turkish delegate was Envar Effendi, who showed himself to be courteous and conciliatory, but one of the men of the Emir Nizam committed an act that brought attention to the Sunni religion; the population assailed the camp of the Embassador; two or three Iranians were killed, everything was pillaged and the Emir Nizam would not have saved his life except through the intervention of Bahri Pasha.

The Turkish government made excuses and payed 15,000 tumans in damages and interests.

In his *Hedayat al-Talibin*, Karim Khan indicates that during the pillage of Karbala the victorious troops respected the homes of the Shaykhis. "All these," he said, "who sought a refuge therein, were saved, and there were accumulated previous objects. None of the companions of Siyyid Kazim was killed, while those who had taken refuge in the sacred tombs were massacred without pity. The Pasha, it is said, entered by horse into the sacred hall."

Discouragement and terror were from then on dominating the Iranians: they did not dare to show their religion nor to proceed with the ceremonies of their cult; the judges were chosen only from among the Sunnis. Siyyid Kazim was profoundly touched by these events. His health was altered and he slowly became weaker. His hair whitened, his forces dwindled and a Monday evening at two and a half hours of the night, in the year 1259 (1843),[35] he died.

Karim-Khan who, on the subject of the taking of Karbala, insists upon the respect that the assailants showed the Shaykhis and to Siyyid Kazim Rashti, does not bother himself at all to declare that it is very probable "that Siyyid Kazim was poisoned in

---

[35] *Translator:* http://en.wikipedia.org/wiki/Sayyid_Kazim_Rashti
Citation: Died 31 December 1843 = 9 Dhu'l-Hijja 1259

Baghdad by this infamous Najib Pasha who, he says, gave him a beverage after the drinking of which he was seized with an intense thirst and died."

It is thus that the Iranians write history!

He was buried behind the window of a corridor of the tomb of the Lord of the believers. This tomb was dug very deeply inclining, at the bottom, towards the interior of the forbidden hall.

Here closes the history of the establishment of Shaykhism, or more or less of its Unity. It will, in effect, after the death of Siyyid Kazim Rashti, divide itself into two branches. One, under the name of Babism, will give it the expansion that seems to have been promised by the force of the movement created by Shaykh Ahmad and which the two masters seem to have awaited, if one believes their predictions; the other, under the direction of Karim Khan, Qajar Kirmani, will continue the battles against the Shi'ite element but will always seek to put itself in the shade by affecting the outer appearance of a perfect Ithna-'Ashari Shi'ism.

NOTES

[1] *Translator:* http://en.wikipedia.org/wiki/Russo-Persian_War_ %281826%E2%80%931828%29
Citation: On 28 July 1826, a 35,000-strong Persian army led by Abbas Mirza, crossed the border and invaded the Khanates of Talysh and Karabakh. The Khans quickly switched sides and surrendered their principal cities — Lenkoran, Quba, Baku — to the Persians. [3] General Ivan Paskevich, Yermolov's subordinate, stated that his commanding officer's actions had started this war.[4]

Aleksey Yermolov, Russia's General Governor of Caucasus, feeling that he did not have sufficient resources to counter the invasion, refused to commit Russian troops to battle and ordered Ganja, the most populous city in the Southern Caucasus, to be abandoned.[5] In Shusha, a small Russian garrison managed to hold out until 5 September when General Madatov's reinforcement arrived to their relief.

Madatov routed the Persians on the banks of the Shamkhor River and retook Ganja on the 5th September. On hearing the news, Abbas Mirza lifted his siege of Shusha and marched towards Ganja.

A new Russian reinforcement under Ivan Paskevich (Yermolov's replacement) arrived just in time to join their forces with Madatov and to form a 8,000-strong corps under Paskevich's supreme command. Near Ganja they fell upon the Persians and forced them to retreat across the Araks River back to Persia. The attack was repulsed but the war was to continue for a year and a half.

The onset of winter weather led to the suspension of hostilities until May 1827, when Paskevich advanced towards Erivan, taking Echmiadzin, Nakhichevan and Abbasabad on his way. The principal war theatre was now Eastern Armenia, whose capital, Erivan, was stormed and captured by Paskevich after six days of siege (October 1). Fourteen days later, General Eristov entered Tabriz, forcing the Shah to sue for peace.

The outbreak of the new Russo-Turkish War revived Persian hopes and hindered peace negotiations, which were conducted by Aleksandr Griboyedov, among others. In January 1828 a Russian detachment reached the shores of Lake Urmia and the Shah started to panic. On his urging, Abbas Mirza speedily signed the Treaty of Turkmenchay (February 2, 1828) which concluded the war.

According to the terms of the treaty, the Khanates of Erivan and Nakhichevan passed to Russia. The Shah promised to pay an indemnity of 20,000,000 silver roubles and allowed his Armenian subjects to migrate to Russian territory without any hindrance. **More importantly, the Shah granted the Russians the exclusive right to maintain a navy in the Caspian and agreed that Russian merchants were free to trade anywhere they wanted in Persia.**

http://en.wikipedia.org/wiki/Russo-Turkish_War_%281828%E2
%80%931829%29
Citation: The Russo-Turkish War of 1828–1829 was sparked by the Greek War of Independence. The war broke out after the Sultan, incensed by the Russian participation in the Battle of Navarino, closed the Dardanelles for Russian ships and revoked the Akkerman Convention... The Sultan had no other choice but to sue for peace, which was concluded in Edirne on September 14, 1829. **The Treaty of Adrianople gave Russia most of the eastern shore of the Black Sea and the mouth of the Danube. Turkey recognized Russian sovereignty over western (Black Sea) Georgia and parts of northwest present-day Armenia (the bulk of Georgia and Armenia had already passed into Russian hands as the result of the two Russo-Persian Wars). Serbia achieved autonomy and Russia was allowed to occupy Moldavia and Walachia**

(guaranteeing their prosperity, and full "liberty of trade" for them) until Turkey had paid a large indemnity. Moldavia and Wallachia remained under Russian protectorate until the end of Crimean War. Archaic slavery was abolished during this period. The Straits Question was settled four years later, when both powers signed the Treaty of Unkiar Skelessi.

[2] *Translator:* http://en.wikipedia.org/wiki/Sayyid_Kazim_Rashti
Citation: Sayyid Kāẓim bin Qāsim al-Ḥusaynī ar-Rashtī (1793–1843) (Arabic: الرشتي الحسيني قاسم بن كاظم سيد), mostly known as Si-yyid Kázim Rashtí (Persian: رشتى كاظم سيد), was the son of Sayyid Qasim of Rasht, a town in northern Iran. He was appointed as the successor of Shaykh Ahmad al-Ahsa'i, and led the Shaykhí move-ment until his death. He came from a family of well known mer-chants. He was a Mullah who, after study of the Islamic writings told his students about the coming of the Mahdi and the "Masih" (the return of Christ) and taught them how to recognize them. Af-ter his death in 1843, many of his students spread out around Asia, Europe and Africa for the search. Upon his death he was laid to rest near the tomb of Imam Husayn in Karbala...the death of Sayy-id Kazim on 31 December 1843...

[3] *Translator:* Also see: 'Our Lord! Send amongst them a Messen-ger of their own (and indeed Allah answered their invocation by sending Muhammad وسلم عليه الله صلى), who shall recite unto them Your Verses and instruct them in the Book and Al-Hikmah, and purify them. Verily! You are the All-Mighty, the All-Wise.' (Quran 2:129) "For this We sent a Messenger to you from among you to recite our Verses to you and purify you and teach you the Book and Wisdom حكمة (Hikma) and teach you things you did not know before." (Qur'an 2:151) "Remember, Allah's blessing on you and the Book and Wisdom He has sent down to you to admonish you. Have fear of Allah and know that Allah has knowledge of all things." (Qur'an 2:231) "He gives wisdom to whoever He wills and whoev-er has been given wisdom has been given great good. But no one pays heed except the people of intelligence." (Qur'an 2:269) 'And He (Allah) will teach him [('Îsa (Jesus)] the Book and Al-Hikmah, (and) the Taurat (Torah) and the Injil (Gospel).' (Qur'an 3:48) "Re-member when Allah made a covenant with the prophets 'Now that We have given you a share of the Book and Wisdom, and then a messenger comes to you confirming what is with you, you must be-lieve in him and help him.' (Qur'an 3:81) 'Indeed Allah conferred a

great favour on the believers when He sent among them a Messenger (Muhammad وسلم عليه الله صلى) from among themselves, reciting unto them His Verses (the Qur'an), and purifying them (from sins by their following him), and instructing them (in) the Book (the Qur'an) and Al-Hikmah, while before that they had been in manifest error.' (Qur'an 3:164) "Or do they in fact envy other people for the bounty Allah has granted them? We gave the family of Ibrahim the Book and Wisdom, and We gave them an immense kingdom." (Qur'an 4:54) 'If only there had been among the generations before you persons having wisdom, prohibiting (others) from Al-Fasad (disbelief, polytheism, and all kinds of crimes and sins) in the earth, (but there were none) — except a few of those whom We saved from among them! Those who did wrong pursued the enjoyment of good things of (this worldly) life, and were Mujrimun (criminals, disbelievers in Allah, polytheists, sinners).' (Qur'an 11:116) 'And when he [Yusuf (Joseph)] attained his full manhood, We gave him wisdom and knowledge (the Prophethood); thus We reward the Muhsinun (doers of good) (Qur'an 12:22) 'They (the angels) said: "Do not be afraid! We give you glad tidings of a boy (son) possessing much knowledge and wisdom." (Qur'an 15:53) 'And from the fruits of date-palms and grapes, you derive strong drink and a goodly provision. Verily, therein is indeed a sign for people who have wisdom.' (Qur'an 16:67) 'Invite (mankind, O Muhammad سلم و عليه الله صلى) to the Way of your Lord (i.e. Islam) with wisdom (i.e. with the Divine Revelation and the Qur'an) and fair preaching, and argue with them in a way that is better. Truly, your Lord knows best who has gone astray from His Path, and He is the Best Aware of those who are guided.' (Qur'an 16:125) "This is part of the wisdom (Hikma / حكمة) Allah has revealed to you. Do not set up other god together with Allah and so be thrown into Hell, blamed and driven out." (Qur'an 17:39) '(It was said to his son): "O Yahya (John)! Hold fast the Scripture [the Taurat (Torah)]." And We gave him wisdom while yet a child.' (Qur'an 19:12) 'We know very well what they will say, when the best among them in knowledge and wisdom will say: "You stayed no longer than a day!" (Qur'an 20:104) "These are the verses of a Wise Book" (Qur'an 31:2) 'And indeed We bestowed upon Luqman Al-Hikmah (wisdom and religious understanding) saying: "Give thanks to Allah." And whoever gives thanks, he gives thanks for (the good of) his own self. And whoever is unthankful, then verily, Allah is All-Rich (Free of all needs), Worthy of all praise.' (Qur'an 31:12) 'See you not (O men) that Allah has subjected for you whatsoever is in the

heavens and whatsoever is in the earth, and has completed and per-
fected His Graces upon you, (both) apparent (i.e. Islamic Monothe-
ism, and the lawful pleasures of this world, including health, good
looks, etc.) and hidden [i.e. One's Faith in Allah (of Islamic Mono-
theism) knowledge, wisdom, guidance for doing righteous deeds,
and also the pleasures and delights of the Hereafter in Paradise]?
Yet of mankind is he who disputes about Allah without knowledge
or guidance or a Book giving light!' (Qur'an 31:20) "[Wives of the
Prophet], Remember what is recited (yuthla / يطلى) in your hous-
es of Allah's Verses (ايات الله / ayaat Allah) and Wisdom (Hikma /
حكمة), for Allah is All-Subtle, All-Aware." (Qur'an 33:34) 'By the
Qur'an, full of wisdom' (Qur'an 36:2) 'And verily, it (this Qur'an)
is in the Mother of the Book (i.e. Al-Lauh Al-Mahfuz), with Us, indeed exalted, full of wisdom.' (Qur'an 43:4) 'Perfect wisdom (this
Qur'an), but (the preaching of) warners benefit them not.' (Qur'an
54:5) "We sent our messengers with clear Revelations, and we sent
down the Book and Balance so that people could uphold justice."
(Qur'an 57:25)

[4] *Translator:* http://en.wikipedia.org/wiki/Ja%27far_al-Sadiq
Citation: Jaʾfar ibn Muhammad al-Sādiq (Arabic: محمد بن جعفر
الصادق) (702–765 C.E. or 17th Rabīʾ al-Awwal 83 AH — 15th Shaw-
wāl 148 AH) was a descendant of Ali from his father's side and
a descendant of Abu Bakr from his mother's side and was himself a prominent Muslim jurist. He is revered as an Imam by the
adherents of Shi'a Islam and as a renowned Islamic scholar and
personality by Sunni Muslims. The Shi'a Muslims consider him
to be the sixth Imam or leader and spiritual successor to Muhammad.[4] The internal dispute over who was to succeed Jaʾfar as
Imam led to schism within Shi'a Islam.[4] Al-Sadiq was celebrated among his brothers and peers and stood out among them for
his great personal merits.[5] He is highly respected by both Sunni and Shi'a Muslims for his great Islamic scholarship, pious character, and academic contributions...He died on 8 December 765.
He was poisoned by Al-Mansur.[32] He is buried in Medina, in the
famous Jannatul Baqee' cemetery. After Ja'far al-Sadiq's death
during the reign of the 'Abbāsids, various Shī'ī groups organised
in secret opposition to their rule. Among them were the supporters of the proto-Ismā'īlī community, of whom the most prominent group were called the "Mubārakiyyah". There are hadīth
which state that Ismā'īl ibn Ja'far "al-Mubārak" would be heir to
the Imamate, as well as those that state Musa al-Kadhim[3][39] was

to be the heir. However, Ismā'īl predeceased his father. Some of the Shī'ah claimed Ismā'īl had not died, but rather gone into hiding, but the proto-Ismā'īlī group accepted his death and therefore that his eldest son, Muḥammad ibn Ismā'īl, was now Imām. Muḥammad remained in contact with this "Mubārakiyyah" group, most of whom resided in Kūfah. In contrast, Twelvers don't believe that Isma'il ibn Jafar was ever given the *nass* ("designation of the Imamate"),[40][41] but they acknowledge that this was the popular belief among the people at the time.[42] Both Shaykh Tusi[40] and Shaykh al-Sadūq[41] did not believe that the divine designation was changed (called *Bada'*), arguing that if matters as important as Imāmate were subject to change, then the fundamentals of belief should also be subject to change. Thus Twelvers accept that Mūsá al-Kāẓim was the only son who was ever designated for Imāmate. This is the initial point of divergence between the proto-Twelvers and the proto-Ismā'īlī. This disagreement over the proper heir to Ja'far has been a point of contention between the two groups ever since. The split among the Mubārakiyyah came with Muḥammad's death. The majority of the group denied his death; they recognised him as the Mahdi. The minority believed in his death and would eventually emerge in later times as the Fāṭimid Ismā'īlī, ancestors to all modern groups. Another Shia branch that emerged around the figure of Ja'far al-Sadiq was the Tawussite Shia. Following the death of al-Sadiq, the Tawussite's denied that he died and instead believed in his Mahdism. Another Shia branch claimed that al-Sadiq's eldest surviving son Abdullah al-Aftah was the Imam to succeed his father. This branch was known as the Fathites. There is little evidence of them surviving beyond al-Aftah's death, since he is commonly believed to have left no descendants.[43]

[5] *Translator:* http://en.wikipedia.org/wiki/Ali_Al-Ridha
Citation: 'Alī ibn Mūsā al-Riḍhā (Arabic: الرضا موسى بن علي) (commonly known as, 'Alī al-Riḍā, Ali Rezā, or Ali Rizā) (ca. December 29, 765 — August 23, 818)[1] was the seventh descendant of the Islamic prophet Muhammad and the eighth of the Twelve Imams, according to Shia sect of Islam as well as an Imam of knowledge according to the Zaydi Shia school and Sufis. His given name was 'Alī ibn Mūsā ibn Ja'far...Once Ali al-Ridha was summoned to Khurasan and he forcibly accepted the special conditions of the succession of al-Ma'mun, al-Ma'mun summoned his brother, Zayd, who had revolted and brought about a riot in Medina to his court in Khurasan. Al-Ma'mun kept him free as a regard and honor to

Ali al-Ridha and overlooked his punishment...'Ali al-Ridha did not outlive al-Ma'mun, and died on May 26, 818, in Persia while accompanying al-Ma'mun at Tus. He was poisoned by al-Ma'mun using grapes. Ali al-Ridha is buried within Imam Ridha Mosque, in Mashhad, Iran.

[6] *Translator:* http://en.wikipedia.org/wiki/Al-Ma%27mun
Citation: Abū Jaʾfar ʿAbdullāh al-Maʿmūn ibn Harūn (also spelled Almamon, Al-Maymun and el-Mâmoûn, Arabic ابوجعفر عبدالله (المأمون) (13 September 786–9 August 833) (المأمون) was an Abbasid caliph who reigned from 813 until his death in 833. He succeeded his brother al-Amin who was killed during the siege of Baghdad(813).[2] ... In A. H. 201 (817 AD) al-Ma'mun forced Imam Rida [pronounced Reza in Farsi] to move from Madina to Merv. Imam Rida, the Eighth descendant of Muhammad, was named his heir. This was not easily accepted by the Abbasid leaders but was widely seen as a political move by al-Ma'mun since he was fearful of the widespread sympathy towards the Ahl al-Bayt. Al-Ma'mun's plan was to keep watch over Imam Rida. However, his plans did not succeed due to the growing popularity of ʿAli Al-Rida in Merv. People from all over the Muslim world traveled to meet the prophet's grandson and listen to his teachings and guidance.

After a debate Al-Ma'mun had set up with the greatest scholars of the world's religions to humiliate the Imam, the victorious Imam informed Al-Ma'mun that his grand vizier, Fadl ibn Sahl, had not been informing him of everything. In Baghdad, the people believed that al-Maʿmūn was unseated, because of rumors spread by Fadl ibn Sahl. Because of this the people of Baghdad were giving their allegiance to al-Ma'mun's uncle Ibrahim ibn Mahdi. Al-Ma'mun set out for Baghdad in 12 April 818. At Tus, he stopped to visit his father's grave. Al-Ma'mun was troubled by the widespread support for the prophet Muhammad's descendant Imam Rida, and the betrayal of his grand vizier. With the aim of gaining Abbasid support and the establish of a new base for his rule in Baghdad, Al-Ma'mun went on to depose of ʿAli Ar-Rida by administering poison, and arranging the murder of Fadl ibn Sahl. On the last day of Safar in 203 AH, Imam Rida died. Imam Rida was buried beside Al-Ma'mun's father Hārūn al-Rashid. Following the death of Imam Rida a great revolt took place in Khurasan, Persia. Al-Ma'mun tried to show himself innocent of the crime but for all he did, he could not get himself acquitted and prove his innocence.

[7] *Translator:* http://en.wikipedia.org/wiki/Taqlid
Citation: Taqlīd is an Arabic verbal noun based on the verb *qalla-da*, literally *to place, to gird or to adorn with a necklace* (qilādah*).*[1]
The term is believed to have originated from the idea of allowing oneself to be led "by the collar". One who performs taqlid *is called a* muqallid,[2] *whereas one who rejects* taqlid *is called a* ghair-muqal-lid. *Sheikh Shaamee Hanafi said it is "to take the statement of some-one without knowing the evidence."*[3]

There are several verses (*ayat*) in the Quran that forbid *taqlid* in matters of religion (5:104–5, 17:36, 21:52–54 43:22–24) though this is interpreted as referring only to fundamentals (*usul ad-din*) and not to subsidiary elements (*furu 'ad-din*) such as details of law and ritual practices that can only be learned through extensive study.

Following the Greater Occultation (*al-ghaybatu'l-kubra*) in 329–941 CE, the Shia are obliged to observe *taqlid* in their religious affairs by following the teachings of a thinker (*mujtahid*) or jurist (*faqih*).[4] As of the 19th century the Shia *'ulama* taught believers to turn to "a source of *taqlid*" (*marja' at-taqlid*) "for advice and guidance and as a model to be imitated."[5]

[8] *Translator:* This is a very similar argument to what Jesus says to the Pharisees when they accuse a woman of adultery and ask him if she should be stoned to death (Gospel of John 8:1–11): "And the scribes and Pharisees brought unto him a woman taken in adultery; and when they had set her in the midst,⁴ They say unto him, Master, this woman was taken in adultery, in the very act.⁵ Now Moses in the law commanded us, that such should be stoned: but what sayest thou?⁶This they said, tempting him, that they might have to accuse him. But Jesus stooped down, and with his finger wrote on the ground, as though he heard them not.⁷ **So when they continued asking him, he lifted up himself, and said unto them, He that is without sin among you, let him first cast a stone at her.**⁸ And again he stooped down, and wrote on the ground.⁹ And they which heard it, being convicted by their own conscience, went out one by one, beginning at the eldest, even unto the last: and Jesus was left alone, and the woman standing in the midst.¹⁰ When Jesus had lifted up himself, and saw none but the woman, he said unto her, Woman, where are those thine accusers? hath no man condemned thee?¹¹ She said, No man, Lord. And Jesus said unto her, Neither do I condemn thee: go, and sin no more."

[9] *Translator:* http://en.wikipedia.org/wiki/Descendants_of_Ali_ibn_
Abi_Talib
Citation: Abu'l-Fadl 'Abbas was the half-brother of the Imam Husayn and the Imam Hasan; their father was 'Ali ibn Abu Talib, the
first Imam; the mother of Husayn and Hasan was Fatima, daughter
of Muhammad, while the mother of 'Abbas was Fatima bint Hizam
al-Qilabiyya, known as Umma al-Banin. 'Abbas was known as the
"righthand man" of the Imam Husayn.

[10] *Translator:* http://en.wikipedia.org/wiki/Ali_ibn_Husayn
Citation: 'Ali ibn al-Husayn (Arabic: علي بن الحسين) (approximately
6 January 659 – 20 October 712)[2] known by the honorific Zayn
al-Abidin ("Beauty/Best of the Worshippers") was a great-grand-
son of Muhammad, as well as the fourth Shi'ah Imam (the third
Imam according to Isma'ilis). His mother was Shahrbanu and his
father was Husayn ibn 'Ali. His brothers include 'Ali al-Asghar
ibn Husayn and 'Ali al-Akbar ibn Husayn. He is also referred to as
Imam al-Sajjad "the Prostrating Imam" and Sayyid as-Sajjadīna wa
Raki'in "Leader of Those who Prostrate and Bow".... He dedicated
his life to learning and became an authority on prophetic traditions and Sharia. He is regarded as the source of the third holiest
book in Shia Islam after the Quraan and the Nahj al Balagha: the
Sahīfa al-Sadjadiyya, commonly referred to as the Psalms of the
Household of Muhammad. Al-Husayn had many supporters such
as Sa'id ibn Jubayr...He migrated to Karbala with his father. He was
the only one of the sons of Hussein ibn Ali who survived the Battle
of Karbala in 680, since he did not take part in the fighting due to
illness.[11]...Al-Husayn resided in Medina until his death on approximately 20 October 712, when he was killed by the Bani Uma-
yyah rulers. By the instructions of Walid Bin Merwan, the governor of Medina, Ali was poisoned by Hisham ibn Abd al-Malik. He
was buried in Jannatul Baqee', the cemetery in Madinah where
other important figures of Islamic history are buried.

[11] *Translator:* http://en.wikipedia.org/wiki/Raka%27at
Citation: A rakat, or raka'ah (Arabic: ركعة *rak'ah*, plural: ركعات
raka'āt), consists of the prescribed movements and words followed by Muslims while offering prayers to God (Allah). After
performing the ablution, and evoking the intention to pray for
the sake of God, the worshipper will stand quietly while reciting
verses of the Quran. The second part of the rakat involves bow-
ing low with hands on knees, as if waiting for God's orders. The

third movement is to prostrate oneself on the ground, with fore-head and nose on the floor and elbows raised, in a posture of sub-mission to God. The fourth movement is to sit with the feet folded under the body. In the concluding portion of the prayers, the wor-shiper recites "Peace be upon you, and God's blessing" once while facing the right, and once while the face is turned to the left. This action reminds Muslims of the importance of others around them, both in the mosque (if the prayer is being offered at mosque), and in the rest of the world. It also refers to a single unit of Islamic prayers. Each daily prayer has a different number of obligatory rakats:

> *Fajr* — The dawn prayer: 2 rakats
> *Dhuhr* — The midday or afternoon prayer: 4 rakats
> *Asr* — The late afternoon prayer: 4 rakats
> *Maghrib* — The evening prayer: 3 rakats
> *Isha'* — The night prayer: 4 rakats, plus 3 rakats of the compul-sory **witr** prayer

The Friday prayer consists of 2 obligatory rakats, and is offered in congregation in place of the afternoon prayer on Friday.

http://en.wikipedia.org/wiki/Witr
Citation: Witr (Arabic: وتر) is an Islamic prayer (*salah*) that is performed at night after *isha'a* (night-time prayer) or before *fajr* (dawn prayer). According to the Hanafi Fiqh witr prayer is *wa-jib*. The status of wajib is very close to that of *fard*. There are a few distinguishing factors of the witr prayer that sets it apart from the *fard* (mandatory) and *sunnah* (recommended) prayers. Witr has an odd number of *rakat* prayed in pairs, with the final raka'ah prayed separately. Therefore, as little as one rakat can be prayed, and eleven at most. This differs from the usual trend of two, three and four rakat of the fard and sunnah prayers.

About the Authors

CHRISTOPHER BUCK, PhD, JD, independent scholar and Pittsburgh attorney, publishes broadly in American studies, religious studies, Baha'i studies, Islamic studies, African American studies, and Native American studies. A former university professor, Dr. Buck previously taught at Pennsylvania State University (2011), Michigan State University (2000–2004), Quincy University (1999–2000), Millikin University (1997–1999), and Carleton University (1994–1996). Buck is author of: God and Apple Pie (2015)—with Introduction by J. Gordon Melton, Distinguished Professor of American Religious History, Baylor University — being the revised edition of *Religious Myths and Visions of America* (2009), acclaimed as "an original contribution to American studies," *Journal of American History* 98.1 (June 2011), p. 280; A*lain Locke: Faith and Philosophy* (2005); *Paradise and Paradigm* (1999), *Symbol and Secret* (1995/2004); *Religious Celebrations* (co-author, 2011); and book chapters: *'Abdu'l-Bahá's Journey West* (2013); *The Blackwell Companion to the Qur'an* (2006/2016); *The Islamic World* (2008); *American Writers* (2004/2010/2015); *British Writers* (2014). Buck has published various journal and encyclopedia articles as well (see https://psu-us.academia.edu/ChristopherBuck), along with over 200 brief articles on the Baha'i Faith at http://bahaiteachings.org/author/christopher-buck. Buck currently practices law as a plaintiff's attorney (see http://pribanic.com/attorneys/christopher-buck/) in Pittsburgh, Pennsylvania, where he lives with his wife, Nahzy Abadi Buck, and his sons, Takur Buck, and Taraz Buck, Ph. D. Email: *BuckPhD@gmail.com*

IAN KLUGE is a poet, playwright and philosophy scholar who lives in Prince George, British Columbia. He has an M.A. and PhD (ABD) from the University of Alberta, Edmonton, and currently teaches courses for the BIHE and the Wilmette Institute. Ian Kluge has published numerous articles about philosophical aspects of the Baha'i Writings. He is also the author of several books, including *Conrad Aiken's Philosophy of Consciousness* and two collections of poetry — *Elegies* and *For the Lord of the Crimson Ark.*

JEAN-MARC LEPAIN is an economist who, in a parallel life, pursues a second career in philosophy and Persian studies. He has studies Persian and Arabic at the Institute of Oriental Languages of Paris and at Teheran University just before the Islamic Revolution. He also studied general philosophy at Sorbonne and Islamic philosophy under Henri Corbin, the famous French iranologist. He has written several books and papers in French and prepared a new translation in French of *Some Answered Questions.* His major themes are individualism, rationality, philosophy of science, neuroscience and neurophilosophy, and spirituality. He lives in Brunei with his wife and two children.

ZAID LUNDBERG (*zaid.lundberg@outlook.com*) is an educator (Löftadalens folkhögskola, Sweden and Wilmette Institute, USA), composer, independent researcher, PhD candidate in History of Religions (Lund University, Sweden) with a bachelor's degree in Psychology (MIU, USA), and a master's degree in History of Religions (Lund University, Sweden). His MA thesis (1996) focused on Baha'i apocalypticism and the concept of progressive revelation (http://bahai-library.com/ lundberg_bahai_apocalypticism&chapter=1) His forthcoming PhD thesis is an analysis of Shoghi Effendi's macro or world critique in a modern western context. He has published over twelve papers in diverse areas (higher states of consciousness, Swedish Baha'i history, globalization, new religious movements, religiogenesis and multi-culturalism) but his main areas of interest and specialization are: the writings and life of Shoghi Effendi, the field and neonym of world critique (previously called "macro critique" or "macro criticism"), theodicy, the concept of evil and rhetorical criticism.

BENJAMIN B. OLSHIN is the Director of the School of Design and Professor of Philosophy, History and Philosophy of Science and Technology, and Design at The University of the Arts. His teaching and research work are interdisciplinary, with publications in the history of technology, philosophy of physics, the history of cartography, and cross-cultural issues in epistemology. He completed an M.A. and Ph.D. at the Institute for the History and Philosophy of Science and Technology (I.H.P.S.T.) at the University of Toronto.

HAROLD ROSEN (www.interfaitheducation.org) is a lifelong student and teacher of religion and philosophy, now serving as a community inter-faith educator in the Vancouver, BC area, and has master's degrees in religion, philosophy and education. He has taught philosophy and religion at various Canadian universities and is the author of several books, including *Founders of Faith: The Parallel Lives of God's Messengers.*

JULIO SAVI studied medicine at the Universities of Bologna and Florence. He lectures widely on Bahá'í subjects and is a member of the faculty of the Wilmette Institute. Dr Savi wrote *The Eternal Quest for God* (George Ronald, 1989), *Remoteness. Selected Poems* (Rome, 2002), *A Nest on the Highest Branch* (New Delhi, 2003), *For the Sake of One God* (New Delhi, 2005), *Towards the Summit of Reality* (George Ronald, 2008), *Unsheathing the Sword of Wisdom* (George Ronald, 2011). Some of his poems have been published in World Order (Wilmette, Illinois). E-mail: *ascanio@iol.it*

MIKHAIL SERGEEV holds his master's degree (1993) and a doctorate (1997) in the history and philosophy of religion from Temple University in Philadelphia. Dr. Sergeev has taught in several universities and colleges of Pennsylvania and New

Jersey. Now in addition to the history of religion he teaches philosophy and modern art at the University of the Arts in Philadelphia. He is the author of numerous articles on the history of religion, philosophy and contemporary art, which were published in Russian and American scholarly journals. He is also the author and editor of seven books, including the monograph *Theory of Religious Cycles: Tradition, Modernity and the Bahá'í Faith* (Brill, 2015).

PETER TERRY studied at the state Universities of Maine and Massachusetts, the University of Chicago, and the conservatories of music in San Francisco and Oberlin. His areas of specialized knowledge are pedagogy, classical music, and comparative religion and scripture. He has published a number of translations from French: *Arabic Bayan, The: From A. L.M. Nicolas' French translation*, by the Báb, English version by Peter Terry (1980); *A Prophet in Modern Times*, annotated English translation by Peter Terry (2008) of selected chapters from A.L.M. Nicolas, *Seyyed Ali Mohammed dit le Bab*, 1905; *The Archaeology of the Kingdom of God*, by Jean-Marc Lepain, translation by Peter Terry (completed 2015) into English of *L'Archeologie du Royaume de Dieu*, 1995; *Seven Proofs, The*, by Báb, The. English translation by Peter Terry (2015) of Nicolas' French translation of The Báb's "Seven Proofs." He has also published numerous papers on Babi and Baha'i topics.

www.ingramcontent.com/pod-product-compliance
Lightning Source LLC
Chambersburg PA
CBHW052032090426
42739CB00010B/1872